Along the Borders

www.penguin.co.uk

Along the Borders

In Search of What Divides and Unites the British Isles

RICHARD COLLETT

doubleday

TRANSWORLD PUBLISHERS

UK | USA | Canada | Ireland | Australia
India | New Zealand | South Africa

Transworld is part of the Penguin Random House group of companies
whose addresses can be found at global.penguinrandomhouse.com.

Penguin Random House UK, One Embassy Gardens,
8 Viaduct Gardens, London SW11 7BW

penguin.co.uk

First published in Great Britain in 2026 by Doubleday
an imprint of Transworld Publishers

001

Copyright © Richard Collett 2026

The moral right of the author has been asserted.

Map bases by Lovell Johns Ltd

Every effort has been made to obtain the necessary permissions with
reference to copyright material, both illustrative and quoted. We apologize
for any omissions in this respect and will be pleased to make the
appropriate acknowledgements in any future edition.

Penguin Random House values and supports copyright. Copyright fuels creativity, encourages diverse voices, promotes freedom of expression and supports a vibrant culture. Thank you for purchasing an authorized edition of this book and for respecting intellectual property laws by not reproducing, scanning or distributing any part of it by any means without permission. You are supporting authors and enabling Penguin Random House to continue to publish books for everyone. No part of this book may be used or reproduced in any manner for the purpose of training artificial intelligence technologies or systems. In accordance with Article 4(3) of the DSM Directive 2019/790, Penguin Random House expressly reserves this work from the text and data mining exception.

Set in 12.1/15.2pt Dante MT Std
Typeset by Six Red Marbles UK, Thetford, Norfolk
Printed and bound in Great Britain by Clays Ltd, Elcograf S.p.A.

The authorized representative in the EEA is Penguin Random House Ireland,
Morrison Chambers, 32 Nassau Street, Dublin D02 YH68.

A CIP catalogue record for this book is available from the British Library.

ISBN: 9781529935882

Penguin Random House is committed to a sustainable future
for our business, our readers and our planet. This book is made
from Forest Stewardship Council® certified paper.

To all my grandparents

Contents

Introduction   1

1   The River Tamar   7
     The Tamar Valley   8
     Launceston   19
     The Northern Borderlands   23

2   Western Cornwall   34
     St Keverne   35
     Cadgwith   43
     Camborne and Redruth   49
     St Just   56

3   The Welsh Marches   60
     Chepstow   61
     Monmouth   68
     Abergavenny   73
     Hay-on-Wye   81
     Llanymynech   85
     Oswestry   89
     The Irish Sea   95

4   The Danelaw   98
     Buckingham   99
     Leicester   102
     Tamworth   115
     Lichfield   123
     Independent Mercia   127

CONTENTS

- 5 The Anglo-Scottish Border — 135
  - Carlisle — 136
  - Gretna Green — 146
  - Hawick — 151
  - Berwick-upon-Tweed — 164
- 6 The Highland–Lowland Divide — 173
  - Inverness — 175
  - Culloden — 178
  - The Inverness Gaelic Society — 183
  - Aberdeen — 188
- 7 Shetland — 193
  - Scalloway — 197
  - Urdale Farm — 201
  - Lerwick — 207
  - Bressay — 213
  - Unst — 218
- 8 Northern Ireland — 223
  - Warrenpoint — 224
  - Pat's Shed — 227
  - Bandit Country — 232
  - Clones — 245
  - Drummully Polyp — 252
  - Derry/Londonderry — 258
- 9 The Kentish Border — 275
  - The Saxon Shore — 276
  - Sandwich — 280
  - Folkestone — 292
  - Dover — 307

Epilogue — 313
Acknowledgements — 319

Introduction

Borderland:

1. A territory at or near a border
2. A vague intermediate state or region
3. An area of overlap between two things

I confess that I'm a border addict. I love standing astride borders, each foot in a different country, the smell of fresh stamps on tattered passport pages, the sharp change of dialects as national flags are caught in the wind. I relish the moment of triumph when you cross from one country to the next, because borders, by their very nature, exist to contain our movements.

I'm not the first traveller to enjoy such kicks. Borders are ancient. Five thousand years ago, the Mesopotamians recorded the first artificial boundaries – territorial claims between rival cities – on clay cuneiform tablets. The Ancient Egyptians documented the border with their Nubian enemies in hieroglyphs on papyrus scrolls, and among the Bronze Age field systems of Western Cornwall, Neolithic Britons laid down simple stone boundaries. Humans have an innate desire to claim plots of land as theirs, to label others as yours. We carve landscapes apart to define our very sense of self and identity. The earliest boundaries slowly evolved into the borderlines that now separate modern nation states, and while these borders are intended as obstacles, people have always found ways to cross them.

Wide rivers and rising mountains, tumbling coastlines and remote islands. High concrete walls and lines of razor wire, blinding spotlights and military checkpoints. Our vision of frontiers often takes extreme geographical or man-made forms, and although there are no customs posts between England and Scotland, and no passport checks between Wales and England, the United Kingdom remains a patchwork of borders, the nation's history etched into the boundaries surrounding us. Hadrian's Wall evokes the lingering memory of ancient divides, and Northern Ireland's 300-mile-long land border recalls the fresh trauma of Ireland's partition a century ago. And then there are the borders that are unseen. How many in the Midlands know they live upon the edge of the medieval Danelaw, without which England may never have united into the nation it became? Travel from Aberdeen to Inverness, and while you never leave Scotland, you cross a linguistic and cultural divide shaped by millennia of bloody, often brutal clashes between Highlanders and Lowlanders.

This book was born on the muddy banks of the River Tamar, the little-known divide between Devon and Cornwall. Few English tourists realize they're crossing one of the world's oldest 'national' boundaries when they holiday in Cornwall, but the Tamar is the ancient border between Celtic Kernow and Anglo-Saxon England, a cultural and political frontier dating back over a thousand years.

During the pandemic, I found myself unexpectedly stuck in Devon, a county I knew little about. I saw ancient divisions resurrected when lockdown laws placed Devon and Cornwall in different tiers, and it became illegal to cross the river.

INTRODUCTION

In the summer of 2021, the gulf between these two counties seemed to widen further when a Cornish action group named 'Kernow Matters To Us' – campaigning against over tourism, second-home ownership and Cornwall's ever-rising cost of living – threatened to block major roads and bridges leading into Cornwall as tourists descended upon the southwest. Mebyon Kernow, Cornwall's 'national' party, called for a devolved Cornish parliament, while some Cornish nationalists even marched for independence. Cornwall was becoming a land apart. I was surprised. Having spent most of my childhood over the 'border' in England – my teenage years were spent in Buckinghamshire, among the rolling countryside of Middle England – I was unaware of the concept of a Cornish 'nation'. Cross over the River Tamar, though, and the black-and-white flag of St Piran flies from rooftops while signs announce in *Kernewek*, the resurrected Celtic language of Cornwall, that you are entering Kernow.

As a travel writer, I've built a career working in regions the Foreign Office typically advises against travelling to. I've tracked down former guerilla fighters in the mountains of Central America and reported on frozen conflict zones on the edge of the former Soviet Union. Separatism is a familiar concept to me, but bridge blocking and nationalist divisions were things I'd believed, in my naivety, to exist only on distant borders, far from the sheltered shores of the United Kingdom. I was always wary of delving too deep into my own country's divisions. I feared what I might find. But as we emerged into a post-pandemic world, the travel journalist within me was stirred to action.

For me, events on the Cornish 'border' that summer revealed the depths of the United Kingdom's identity crisis, one that's deepened throughout my lifetime. Perhaps it began under the Blair government, when Scotland, Wales and Northern Ireland gained devolved parliaments. It may well have begun long before this, when the British Empire – arguably the strongest thing holding the idea of Britishness together – unravelled after the Second World War.

I was born in Scotland to English parents, and within my own living memory, Britain has visibly fragmented. I remember the Scottish referendum well. I spent a long night nervously awaiting the result, relieved when independence was thwarted by a narrow margin. Brexit revived calls for an independent Scotland, and the Scottish National Party's campaigns have inspired similar calls in Wales, where Plaid Cymru ('The Party of Wales') is now winning more parliamentary seats than ever before. England's northern regions, including Yorkshire and Northumbria, are calling for increased devolution from Westminster; right-wing politicians likening small boats and refugees to an invasion force have politicized Kent's maritime border with France; and across the Irish Sea, Brexit resurrected very real fears that a hard border could reignite the Troubles.

It's an identity crisis I'm enduring on a personal as well as a national level, as I question what place my own mixed British identity holds in a kingdom less united by the day. Was the Union I'd known my entire life really ready to break apart? The Brit in me was terrified of such a break-up, but the Scot in me also understood the burning desire for autonomy, independence and a stronger sense of self – desires I'd seen all too often in breakaway territories and civil-war ravaged countries elsewhere in the world.

I wanted to confront my own nation's deep-seated identity

INTRODUCTION

issues head on. I resolved to plunge myself into the United Kingdom's borderlands, not only in search of what divides us, but what unites us. Nationalities are often strongest on the border, where people define themselves in opposition to neighbours, but borderlands are also the spaces in between, where centuries of history merge and collide, moulding the continuous links holding the UK's home nations together. It was in the borderlands that I hoped to uncover the roots of a uniting British identity I feared could soon be lost.

This book chronicles my multi-year journey, over land and sea, through the United Kingdom's borderlands. From the River Tamar, I travel to Cornwall, the Welsh Marches, the Midlands, the Anglo-Scottish border, the Scottish Highlands, Shetland, Northern Ireland and the Kentish coast. This is not just a book about the United Kingdom's borders and boundaries: it's about the people that live in these multicultural borderlands, and the resilient borderers who've shaped the history of a diverse nation we all call home. Ultimately, this is a book about how our borders and boundaries are bridged, and how they bring us together.

1

The River Tamar

The Cornish are the last of an ancient race, their moribund way of life slowly disappearing.

Philip Payton, *Cornwall: A History*

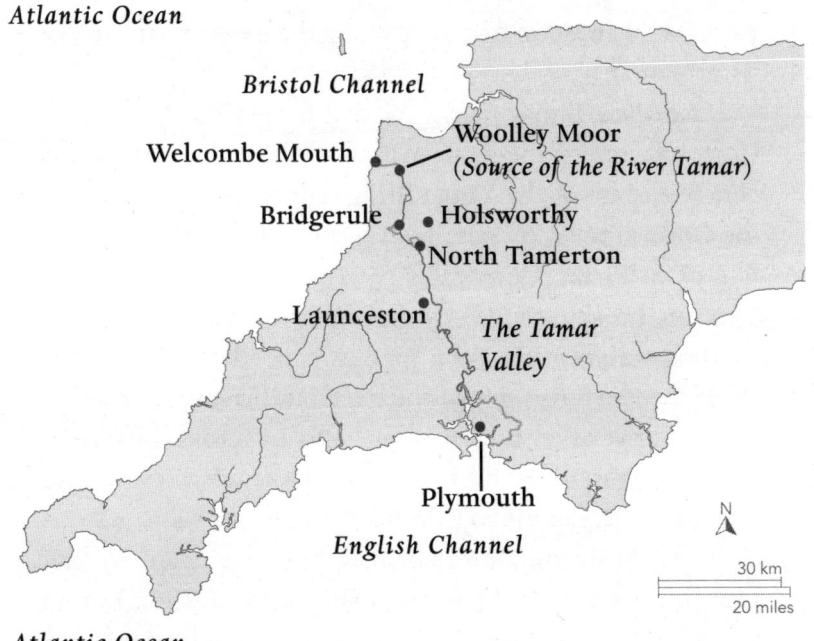

The Tamar Valley

It was a grey October morning when my journey began at Plymouth station. My partner Claire and I hopped on the twice-hourly train service north into the Tamar Valley, and after winding through terraced suburbs and past naval dockyards, we were soon trundling along the eastern bank of the River Tamar.

The River Tamar marks the divide between Devon and Cornwall, and on the western bank of the river – beyond the concrete spans of the Tamar Bridge connecting Plymouth to the Cornish town of Saltash – I spotted the black-and-white flag of St Piran (Cornwall's patron saint) flying proudly. The sun, breaking suddenly through the clouds, glinted off swirling waters as the train sped us beneath the bridge and along the Devonian side of the river, but I knew from countless trips over the 'border' that halfway across the Tamar Bridge, you're greeted by words of *Kernewek*: *Kernow a'gas dynergh*, or 'Welcome to Cornwall.'

To Cornish and Devonian alike, the River Tamar is not just another county boundary. This is the ancient border between Celtic Kernow and Anglo-Saxon England. Here at its widest extent, where dark churning waters frothed wildly on our left-hand side, I could see why Athelstan, king of the Anglo-Saxons, had decreed in 936 that the river should be the border between the Cornish and English.

To this day, the Cornish claim that the River Tamar is

one of the oldest 'national boundaries' in the world (older even than the Anglo-Scottish border, which was established in 1237), and I wanted to uncover the cultural and political divisions the River Tamar has forged. The river would be our constant companion on the first leg of my journey into Britain's borderlands, as we travelled north from Plymouth, first into the Tamar Valley, then to Launceston, the medieval gateway to Cornwall, and finally on to the blustery shores of the Bristol Channel.

The Tamar stretches for sixty-one miles from source to sea, and Cornwall is otherwise only connected to the rest of mainland Britain by a thin sliver of land some four miles long in the north – effectively making it an island. Separated from Wales by the Bristol Channel, the Cornish peninsula kicks westwards into the ferocious waves of the Atlantic Ocean. The jagged northern coastline is assaulted by storms, leaving sheer cliffs covered in low-lying scrub that rise and fall by hundreds of metres as the peninsula narrows on its way to Land's End. The southern shores are calmer, sheltering fishing fleets in deep-water harbours as the coast reaches back east towards Plymouth Sound, where the muddy banks of the Tamar separate Cornwall from Devon.

Starting as a trickle of spring water in a soggy field in northern Cornwall, the River Tamar courses south through farmland and forests. Crossed by medieval packhorse bridges built from Cornish or Dartmoor granite, the river swells into a formidable natural barrier as it passes Iron Age hill forts, the ruins of forlorn Roman camps and the ragged round keeps of Norman castles constructed to conquer an unyielding people.

Great bends in the river constrain the isolated gorges and

derelict tin mines of the Tamar Valley, where Anglo-Saxons fought Britons in bloody frontier battles that decided the fates of fledgling nations. Concrete viaducts span muddy, tidal banks and swirling brown waters maroon entire peninsulas between crashing tributaries before the River Tamar collides with Plymouth Sound, then flows into the English Channel.

In twenty-first century Britain, a resurgent Cornish 'nation' proudly flies the flag of St Piran, has revived its ancient language and asserts its identity, often in opposition to the English. But I also knew that our first destination, the Tamar Valley – which straddles the frontier just a few miles north of Plymouth – has proven to be a model of cross-border cooperation rather than regional separatism. This is a borderland where culture, history, languages and politics from two sides of a dividing line coexist. I wanted to know if rather than being a divisive border, the River Tamar brought people together.

As we trundled deeper into the Tamar Valley – where forested hills replaced Plymouth's urban sprawl – I recalled the folkloric, cross-border legend of two giants named Tavy and Torridge, who both fell in love with a water nymph named Tamara. Frustrated by the affections of her suitors, Tamara's father magicked his daughter into a river. Longing for his lost love, Tavy desired nothing more than to flow by Tamara's side forever and, by choice, transformed himself into a wide waterway as well. Torridge wandered the moors of northern Cornwall, searching in vain for Tavy and Tamara. Unable to bear the agony of loss, Torridge also turned into a river, but he was destined to flow northwards, forever alone.

THE RIVER TAMAR

The triangular wedge of land where the giant Tavy meets water nymph Tamara is the Bere Peninsula, where we jumped off the diesel-powered train at the single-platform station in the village of Bere Ferrers. Bright floral arrangements and vintage Great Western Railway posters decorated the red-brick Victorian station, where Clive Charlton, a local rail enthusiast and former University of Plymouth lecturer, met us with an inquisitive smile.

Dressed in a light-blue rain jacket in readiness for the grey clouds above to burst, Clive was holding a battered guidebook to the Bere Peninsula and a well-thumbed copy of the *Friends of the Tamar Valley Journal*, a quarterly local publication he occasionally edited. For much of his working life he had taught geography, but now retired, he spends his days volunteering for the local railway society that maintains the Tamar Valley Line – the gloriously scenic, twelve-mile-long line stretching north from Plymouth to the Cornish riverside village of Gunnislake.

'This is one of the most isolated places in the Tamar Valley,' he said, guiding us past rows of whitewashed granite houses to an old riverside quay on the River Tavy. 'I don't always see this as a border, though,' he added. We looked downriver, where I could see the Tavy merging with the Tamar a short distance away. 'But over there. They'll tell you this is the Cornish frontier. And I suppose it is a frontier of sorts, isn't it?'

The Bere Peninsula is in Devon, but it's right on Athelstan's historic boundary with Cornwall. This is where the broad borderlands of the Tamar Valley begin in earnest, as the river carves its path between Devon and Cornwall. A lack of roads had forced us to leave our car behind in Plymouth, and if we'd stayed on the train, it would have whisked us north and over the 37-metre-tall archways of the Calstock Viaduct. There, in the heart of the Tamar Valley, the remains of a Roman fort large enough to shelter five hundred soldiers were discovered in 2007.

Even two thousand years ago, the Tamar Valley proved to be a formidable natural borderland. Aside from two smaller and equally forlorn outposts excavated near Fowey and Bodmin, the River Tamar marked the westerly extent of the Roman advance into Cornwall. Roman influence was limited – the Romans traded for tin and other valuable minerals found in abundance across the peninsula, but never truly conquered Cornwall – yet the Cornish people still trace their origins to the exodus of the Roman legions from Britain in the early fifth century.

In the dying gasps of an empire that once ruled from Anatolia to Africa, warring tribes carved Roman Britain into disparate kingdoms. Invading Anglo-Saxon warbands saw opportunity in disorder, and by the ninth century, these Germanic invaders – or the English, as they eventually called themselves – had settled westwards, right up to the banks of the River Tamar where we were now.

The Cornish peninsula became a natural refuge for Britons fleeing Anglo-Saxon swords, and in 936, Athelstan made his declaration that the Tamar would be the border between Celtic Cornwall and Anglo-Saxon England. The Cornish are a more ancient people than the English, but with the river as a frontier, they were forever defined in opposition to the powerful Anglo-Saxons who now dominated Britain.

Historians are not sure if the Anglo-Saxon takeover of Celtic lands was a violent bloodbath or a slow integration of cultures. In 838, a great and presumably bloody battle was fought between Anglo-Saxons and a Cornish army allied with Vikings at a place called Hingston Down in the Tamar Valley. The Anglo-Saxons won the day, but they still retreated into Devon, rather than risk advancing into the barren moors beyond. Writing later, in the twelfth century, medieval historian William of Malmesbury told of the violent expulsion of the Cornish from Exeter two hundred years earlier in almost genocidal terms, describing Athelstan as 'purging' Devon of its 'contaminated race'. Many survivors fled Britain entirely, crossing the English Channel as refugees to settle a land that came to be called Brittany.

Given that ancient pre-Anglo-Saxon legends like that of Tavy, Tamara and Torridge are told on both sides of the River Tamar, Britons surely intermarried and adopted Anglo-Saxon customs and languages. Peaceful or violent, though, the Britons were displaced to such an extent that Cornish history is viewed almost entirely through the prism of English historians, and almost no records remain of the last Cornish monarchs who fought the Anglo-Saxons (although one contender for the title of 'Last King of Cornwall' is King Donyarth, who drowned in a river, having allied with a Viking army to fight Alfred the Great). Even the name Cornwall speaks to this othering. The Cornish refer to their country as Kernow (meaning 'horn' or 'headland'), while the English name 'Cornwall' is a corruption of this Celtic word for headland (*corn*) and an Old English word for foreigner (*wealh* – the same word from which 'Wales' is derived).

While this history still weighs heavily on the minds of the Cornish today, who I often find will do anything to prove they're *not* English, for Clive, the Tamar Valley isn't necessarily a frontier between nations, but a place where dividing lines have blurred. Separated from much of the surrounding counties by sheer cliffs, steep-sided hills and the wide banks of the river, it's no wonder Clive views the Tamar Valley as what he called, in geography-speak, a 'liminal space or a zone of transition', where two cultures merge together.

Bere Ferrers, his home village, speaks to multiple identities crashing and colliding on the banks of the River Tamar. The word 'Bere' is derived from another Celtic word for peninsula, while the second part of the name refers to the Norman 'de Ferrers' family who were given the village following William the Conqueror's invasion of England in 1066. It's a stark reminder that this isn't just a river, but a border holding two nations' histories within its mud and blood-soaked boundaries.

But borders are never the static lines we see drawn on maps, and for centuries, the Cornish 'frontier' remained remarkably porous. In the graveyard of St Andrew's Church, built in the tall Norman style by the de Ferrers family, Clive showed us cracked and faded headstones, where English surnames like Brighton, Dart and Williams mixed with Cornish and Norman names like Tremayne, Trevethan and de Burgh.

The relative isolation of villages in the Tamar Valley meant that historically, people had to get along with those on the other side of the river. Before the arrival of the railway, for example, it was quicker for a Devonian to cross the river and do business in Cornwall than it was to travel all the way south to Plymouth. The River Tamar was once full of flat-bottomed 'Tamar barges', which navigated tidal waterways with ease. They would stop off on either side of the river – much like the train does today – picking people up, setting them down and allowing communities on both sides to mingle, mix and marry.

'The Tamar was the glue sticking the two sides together,' Clive said, as we looped back through the village, where flyers for an autumn apple festival covered the windows of the rustic Plough Inn. 'And the barges and the trains took no notice of Devon and Cornwall. They went where they had to.'

This sense of unity continues today. The Tamar Valley encompasses several cross-border institutions, including the Tamar Valley National Landscape Area of Outstanding Natural Beauty, and parts of the UNESCO World Heritage-listed Cornwall and West Devon Mining Landscape. The Tamar Valley Line's 'Rail Ale Trail' allows you to hop on and off at pubs on either side of the river (a group of rowdy teenage punters were doing just that later in the day). The Tamar Valley River Festival, held upriver in Calstock every October, attracts artists, musicians, craftspeople and families from Cornwall and Devon, and the spirit of the old Tamar barges was revived with the reopening of the historic Calstock Ferry (now solar-powered) in 2025, which connects the Bere Peninsula with Kernow.

Clive added that people along the border often hold multiple identities – be they English and Cornish, or Cornish and British – but he also made it clear that his opinion was one of an Englishman. In large parts of Cornwall, he readily admitted, the River Tamar was increasingly seen as a sharp dividing line, rather than a transitional space.

Clive, whose wife is Cornish, explained how they used to

live in Saltash, the town directly connected to Plymouth by the Tamar Bridge we'd passed earlier on the train. Clive is convinced that people in Saltash now see the river itself as a stronger and more divisive border than they used to, largely because of the resurgence of Cornish identity.

'People like identity,' he said, as he theorized the reasons behind this shift. 'And there's this modern idea of Cornishness that's emerging, even in places like Saltash. Cornish identity has been enlarged through political and cultural campaigns, television and radio shows. If I still lived in Saltash, I'd probably adopt the Cornish identity myself. There's a huge Cornish profile there, and it's getting bigger. We'd be Cornish nationalists by now!'

Identity is strongest in opposition to something else, and in borderlands, different nationalities can become more defined. While Cornishness is on the rise, so too is the sense of a Devonian identity as being something more than English. 'My son is a bit of a Devon nationalist now,' Clive said with a shake of his head. 'He has that green, black and white Devon flag on his car.'

Having grown up in the town of Buckingham, not far from the concrete and roundabouts of Milton Keynes, I felt a longing for such a robust sense of identity. I don't know anyone who's ever stickered a Buckinghamshire flag on their car – probably because it rather distastefully depicts a chained swan on a black and blood-red field. The sense of local identity in Home Counties like Buckinghamshire has always seemed loose to me, while on a national level, there's no doubt that flying the English flag outside one's home conjures up images of far-right nationalism rather than the humbler patriotism I associate with the Union Jack. Here in the southwest, though, both sides of the River Tamar have zero shame flying their respective flags.

From the other side of the border, Celtic culture seemed more readily defined than its English counterpart. This was one of the reasons Claire had joined me on this journey along the Cornwall–Devon border. She was also searching for a sense of identity in a fragmented United Kingdom. When the pandemic struck, we'd both been living and working in Mexico. Our initial plan to see out the lockdown eating tacos and drinking mezcal didn't pan out, and we soon found ourselves in her grandmother's vacant house in Exmouth, Devon. We were there because we had nowhere else to go, but we soon fell for the town's long sandy beach, red sandstone cliffs and seaside spirit.

The long quiet weeks in the Devon house had reignited Claire's interest in her Cornish heritage. She spent evenings delving into birth, death and marriage certificates on the genealogy website Ancestry, uncovering tales of humble miners and noble Cornish gentry alike. Although Claire had grown up in London, her grandmother was originally from the former mining town of Camborne in western Cornwall, and her dad had always told her southwestern stories. Despite spending most of his life outside of the 'homeland', her dad is a proud Cornishman. He keeps a stash of Cornish Proper Job beers in his fridge in Kent and said he'd never known any other county in England with such an appreciation of its own identity as Cornwall, except perhaps Yorkshire.

But ever since the Great Western Railway bridged the River Tamar in the 1850s, British tourists, travellers and even Cornish emigrants have often romanticized Cornwall, remembering childhood holidays to sandy beaches or half-term breaks spent in briny fishing cottages. Perhaps that's because myths and legends have lingered on in Cornwall.

On the moors that rise between coastlines, ancient standing stones and menhirs sit under starry night skies that have changed little since the first Britons gazed upon them. Legends of battling giants, petrified maidens and Cornish *piskies* abound in a mist-strewn landscape. Cornwall is not just the fabled land of King Arthur, who is said to have been conceived at Tintagel Castle: the tale of Jack and the Beanstalk also has its origins in the giants of Cornish folklore. Another giant named Comoran is said to have built St Michael's Mount on Cornwall's southern shores.

It's easy to be swept up in folkloric tales of warring giants and legendary kings, but it's even easier to forget these stories trace their origins to a mythical Cornwall that never really existed. The reality of life in modern Cornwall is far from romantic, as the housing crisis and economic stagnation have shown – Cornwall is consistently ranked as one the poorest regions in the United Kingdom. This itself has contributed to the rise of a stronger Cornish identity and the rise of nationalist sentiment from parties like Mebyon Kernow.

Clive's transitional space in the Tamar Valley is thinning out at the expense of these stronger regional identities, and he admitted his beloved borderland identity is in decline. For Clive and his wife, this is a problem. They are neither entirely Cornish nor wholly Devonian, just as I am neither fully English nor wholly Scottish. Their home is the Tamar Valley, a valley crossing borders and boundaries.

'Where does one border really begin and another end? Who gets to decide?' Clive asked, as he walked us back to Bere Ferrers station. 'I keep fantasizing about making a

Tamar Valley flag. It could be black and green – a bit of the Cornish flag and a bit of the Devonian!'

Launceston

The Norman castle in Launceston casts a long shadow over its medieval streets. A rounded keep, made no less fearsome by its crumbling stone walls, occupies the highest point in Cornwall's former county town, rising above a second layer of walls and towers to form a formidable defensive ring designed to keep out even the most determined of Cornish warriors from the west.

Launceston is almost exactly halfway along the Devon and Cornwall border. As the traditional gateway to the west, I was here to discover how a Cornish cultural revival was strengthening local identities along the border.

After taking the train back to Plymouth, we'd driven north the next day, bypassing the Tamar Valley on its eastern flank, and passing through Devon villages with Anglo-Saxon names like Lifton ('-ton' is an Anglo-Saxon suffix for town) and Tinhay (*hay* is an old English word for an enclosed space). Once we were west of the River Tamar, Cornish names like Trebullett (*tre* is Cornish for settlement), Lewannick and Petherwin immediately jumped off the map as we found ourselves in a stretch of borderland becoming less hazy by the mile.

'Travellers coming out of Devon, lift up their hearts at the sight of Launceston!' recited Rob Tremain loudly and rather dramatically, greeting us with poetic lines by Sir John Betjemen at the top of Launceston's multi-storey car park. 'The Tamar is crossed, and here, at last, is the Duchy.'

Wearing a face mask made of Cornish tartan and carrying a tote bag emblazoned with the flag of St Piran, Rob was a caricature of Cornishness. Born and raised in Launceston, he's a former mayor and town councillor. He's also been the town crier for over forty-five years, after taking the job for what he thought would be just one day, when no one else was willing to ring the bell and shout 'Oyez, oyez, oyez.'

Rob has devoted himself to the Cornish cause. He was in his element showing us around his 'beloved *Lanson*', regaling us with stories of his time spent working at Tintagel Castle, the ancient seat of Cornish kings not far away on the north coast, where tales from Cornish mythology had cemented his love for Cornwall. This patriotism inspired him to almost single-handedly found Launceston's St Piran's day parade, a celebration of Cornwall's patron saint and all things Cornish which he leads every year, on 5 March. Rob was also president of Launceston's Old Cornwall Society, a group promoting and preserving Cornish history, and he successfully petitioned English Heritage to fly the Cornish flag from the ramparts of Launceston Castle, instead of the English cross of St George. If there was ever an example of how national identities become *more* defined on the border, Rob is it.

'The Cornish called this *Castle Terrible*,' Rob said ominously as he showed us into the castle's grounds, where disintegrating battlements faced westwards towards Cornish fields arrayed across a green valley. 'They used to hang Cornish agitators and rebels here.'

Built in 1068 by Robert de Mortain, the half-brother of William the Conqueror, Launceston Castle's round keep and stone walls were intended to subdue a semi-independent people the Anglo-Saxons had never truly conquered. Mortain replaced Anglo-Saxon lords with Breton nobles descended from refugees who'd fled Anglo-Saxon advances centuries earlier, and at the time, they spoke a language remarkably akin to Cornish.

The Cornish never entirely yielded to the Normans either. Instead, the Anglo-Normans created a distinct system of feudal overlordship particular to Cornwall. Successive heirs to the English throne were granted wide-ranging powers of taxation and control as the 'Earl of Cornwall', and in 1337, King John upgraded this to a dukedom, a rare political entity (the only other similar system is the Duchy of Lancaster) allowing the heir to the throne to generate an independent income at the expense of the Cornish. Despite its feudal roots – and the lingering spectre of Anglo-Saxon and Norman subjugation – it's a system often cited by Cornish nationalists as proof that Cornwall is indeed separate from England.

It's a system that still exists. Prince William, the current Duke of Cornwall, owns vast tracts of land and possesses the right to levy ancient taxes across the Duchy, a fact which Rob sees as a continuing form of subjugation. 'They're automatically "the prince" of Cornwall,' he said scathingly, as we walked through one of the castle's stone gates, and on to a narrow high street hemmed in by tall red-brick buildings occupied by bakeries, coffee shops and estate agents. 'The Duke of Cornwall is the owner of all mineral rights here, too, so if I find copper in my garden it goes to the Duchy!'

The Cornish never truly accepted the rule of English monarchs, but despite a series of bloody rebellions that sought to protect Cornish rights (two in 1497 and the last in 1549), centuries of English rule led to what Rob would call the forced Anglicization of Cornwall. This is most evident in shifting linguistic lines, as *Kernewek*, the ancient language of Cornwall, was pushed westwards, away from the banks of the River Tamar. Closely related to Welsh and Breton, the language clung on in the far west, but by the eighteenth century it was all but extinct, with the last native Cornish speaker traditionally being cited as having died in 1777. The language was revived by scholars in the twentieth century, at a time when Cornwall was attempting to reassert its fading Celtic identity in the wake of an economic crisis that resulted in the mass exodus of as many as 250,000 Cornish residents between 1861 and 1901.

In 1928, Cornish revivalist Henry Jenner founded a movement named Gorsedh Kernow (or in English, the 'Cornish Bards'): a group of poets, artists and storytellers tasked to 'maintain the national Celtic spirit of Cornwall' in the way of the Celtic bards of old. The organization still exists, and indeed, the 'Cornish revival' has picked up pace, with the number of Cornish-language speakers on the increase. In 2022, the Cornish-language singer Gwenno Saunders released an album entirely in Cornish, while the emergence of bilingual primary schools means that for the first time since the late eighteenth century, there are fluent bilingual speakers of *Kernewek* who have learnt the language from birth.

In Launceston, I saw buses with English and Cornish writing emblazoned across their red bodywork. And while you're unlikely to hear Cornish spoken unless you're actively seeking it out (the 2021 census recorded just 563 fluent Cornish speakers across Cornwall), Cornish language lessons are held once a week in the town's Methodist church, and flyers advertised *Yeth an Werin* (roughly translating to 'informal meetings of Cornish speakers') in local pubs.

The resurgence of Cornwall's sense of self is evident in other ways in Launceston. Rob, whose commitment to preserving Celtic culture saw him initiated as one of the Bards of Gorsedh Kernow, is now leading the slow but assured revival of Cornishness in the borderlands. As he guided us through streets sprawling outwards from Launceston Castle, he enthusiastically described how the St Piran's Day parade fills the town with Cornish bagpipers, singers and dancers. As we walked through Launceston, we saw Cornish flags and Union Jacks lining the high street. The local Tesco was even packed with traditional (but admittedly touristy) Cornish goods like pasties, Rattler cider and clotted cream, which we found in a dedicated Cornish section at the front of the supermarket.

The liminal space of the Tamar Valley ends in Launceston, the gateway to Cornwall, where the town's border location inspires locals like Rob to take up the Cornish revival in earnest. 'This little land of Cornwall, it's not an English county,' Rob sternly reminded me as we set off on the last leg of our journey into the Cornish-Devonian borderlands. 'We're proud to be British, but we're not English, we're Cornish.'

The Northern Borderlands

We left Rob in the multi-storey car park, driving our Renault Clio through Launceston's narrow medieval streets and on to the road back east, continuing our journey along the border.

This wasn't the modern A30 dual carriageway, but an ancient highway traversed by Britons and Dumnonians (the Celtic tribe who ruled much of the southwest after the fall of the Roman Empire), by the last Cornish kings and their Anglo-Saxon conquerors, and by the earls and dukes of Cornwall.

Driving over Polson Bridge, a couple of miles east of Launceston, we left Cornwall and re-entered Devon. Although it pales in size compared to the modern bridges spanning the River Tamar to the south, Polson Bridge has long been a symbolically significant crossing. In bygone times, Cornish rebels marched over on their way to fight English kings, and in a curious medieval tradition that's survived into the modern era: once a year at the bridge Cornish gentry present their duke with a pint of cumin, an ash-wood bow and a grey riding crop.

It's also been the scene of bridge blocking, that most popular of southwestern protests. One such protest broke out in 2016, when Cornish councillors and patriots – led by the Grand Bard of the Gorsedh Kernow, who was dressed in a flowing, druid-like blue robe – marched on to the bridge amid a stream of Cornish flags and songs. The march was part of a wider campaign against an ill-thought-out plan, conjured up in Westminster, to unite the two counties as one parliamentary constituency under the name 'Devonwall'. Rob had been in the thick of the action, and I was intrigued, because it hadn't just been the Cornish fighting to preserve their old border, but Devonians, too. Neither side wanted a giant, cross-border administrative region. Devon and Cornwall cherish the strength of their local identities, and so the Devonwall plan was scrapped.

Beyond Polson Bridge, the border became a ragged

patchwork of confused boundaries I now wanted to unravel. No longer constrained by wide banks as the River Tamar narrowed, the border followed its own path, leaving entire parishes on the 'wrong' side of an ever-confused borderland. The further north we drove, the more nauseating it became to follow the border, and I held on as Claire swerved the car around a tight bend flanked by stout oaks. We emerged from the shadows of a sunken hollow, an old track used by Devonshire drovers for a thousand years, and she slammed on the brakes as a Range Rover hurtled into view. The driver reversed into a passing place where trees gave way to open fields, and we continued onwards, as I desperately tracked dashed borderlines on the map and shouted directions to Claire.

A packhorse bridge took us over the River Ottery – a tributary of the Tamar which Cornish historian Philip Payton calls 'an ethnic and linguistic border', and into North Petherwin, a Cornish parish historically in Devon until its transfer to Cornwall in 1966.

We crossed eastwards, but there were no signs marking what should have been our re-entry into Devon. Instead, we found ourselves in North Tamerton, the only parish in Cornwall that extends east over the River Tamar. A tiny parish of flat green fields, the odd farmhouse turned holiday cottage, and nothing much else, North Tamerton was once the home of an eccentric opium addicted reverend named Robert Stephen Hawker, famed for composing the unofficial national anthem of Cornwall.

An epic ballad of rebellion, 'The Song of the Western Men' tells of Cornish rebels marching into England to set right an injustice. It's still sung with a tear in the eye at rugby matches, sea-shanty festivals and late-night pub lock-ins across Cornwall.

Claire – whose dad taught her the song when she was young – sang as we drove through the village:

> *A good sword and a trusty hand!*
> *A merry heart and true!*
> *King James's men shall understand*
> *What Cornish lads can do.*
> *And have they fixed the where and when?*
> *And shall Trelawny die?*
> *Here's twenty thousand Cornishmen*
> *Will know the reason why!*

Somewhere along the country road the song ended, Devon began and we found ourselves in Bridgerule, a village cut in two by the River Tamar. We'd arrived on the eastern bank of the river, but since the Devonian village largely sits on the western bank, Bridgerule has long been a source of grief for Claire's dad. On the other side of a narrow packhorse bridge, a sign outside the Bridge Inn proclaimed it to be the only pub in Devon *west* of the River Tamar. Claire sent her dad a photo. He replied quickly, exclaiming that, clearly, the pub was breaking international law. For Claire's dad, and the vast majority of Cornish people you'll ever meet, anything west of the River Tamar is Cornish – and how dare the English encroach on their territory.

It was a slow weekday afternoon; the pub was closed, and there wasn't a local in sight. Instead of enjoying a pint of Doom Bar on the banks of the Tamar, we followed a maze of country lanes east to the market town of Holsworthy, where we popped into the local museum to find out what effect these confusing boundaries have had on local identities.

When we walked through the door, the museum's curator, Diane Green, was pacing around, hectically collecting frayed papers and dusty maps. Holsworthy Museum is home to five cluttered rooms of 'nostalgia and local history', and after I'd phoned ahead the day before, Diane had helpfully trawled through the archives, finding documents charting local boundary changes over the centuries.

Diane, an excitable volunteer who selflessly sacrifices her time to help with curious projects like my own, showed me a map dated 1809. 'All the parishes are on the wrong side!' she said, in a sort of 'huzzah' moment, as if we'd pinpointed the location of the Holy Grail rather than a few shifts in local administrative boundaries. I was just as excited as her. 'North Petherwin is shown within Devon, but now it's in Cornwall,' she continued, tracing lines over the old map. 'I don't know how it came to be in Devon!'

We enthusiastically followed the map's boundary lines north. 'North Tamerton is really peculiar,' she continued in a tone filled with genuine intrigue, her glasses slipping down her nose as she peered closer at the map. 'The postal address is Holsworthy, which is Devon. You write a letter to Devon, but it's actually going to Cornwall. They used to have awful arguments with the phone directory. It's in Cornwall, even though it's always been east of the River Tamar.'

Her finger halted on Bridgerule. 'I live on the west side of Bridgerule,' she explained, happy we'd taken the time to visit her village earlier. 'The county border goes diagonally across our back garden, then around our house. The property is in Devon, but the road is in Cornwall. We get all sorts of problems with councils arguing over responsibility for things.'

While the Cornish, as Claire's dad had already shown us, believe the River Tamar to be an immovable border, history has shown the opposite. In reality, it's always been a porous frontier, a borderland of shifting allegiances and changing boundaries. The northern stretches of the River Tamar aren't the only plots of land to have changed hands over time: the Rame Peninsula, southwest of Plymouth, has long been a source of contention between Devon and Cornwall. Bounded to the north by the River Tamar, where the waterway empties into Plymouth Sound, and to the south by the English Channel, parts of the Rame Peninsula were held by an Anglo-Saxon earldom for centuries, despite being on the 'wrong' side of the border. The small village of Kingsand, perched on the peninsula's eastern shores and facing towards Plymouth Sound, remained a Devonian exclave until 1844, when it was returned to Cornwall as part of the Counties (Detached Parts) Act, a Victorian effort to straighten out administrative lines on the map.

Diane explained how until 1844, counties were a mishmash of enclaves and exclaves dating back to feudal times, when lords claimed ownership over individual parishes and parcels of land. Parts of Durham had been in Yorkshire and Northumberland; Buckinghamshire had exclaves in Hertfordshire; and villages in Devon were geographically located in what should have been Dorset or Cornwall, just as we'd seen during our drive along the border.

Then, with the stroke of a Victorian administrator's pen, boundaries were redefined, and people found themselves in new jurisdictions. Along the Cornish-Devonian border, where regional identities were strong, it may have felt like villages had moved countries rather than counties.

With so many shifting boundaries along the border's length, I asked Diane if there were strong Devonian or Cornish identities along the northern banks of the River Tamar. 'It depends on who you speak to,' she said, after some thought. 'There's a peculiar border identity. In Bridgerule and Holsworthy, for example, we eat our cream teas the Cornish way. We spread the jam, then put on a dollop of cream. I never realized until I visited Barnstaple in North Devon where they do it differently.'

Diane theorized that Bridgerule ended up in Devon purely because the local church was on the eastern side of the River Tamar. Neither side had any say in the boundary changes, and many residents have never lost their sense of Cornishness. Unfortunately, she added, this sometimes caused tensions.

'The lady who runs the pub in Bridgerule,' Diane switched to a low murmur, as if we were conspirators. 'She told me she once went to another pub over the border and was met with outright hostility. She said: "I'm a local." They asked where she was from. She said: "From Bridgerule, two miles away." They said: "That's Devon, so get out of the pub. We don't like incomers."'

Hearsay or not, the anecdote showed how nationalism dilutes cross-border unity. 'There's a lot of nationalism in Cornwall, some of it nasty,' she continued, before telling us how the revival of the Cornish identity was strengthening her sense of a Devonian identity. 'They want their own parliament, and I can't blame them. Westminster is so far away.

But if the Cornish get their own parliament, we should get one here in Devon.'

Like Cornwall, Devon has its own share of problems, and Diane seemed happy to vent her frustrations about Holsworthy, telling me how the 800-year-old market has all but gone, charity shops line the high street and house prices have shot up, despite there being few employment opportunities outside of agriculture. 'What are locals supposed to do?' she asked, as we helped her collect the maps as she prepared to close the museum for the day. 'It's all gone downhill. But it has everywhere in Britain, I suppose.'

It was a bleaker outlook than I'd hoped, but I was reminded that while my focus had largely been on Cornwall, Devon is just as proud to wave its flag. Regional identities in the southwest are strong, and the Cornish-Devonian rivalry is age-old. I hope, though, that rivalry remains friendly, rather than descending into petty disputes about which side of a boundary someone comes from.

We spent the night in a field outside Holsworthy, where a farmer had built shepherd's huts overlooking the borderlands. 'Oh, if I was over the border in Cornwall, I could charge an extra £20 a night,' he mused, as he showed us to our wooden hut. 'It's a strong tourism brand they have over there these days.'

We awoke to find a thick blanket of fog stretching westwards towards the River Tamar and jumped in the car to escape the chilly morning frost. I wanted to find the source of the Tamar – the source of the division between Devon and Cornwall – which supposedly lay a few miles further north, at a place called Woolley Moor. We found the moor, where the Tamar begins in a muddy, waterlogged field, but the road next to it was deluged with brown flood water. The source remained hidden behind hedgerows, and no footpaths led to the spring feeding a river that's divided two nations.

At the time of my first visit, no signs even noted that the source was near by. It felt so anticlimactic, disrespectful even, that the source of this great waterway – which has such a strong hold on the hearts and minds of the Cornish – was so close, yet not even marked.

I was reminded of a tale I'd been told by a seasoned West Country journalist, which hints at the more extreme depths of nationalist feeling some in Cornwall hold for their border. He said he'd once reported a story from this exact spot, some time in the 1980s, when a group of Cornish men drove a digger to the river's source and were arrested after attempting to dig a channel north. Their grand plan was to connect the Tamar to Marsland Water, which flows towards the Bristol Channel. If the conspirators had succeeded in their ambitious work of nationalist engineering, they'd have turned much of Cornwall into an island. Or so I was told. Unfortunately, I've never been able to verify the story.

Years later, when I returned, I was happy to see that a granite monument now sits on the roadside, alerting passers-by that here at Woolley Moor the River Tamar begins its long journey south to Plymouth Sound.

The growing mass of dark clouds spurred us onwards, and the stark, sullen landscape of the Marsland Valley marked the end of the border. Natural folds formed by the movement of tectonic plates several ages ago had left an undulating *combe* (an Old English word for 'valley') with steep, barren sides. The western side of the valley was in Cornwall, of course, and the east in Devon. The border's northern reaches are unpopulated compared to the south. The land is dotted with isolated farms and small hamlets hidden away in *combes* like this. There are no great ports – just small fishing harbours carved from granite cliffs, as boundaries blur along a harsh coastline, uniting those on either side of the border through sheer isolation.

We trudged through never-ending mizzle until we reached a wooden sign planted into the rocks. *Welcome to Kernow*, I read, before we crossed the river and dragged ourselves uphill to the northernmost point of the border. 'My gran used to tell me that this wasn't the "real" Cornwall,' Claire said, as we stared across to grey clouds in the Bristol Channel. 'She always said the real Cornwall was in the west.'

Claire's gran was right, of course, because the borderland we'd just travelled through was not quite Devon, nor Cornwall, but a middle land where local identities have traditionally coexisted to the point of merging. This mixed identity struck me vividly in the Tamar Valley, where Clive, the ever-avid geographer, had dreamt of a cross-border flag for his beloved community. It's this hazy in-between which I believe inspires the strength of the British identity: an identity uniting all on different sides of its borderlines rather than dividing them.

But like Britishness itself, this middle land is diminishing. Protests against second homes and economic disparity have become common occurrences further west, in places like St Austell, St Ives and Truro, Cornwall's capital. There are marches, as action groups and campaigners suggest that independence (or more realistically, a devolved parliament) would be a solution to economic problems.

Launceston, and its diehard town crier Rob Tremain, had demonstrated the strength of a resurgent Cornish identity stretching to the banks of the River Tamar. Rob would say this is how things should always have been. But while stronger national identities play an integral role in modern, multicultural Britain, they also leave less room for the more complex identities in between, in places like the Tamar Valley, or among the shifting boundaries around Holsworthy where we'd seen how nationalism can divide.

In borderlands, the only constant is change. The River Tamar was never the immovable barrier that Athelstan envisaged, and the boundaries between Devon and Cornwall have shifted backwards and forwards over the centuries. Like the borders that define it, so too will the United Kingdom evolve, and – depending on the politics and desires of its people – perhaps even devolve further.

Now, it was time to travel west into deepest Cornwall, where *Kernewek* is being revived and where the Cornish identity is surely strongest. On Britain's most south-westerly frontier, where the sun sets at Land's End, I hoped to find what it meant to be Cornish, and perhaps, to discover if the Cornish truly did want independence.

2
Western Cornwall

They shall have a name perpetual and fame permanent and immortal.

> Memorial to An Gof and Thomas Flamank, leaders of the 1497 Cornish rebellion, on the site of their defeat at Blackheath, London

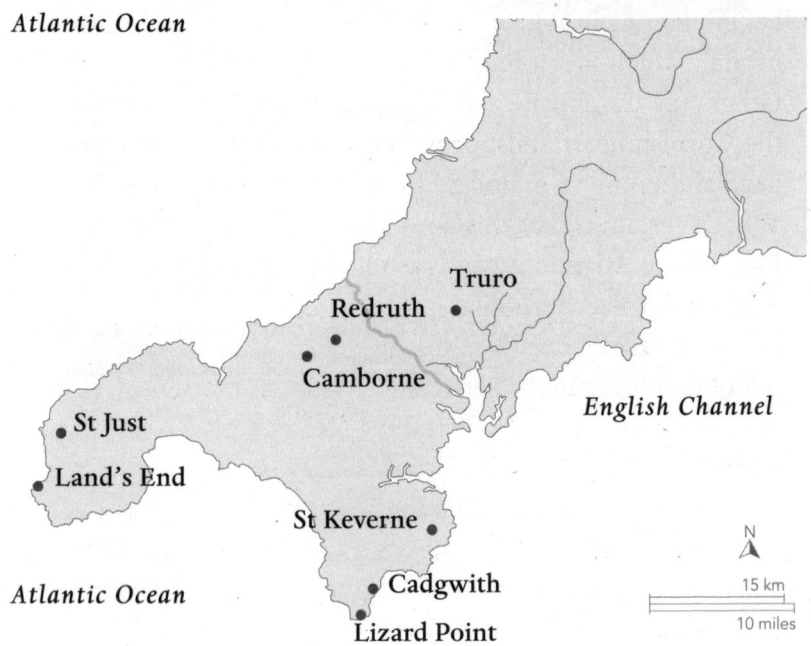

St Keverne

It was another grey October day when we crossed the Tamar Bridge. *Kernow a'gas dynergh*. The ancient words of *Kernewek* flashed past as the A38 swept us ever westwards, across an invisible boundary that splits the Cornish peninsula between east and west. No one's sure exactly where this 'border' begins. Some say Truro, Cornwall's only city and its de facto capital, which lies some fifty miles from the River Tamar. Others say Camborne and Redruth, twin mining towns in the Cornish heartlands; or perhaps the Lizard, an isolated headland home to mainland Britain's southernmost point. What's certain is that this borderland culminates at Land's End, where Atlantic waves crash into granite cliffs on Britain's southwestern frontier.

A bastion of Cornish culture, Britain's extreme southwest is a borderland caught between the Atlantic Ocean and the constant pressure of Anglicization. The last holdout of the Cornish language, linguistic maps show the slow retreat of *Kernewek* westwards through the centuries. As the language withered, it was here in the west where the disaffected Cornish roused medieval rebellions. In more recent times, it's in western Cornwall – a land of pastel-coloured fishing villages and glorious sandy beaches, beloved by legions of holidaymakers – that economic stagnation and overtourism are fermenting nationalist sentiment and inspiring a resurgent Cornish identity.

The next leg of my journey would take me across this cultural and linguistic boundary into western Cornwall. As I searched for the 'true' meaning of Cornishness, I wanted to know why so many campaigned for devolution, what drives Cornish nationalism and – in extreme circles – why a minority desires independence. I would start on the Lizard, where bloody rebellion tore Britain asunder five centuries ago, before tracing Cornwall's western divide north to Camborne and Redruth, where among old miners' cottages support for Mebyon Kernow, Cornwall's nationalist party, is strongest. Finally, I would drive west to St Just to see the Cornish revival in full swing, just a stone's throw from Land's End, where Britain ends – or perhaps, where Cornwall begins.

Rain spattered St Keverne's village square. A damp Cornish flag hung limply above the churchyard's weather-beaten headstones, and a muddy tractor sprawled across two parking spaces outside Londis. Set among rolling Cornish countryside on the Lizard (mainland Britain's most southerly landmass, some seventy miles west of the River Tamar) St Keverne is, on first inspection, an unremarkable village. Cottages, some thatched, lined tight streets, and the corner shop advertised an upcoming harvest festival in colourful typefaces. But on a hot summer's day in 1497 – far removed from the endless autumn rain we experienced – a humble blacksmith named Michael Joseph rallied a crowd on the green-hued, serpentinite steps of St Keverne's churchyard.

Decrying King Henry VII's debilitating taxes, Michael Joseph – or An Gof, as he's known in Cornish ('the Blacksmith') – teamed up with Thomas Flamank, a learned lawyer from Bodmin. Together, they marched an army of some 15,000 Cornishmen and Devonians into England. At Blackheath – a few miles outside London's city walls – the ragtag rebel army of farmers and tin miners met a bloody end in battle against King Henry VII's mounted knights. Thousands were killed, and the two ringleaders were dealt a grizzly death – they were hung, drawn and quartered for treason. An Gof is said to have claimed to a baying crowd before he died that he'd have 'a name perpetual and a fame immortal', and though England has forgotten, Cornwall remembers.

Before parking in the square, we'd stopped on the sloping hill leading down to the village for a photograph with An Gof and Flamank. They've found immortality in statue form. The blacksmith's muscled arm is raised high, his foot placed firmly on an anvil. Flamank clutches a scroll in one fist, his other arm resting on An Gof's shoulder. Tourists drive by, oblivious, on their way to holiday homes on the Lizard's salty coastline. It's an episode of British history I had never learnt about in school, but here in Cornwall, this little-known rebellion fuelled the fires of Cornish nationalism. By digging into the Lizard's rebellious past, I hoped to uncover the smouldering nationalist embers now stoking Cornwall's reawakening. There was no better place to start than St Keverne, where An Gof led a rebellion five hundred years ago.

We hurried inside the Three Tuns, a cosy pub next to the church, where stalwart regulars sipped pints of Doom Bar and nibbled on lemon drizzle cake from the pub's weekday charity bake sale. We found Karen – a local teacher, head of St Keverne's history society and a lifelong supporter of

Mebyon Kernow – sitting at a wooden table strewn with history books and newspaper cuttings.

Like Rob Tremain, Karen is a Bard of the Gorsedh Kernow, an honour recognizing her lifelong service to Cornish culture and history. She was dressed in a neat pink sweater and had the air of a stern teacher; the kind you'd never answer back to in class. She confidently strode through the pub, saying hi to the regulars, and returned moments later with a plate of cake.

I'd asked Karen if she could help us understand what drove Cornwall to bloody rebellion all those years ago. After ordering a round of pints and a pot of tea for us all, I was surprised when our conversation began not in 1497, but in 1997. In a booming voice that reverberated off the pub's timbers, she reminisced with excitement about how in 1997 she'd taken part in Keskerdh Kernow 500, a grand recreation of An Gof and Flamank's march to London.

'The five hundredth anniversary of the great Cornish rebellion of 1497 was a glorious day,' a triumphant Karen recalled as she shared out lemon drizzle. 'We all assembled outside the churchyard, just like An Gof and his rebels, and marched out of the village, east towards England.'

Karen had kept faded clippings from local newspapers, showing a crowd of hundreds waving Cornish flags as a piper led them out of St Keverne. She'd marched for a week through Cornwall. Around forty others marched 300 miles, all the way to London. Hundreds more, including Karen, rejoined the march in Blackheath, where the swelling ranks of the procession lowered their flags and unveiled a memorial by the mass grave of rebels killed in battle.

'Here on the Lizard, and further west towards Penwith,

we were the last of the Cornish speakers,' Karen said, explaining wistfully how western Cornwall had been a tinderbox of rebellion waiting for a spark. 'In the fifteenth century, English was replacing Cornish. The Cornish gentry, all the people with wealth and power, were Anglicized, so it's no accident the rebels were from Cornish-speaking areas.'

Fuelled by the losses at Blackheath, the disaffected Cornish were stirred into a second rebellion in 1497, when Perkin Warbeck – a pretender to the English throne, who claimed to be the son of the deposed King Edward IV – raised another army and marched over the River Tamar. The rebellion came to an ignominious end when Warbeck was routed outside Taunton. In 1549, another great rebellion painted Devon's rolling hills and Cornwall's granite cliffs red with blood, when Cornish and Devonian alike rose up in arms to protest the new religious order imposed upon them by the Tudor boy king, Edward VI, who planned to install a new English-language prayer book in churches.

The Devonians saw the new Protestant prayer book as an attack on their Catholic faith, while the Cornish saw it as an attack on both their faith and their language. The Prayer Book Rebellion lasted two and a half months. By summer's end, six thousand rebels lay dead, and I was shocked when Karen said that in Clyst St Mary – a Devon village about a hundred miles from St Keverne – royalist soldiers relieving the siege of Exeter executed, in cold blood, some six hundred Cornish and Devonian prisoners of war. The new prayer book was imposed, and Cornish churches were forced to perform services in English.

St Keverne was swept up in this rebellion, too. The parish priest, Robert Raffe, was hanged from the church steeple. The

Prayer Book Rebellion's upheavals marked the downward spiral of Cornwall's distinct Celtic language, but it lingered on in the Lizard, where I heard snatched words of Cornish dialect drifting across the Three Tuns. Five hundred years later, the march to Blackheath demonstrated the strength of the Cornish revival, but centuries of Anglicization have left St Keverne divided, and Karen was furious that her own steely love for Cornwall isn't always shared by her fellow villagers.

'We had to fight,' she said, describing the battle to erect An Gof's statue in martial terms. 'Some councillors said he fought against the king, against his country, that he's a traitor and his statue couldn't be next to the war memorial. That's why the statue is at the top of the village, not in the village square. It divided the village, and that's because not everyone was taught the history of the rebellions, even here in Cornwall.'

Disheartened by a lack of understanding, recognition and knowledge of Cornish history, Karen wants Cornwall to change its Anglocentric school curriculums. 'People in England don't understand that Cornwall is separate,' she said, as I took a deep sip of my pint, buckling up as Karen gave the now-nervous Englishman in me a hard lesson in Cornishness. 'Never use the "C-Word". Never call Cornwall a *county*. It's not. You *can* call it the Duchy of Cornwall. It gives you more of an air of separatism. That's important to *us* at present.'

By 'us', Karen meant Cornish nationalists like herself. She's adamant Cornwall should run its own affairs. She blames English immigration to Cornwall for what she sees as the Duchy's failure to unite on issues like devolution, which was consistently rejected by a Conservative-majority council until a 'Devolution Deal' was finally struck in 2023. The deal provides Cornwall with increased autonomy in certain areas of local government, including green energy, adult education and access to funding that supports Cornish culture and language, to protect Cornwall's distinct identity. For many – including Karen – the deal didn't go nearly far enough, and there are continued calls for a fully devolved Cornish Assembly, or Senedh Kernow, which would have the same devolved powers as the Welsh and Scottish parliaments to create laws in areas as wide-ranging as health, education, agriculture, justice and even taxation.

'I'm in the minority,' said Karen, fired up by the elusive dream of an independent Cornwall. 'Most people here, even on the Lizard, don't see Cornishness as a thing any more. The problem is that half the population aren't local. I feel like a foreigner in my own land. I'd say that English people coming into Cornwall is a form of modern colonialism. They're Tory voters, they buy expensive houses, and they don't see Cornwall as a distinct place.'

A modern day An Gof, Karen regularly takes part in independence marches, organizing what she sees as the last stand of her Cornish homeland in the face of English expansionism. She'd be quite happy if the River Tamar's bridges were blocked and the Torpoint Ferry from Plymouth run aground. I was slightly unsettled. Although Karen had the best interests of her beloved Cornwall at heart, and despite her infectious Cornish pride, I wondered if there was a touch of xenophobia aimed at her English neighbours. I finished my pint before asking: 'So, who has the right to call themselves Cornish?'

'Everyone wants a sense of identity,' she replied, which

I wholeheartedly agreed with. 'If you've got a way to link yourself to a defined sense of identity, you take it. But if I'm brutally honest with you, a Cornish person is someone who was born here, who has Cornish forebears.

'But the other part of me says that if you feel Cornish in your heart,' she added, noticing our discomfort at the increasingly anti-English tangent we'd taken. 'If you really love Cornwall, and you love its history and culture, then you're welcome here.'

She announced she needed to prepare for a march the next day in St Austell with Yes Kernow – an organization inspired by the similar Yes Cymru and Yes Scotland campaigns advocating for independence in their respective Celtic lands. After finishing the cake, we bid farewell and hopped in the car for the short drive south to Lizard Point.

Karen's fiery nationalist rhetoric stayed with us as we navigated slender lanes before bursting on to the peninsula's windswept coastline. I mulled over her view that only those born and raised in Cornwall were truly Cornish. Claire, who is half Cornish, would fail Karen's test. In Scotland, by the same measure, my Celtic claims would have no grounding at all. I'd only been born in Aberdeen and spent little time there before I moved south of the border with my English parents.

Karen is right to stand up for Cornwall's identity, but hard-line principles serve to alienate Cornish supporters like us who don't have the luxury of such neat national divisions. Unlike Karen, who is unwavering in her national beliefs, identity often isn't confined to one place alone. It drifts across Britain's boundaries. For us to exclusively choose one side of our identity would be to surrender the other.

In the southwest, the lines between England, Britain and

Cornwall have blurred for centuries. As we parked outside a busy ice-cream parlour by Lizard Point, I wondered if An Gof, Flamank and the tens of thousands who died in the Cornish rebellions would agree with Karen. Perhaps they'd embrace anyone who supported the Cornish cause, regardless of where they were born or raised.

Lizard Point is a true national frontier. These days, you might spot the red sails of a Cornish lugger, or the belching funnels of a cruise ship as seals slap around on the rocks below. If you were here on 29 July 1588, you'd have seen rigging and cannons as the Spanish Armada sailed past to make war on England. We bought ourselves a few scoops of Roskilly's Cornish ice cream (made in a dairy outside St Keverne) to sweeten the soured mood, then hopped back in the car for another short drive through narrowing country lanes overshadowed by thick hedgerows and a thicker sense of claustrophobia. We arrived abruptly, some twenty minutes later, on the Lizard's sheltered southeastern coast. Three hundred years of history creaked beneath our feet as we checked into Cadgwith Cove Inn. We hauled our bags up the rickety stairs and collapsed on the bed, badly in need of rest before we explored Cornwall's maritime identity in one of the Lizard's age-old fishing villages the next day.

Cadgwith

We were woken by squawking seagulls. I pulled back the yellow curtains and sunlight burst into the cramped room. Down on the shingle beach, clanking tractors pushed fishing trawlers into the rolling surf. Despite the early-morning noise, with clear skies and calm seas, Cadgwith was like a Cornish postcard.

In the Cadgwith Cove Inn's nautical-themed breakfast room, a placard on the stone wall joked that Cadgwith is a 'drinking village with a fishing problem'. Lobster pots and rusting anchors spoke of the village's fishing traditions, and I felt like I was on a fishing schooner as the smell of frying mackerel wafted through from the kitchen.

On a peninsula surrounded by water on three sides, Cornwall's maritime identity is intertwined with its wider 'national' identity. Cadgwith, with its picturesque stone harbour, perched on Britain's southern frontier, is the epitome of a Cornish fishing village. Given the steady decline of the United Kingdom's fishing communities, I wanted to know if this vital component of Cornwall's heritage can survive in an age of industrial trawlers and fishing quotas.

Fuelled up on fresh fish caught in the English Channel, we strolled out on to 'the Todden', a short strip of granite and serpentinite rocks glistening with seaweed that divides the northern and southern beaches – for Cadgwith is a tale of two beaches. From our slight vantage point on the Todden, we watched a woman in a frayed cable-knit sweater throw a bucket of fish guts over the rocks. On the southern side, a couple cracked a bottle of breakfast bubbly on the patio of a seafront holiday home, and cold-water swimmers donned wetsuits next to stacks of kayaks and paddleboards piled up on the shingle.

Fish blood is ground into the very mortar holding Cadgwith's creaking buildings together. The grime and guts of a working harbour mix with the leisurely life of holidaymakers, and I chuckled at another comedy sign outside the

Cadgwith Cove Crab – selling crab sandwiches for £8.50 a pop – which said, 'Beware the locals; don't feed.' Boats have launched from these beaches for hundreds of years. Cadgwith's boom years came when vast shoals of pilchards – a type of sardine – arrived off the coast of Cornwall, seemingly out of nowhere, in the 1750s. They were caught using huge seine nets (the largest recorded haul in Cadgwith was 1.3 million pilchards on a single day in 1845) then salted, pressed into barrels and shipped off to be sold to Catholic countries with a penchant for Fish Fridays. But as abruptly as they'd arrived, the pilchards disappeared. No one's quite sure why (perhaps it was overfishing, migration or a combination of both), but by the late nineteenth century, pilchard fishing was no longer viable. This, alongside the increasing mechanization of the fishing industry throughout the twentieth century, threw Cadgwith's small fleet into decline.

We left the beach to follow the South West Coast Path. A few miles of tramping up and down steep pathways and gorse-covered cliffs brought us to the neighbouring village of the Lizard, where we met Nigel Legge, a semi-retired fisherman and artist who'd agreed to tell us more about the local fishing heritage. We found him in a workshop strewn with bundles of fresh willow sticks, salt-stained fishing nets and half-finished paintings. Nigel, who looked every part the fisherman in his worn cable-knit jumper – the unofficial uniform of Cornwall's fishing community – and thick beard, had fished out of Cadgwith's harbour for decades. Now he spends his days handcrafting 'withy pots', a traditional willow lobster pot used by Devon and Cornwall's fishermen for over a thousand years.

Nigel was busy weaving. He gruffly explained how the

pots he makes are largely sold as ornaments or television props these days. Few fishers use them any more, given the ready availability of robust plastic and metal fishing gear. He also explained how Cornwall's small fishing fleets, based in traditional harbours like Cadgwith, struggle to compete with large trawlers working out of big ports like Newlyn and Falmouth. Nigel, his hands scarred by decades of hauling lines and weaving tough willow, said that Cadgwith is still one of the luckier fishing villages.

'There are far less boats down there than when I was a boy,' he said in a heavy Cornish accent, not taking his eyes off the willow he was bending into a bell shape. 'Everyone's involved in crab and lobsters now. That's where the money is, but some of the bigger boats still go fishing.'

With high overheads, strict bureaucracy, complex fishing quotas and depleted stocks to deal with, Brexit made a tough business harder, with Cornish fishers now struggling to sell their catch over the resurrected maritime borders separating Cornwall from Europe. It's a bitter irony, given Cornwall voted in the majority to leave the EU. Many in Cadgwith have now turned to tourism. Nigel runs coastal tours in his fishing boat, and fishers sell their catch directly to pubs, hotels and tourists. It's a catch-22, though. As more tourists fell for Cadgwith's pretty harbour, developers bought up fishing cottages, forcing many young fishers out of a local property market where their ancestors had lived for centuries.

Things came to a head when the old cellars and Winch House on the seafront opposite the Cadgwith Inn were eyed up by developers. The ancient buildings, used for storage and maintenance, are vital to Cadgwith's fishing fleet, so the village banded together and raised a staggering £300,000 to save them. Like the Cornish rebels of old, Cadgwith refused to surrender, and the buildings are now owned by the Cadgwith Fishing Cove Trust for community use.

We left Nigel weaving withy pots and hiked back to Cadgwith before the sun set in a blaze of purple and red over the harbour. That Friday night, as drinkers spilt into the Cadgwith Cove Inn, we had a glimpse into a traditional way of life now so alien to many of us.

Distracted by the sight of one of Nigel's paintings hanging behind the beer taps, I smacked my head on the low hanging timber door frame leading into the bar. Dan the barman poured me a welcome pint of Tribute as I nursed the bump. He's proud of his own Cornish heritage, but prouder still that the village had saved its fishing sheds. 'It was an epic fundraiser,' he said, effortlessly pouring pints. 'Otherwise, it would all have been lost.'

I chuckled at yet *another* comedy placard, this time warning visitors 'against the danger of seasickness while listening to the nautical chat in the bar', and we sat down for dinner on a wooden barrel perched next to a steering helm. 'All fresh from the fishermen over the road,' said Dan when he brought over the seafood special, consisting of mounds of crab linguine topped with an entire seabass. 'They wouldn't come in to sing for us if we didn't buy their fish. Grab a seat outside right after dinner or you'll be standing all evening!'

Cadgwith's singing fishers bellow out sea shanties and Cornish yarns in the pub's front yard every Friday night. It's a tradition known as St Inebriates' Night. Named for a completely made-up Irish monk, locals gleefully explain to gullible visitors like me how Saint Inebriates was shipwrecked, and arrived at Cadgwith's pub on a raft made of empty beer barrels. Saint Inebriates would've been proud as the pints did the rounds on the cold patio just metres from the beach. After young and old alike sang (or shouted) 'Drunken Sailor', the lady standing next to us – a nurse from Devon – told me she'd been visiting the Cadgwith Singers every year since she was sixteen. One summer in Cadgwith, she fell in love with a Cornish fisherman. Her heart was broken when he went to work at sea in the Isles of Scilly, and they never met again. At the bar, when someone bought me a pint of beer and asked if I'd found my sea legs yet, I concluded that yes, Cadgwith was a drinking village with a fishing problem.

By 10 p.m., the singers had pints in each hand. As the booze flowed thick as the English Channel's salty waters, we shed a tear when the solemn 'Song of the Western Men' was sung. More tears were shed all around as the Cadgwith Singers rounded off the night with a heartfelt rendition of 'Cornwall My Home'. Everyone who knew the words sang out: 'Because I was born here, and here shall I die. This is my Cornwall, and this is my home.'

Dan kicked everyone out at midnight. We stumbled up the creaky stairs and woke the next morning with hoarse throats and sore heads. In Cadgwith, the salt hangs heavy in the air, and the smell of fish lingers on clothes long after you've left. The village remains a bastion of Cornishness, and with tangible links to a maritime heritage stretching through the centuries like a tangled but ever-enduring fishing line, I was envious of their robust sense of place and identity. With full hearts and weak stomachs, we skipped the mackerel that morning. We checked out of the Cadgwith Inn and drove north to Camborne and Redruth.

Camborne and Redruth

Driving north, I now wanted to see Mebyon Kernow's heartland, where elements of a disgruntled electorate have welcomed calls for devolution and are drawing on their distinct Cornish identity to develop new cultural and economic opportunities in some of Cornwall's most impoverished areas.

Camborne, which sits approximately twenty miles north of the Lizard and three miles south of Cornwall's northern coastline, is no more than a ten-minute drive from its twin town of Redruth. Every year, thousands of spectators watch a brutal rugby derby fought between the two. The rivalry is fierce, and if you call a Cambornite a Redruthian – or vice versa – you'll be chased out of town. Call anyone English, though, and you'll incite another Cornish rebellion.

The twin towns were at the forefront of the industrial revolution. On Christmas Eve 1801, Cornish inventor Richard Trevithick made history when he drove himself and six friends up Camborne's Fore Street in the world's first steam-powered passenger vehicle, an invention that would forever revolutionize train travel. Redruth and Camborne were once pillars of the Cornish mining industry, too. Given that Britons were refining tin on the Cornish peninsula eight thousand years ago, mining was long integral to Cornwall's identity. The skills of the tin miners were held in such high regard that in 1201, King John I allowed Cornish tinners to create administrative areas called 'Stannaries', forming what was effectively a local parliament for Cornwall's miners.

The Stannaries were hugely powerful, holding the right to levy taxes and pass judgments in court. Although this power was later curtailed (the last Stannary Court sat in Truro in 1753), the Stannaries were never legally revoked, and like the 'Duchy', the peculiar system is held up as another example of Cornwall's historical independence from England. However, there are no tin miners left for the Stannaries to preside over. Cornwall's last tin mine shut down in 1998, and the low-lying valley between Camborne and Redruth is littered with the hulking stone remnants and broken wheelhouses of the King Edward Mine, which closed its shafts in the early twentieth century.

Crumbling chimneys blighting Cornish landscapes are a reminder of a past identity whose demise has left Cornwall with unplugged economic gaps. Far from the holiday homes and celebrity chef-run restaurants on the coast, I was astounded to discover that Camborne has the highest rate of food-bank usage in the UK. Poverty feeds nationalism, so no wonder Mebyon Kernow's calls for autonomy are welcomed in one of the most economically deprived regions in Northern Europe.

Cornwall's national party have consistently held multiple seats on both Camborne and Redruth's town councils, and in 2022, Camborne elected a Mebyon Kernow candidate as mayor. I once interviewed one of Camborne's Mebyon Kernow councillors, Ryan Congdon, who explained how the party's goal wasn't necessarily independence, but rather full devolution within Britain. When we spoke, he highlighted Camborne's housing crisis, Cornwall's unsustainable tourism industry and the decline of traditional industries like fishing, agriculture and mining as huge factors in local discontent and economic degradation. With more autonomy, he believes Cornwall could apply local solutions to local problems, including tourist taxes and stricter rules on second homes.

Having seen people in his constituency living in Portakabins, Ryan was also concerned with the loss of Cornwall's cultural heritage, as more young people are forced to leave as house prices become increasingly out of sync with local wages. Mebyon Kernow was initially founded in 1951 to promote Cornwall's Celtic Revival – before it began dabbling in more serious nationalist politics – and to preserve the distinct Cornish identity Ryan fears for. This includes, of course, *Kernewek*, and in Camborne, I was excited to visit Kowsva, Cornwall's first dedicated Cornish-language bookshop, which we found next to a preserved tin-mining shaft on the road towards Redruth.

'*Dydh da!*' came a greeting in *Kernewek* when we peeked our heads inside Kowsva (which means 'talking place') for a look. 'Interested in learning Cornish?' I looked around the bookshop with intrigue, where Cornish bunting lined shelves stacked with Cornish-language literature, including translated *Tintin* comics, a *Cornish Grammar for Beginners* and recipe books.

'I'm learning Cornish myself,' said Emma, the chirpy volunteer shop assistant. 'I know the basics, and I'm just about conversational, but it's tough. I started because I wanted to understand what all the place names meant around me, so I could understand Cornwall.'

Kernewek is an older language than English, but the

dominance of the latter led to its demise. Cornish nationalists will have you believe that *Kernewek* died out completely due to deliberate English suppression following the Prayer Book Rebellion, but this extinction myth isn't quite true. Although Dolly Pentreath, a fishwife from Mousehole (a fishing village in western Cornwall, a few miles west of Penzance) who died in 1777, was immortalized in Cornish lore as the last native Cornish speaker, the language survived in remote, rural villages in the west, while words and phrases carried over to form the Cornish dialect of English you hear today.

Kernewek survived in place names, too – like Redruth (which means 'Red Ford', although not in the way you think: *red* is derived from a Cornish word for ford, and *ruth* alludes to the red iron ore found in the stream) or Carn Brea, the 'hill top' overlooking Camborne – which is why Emma was keen to learn the language, to better understand the land around her.

The revival of the language was kick-started after antiquarian Henry Jenner pieced together *A Handbook for the Cornish Language* from salvaged medieval texts in 1904. It's remarkable the language was revived at all, and it's faced serious challenges to get where it is today, not least because of the small number of speakers and battles over spelling, grammar and pronunciation.

'There are maybe five hundred fluent Cornish speakers now,' said Emma, adding that the language was reclassified as being no longer extinct in the 2000s. 'But you know, everyone speaks a word or two, even if they don't think they know Cornish.'

Championed by Cornish cultural and political groups like the Gorsedh Kernow and Mebyon Kernow, there are now

Cornish-language playgroups where children are brought up bilingually, while council-funded programmes provide the tools and resources to teach classes in primary and secondary schools. There are Cornish-language weekends, festivals, pub meetups and walks across the Duchy, all aimed at various levels of learning and ability. Emma added the next step is to get *Kernewek* on the language-learning platform Duolingo, where anyone can learn it.

'You should visit Kresen Kernow today as well,' said Emma, as we left her to help an elderly man looking for a *Kernewek* dictionary. 'The *Ordinalia* is back in Cornwall, after five hundred years!'

Kresen Kernow ('the Cornwall Centre') is a fledgling 'national' project housing Cornwall's archives within a revamped red-brick brewery in the centre of Redruth, abandoned two decades earlier after an arsenic contamination. Thankfully, the arsenic has been cleaned up. Walking into the modern, brightly lit centre after the short drive, I found myself in an antiquarian's paradise Henry Jenner would've loved, surrounded by tens of thousands of books, maps, documents, scrolls and photographs, each telling a small piece of Cornwall's story.

On Emma's advice, we'd come to see a faded fourteenth-century manuscript of the *Ordinalia*, a trilogy of epic religious plays written in medieval Cornish and intended to be performed by the masses, for the masses. The plays marked the zenith of *Kernewek*, with Latin stage directions and snippets of French telling not of a borderland dominated by England, but of a cultured, medieval Cornwall in touch with the continent. Directed by the 'Ordinary' – a director whose job was to push, shout and cajole a ragtag cast of drunken parishioners on to the stage – the plays were held on feast days, bringing biblical stories to life within a *plen-an-gwery*, a type of ancient, open air amphitheatre unique to Cornwall.

'The plays are two hundred years older than Shakespeare,' said Tamsin, an enthusiastic archivist from Truro who showed us into Kresen Kernow's *Ordinalia* exhibition. 'But they were lost before their time.'

The *Ordinalia*, which drew inspiration from banned gospels, wasn't afraid to poke fun at the authorities, and the plays were outlawed in the sixteenth century. Tamsin showed us one of the few surviving manuscripts, now protected behind perspex in a purpose-built, temperature-controlled room. It is thought to have been transcribed by monks at Glasney College, a monastery near Truro that compiled Cornish literature until its dissolution during the Reformation.

'The manuscript is normally stored in Oxford's Bodleian Library. They've been there for centuries,' said Tamsin, who lives and breathes Cornish history, day in, day out in the archives. 'It took years of planning and meetings to finally get the *Ordinalia* back in Cornwall, once we'd built the facilities here to safely display it.'

Centuries on, the unfamiliar consonants of *Kernewek* stood out through the glass. For the first time in hundreds of years, the manuscript had returned to its rightful home in Cornwall, a sure sign that *Kernewek* truly had been resurrected from near death. Kresen Kernow – a modern hub for Cornish culture and history – is breathing much-needed life into a run-down area of Redruth, and Tamsin was keen to give us the grand tour.

Having previously worked in what she called the dingy archives in Truro, she happily explained how she now had twenty-four miles of shelves and enough space for twenty years' worth of expansion in the state-of-the-art facility. Tamsin wants everyone to become 'amateur archivists', and she was overjoyed that Cornwall now had a dedicated space where anyone can research their family trees, and – if they have the desire – dig into twelfth-century land grants, fourteenth-century church tithes and even see a rare charter signed by Queen Elizabeth I.

Unfortunately, not everyone would have the chance to see the *Ordinalia* manuscripts. A few weeks later they would return to the shelves of the Bodleian Library. It felt wrong, Cornish plays locked away in an English library where they would never be displayed as proudly as they were here in Redruth.

We left Tamsin sorting through stacks of nineteenth-century maritime correspondence and set off from Redruth, past the granite cottages built for miners that line Camborne's high street and on to the A30. By looking to its past – to a golden age of *Kernewek* culture, literature and language – the Cornish heartland was drawing on its distinct identity to develop new cultural opportunities for future generations. The twin towns show the positive side of embracing Britain's multicultural past, and as much as I was disheartened by the economic malaise Mebyon Kernow was tapping into, as we drove deeper into the ever-narrowing Cornish peninsula, a glimmer of hope followed us west.

St Just

Six miles north of Land's End, in the Penwith town of St Just, centuries of Cornish history are stamped into granite flagstones and the street signs are bilingual. The Star Inn, with its slate roof, timber beams and a bar draped with Celtic flags, was doing a steady trade as people waited for the *Ordinalia* to begin.

Roman soldiers were checking tickets at the entrance to one of Cornwall's last surviving medieval amphitheatres. A red devil on stilts entertained the crowd as picnic blankets and camping chairs were set up on the grass. Coinciding with the manuscript's return to Cornwall, the *Ordinalia* trilogy was being performed back-to-back, and we were just in time to watch the final play.

This was history brought to life. I could imagine a fourteenth-century village turning out for a drunken weekend of eating, singing, dancing, bad acting and free-flowing mead. The acting in this modern rendition, though, was brilliant, with paid, professional actors funded by Cornwall Council starring alongside enthusiastic amateurs. Far from being the quaint religious tale I expected, there were Cornish fishermen complaining about fishing quotas and government bureaucracy, against a backdrop of extreme pyrotechnics. A few monologues were delivered in *Kernewek*, and most of the singing was in Cornish, but much of the performance was adapted from a newer English translation, rather than medieval manuscripts. That mattered little to the crowd, who lapped up whichever language flittered on the evening breeze.

'You've heard our language, our dialect and our singing in stories passed down for centuries,' said the Ordinary – a confident Cornishwoman who was dressed in a top hat and holding a long black cane – before the curtain dropped on the Resurrection after two hours of theatrics. 'But this isn't where our story ends. We are passing our language on to the next rendition of the Cornish *Ordinalia*.'

The performance of these once-banned medieval plays in their entirety was a huge milestone for the Cornish cultural revival, demonstrating the progress made since Henry Jenner scratched together his *Handbook*. It was a triumphant night for Cornishness, but like the *Ordinalia*, our story didn't end here. The next day, we had one final stop.

We drove south, meeting the last stretch of A30 as it reached west towards Land's End. After passing the First and Last, an old coaching inn on the road to Land's End, we found ourselves in what seemed like the largest car park in Cornwall. Coaches disgorged battalions of passengers, and after paying £5 for the privilege of parking, we walked through grand Corinthian columns and into the Land's End Landmark.

We hurried past the obligatory pasty shop, the Land's End Hotel and the First and Last Post Box to stand at the most south-westerly point in mainland Britain. I zipped my raincoat tighter because here, on the edge of Britain, the south-westerly winds were whipping the waves below into a frenzy as grey clouds massed above us. Beyond the jagged rocks, which reached into the sea like a grasping hand, lay King Arthur's mystical land of Avalon. Brave the rough three-hour crossing, and you'd find yourself in the Isles of Scilly. Here at the end of our Cornish journey, though, we weren't concerned with myths and legends.

'Where's the real Cornwall, then?' I asked Claire. Her gran had always said it was here in the west, but, clearly, we'd gone too far. The flag of St Piran might fly from Land's End, but the Land's End Cafe advertised itself as 'The First and Last refreshment in England'. They hadn't received the memo that Cornwall *isn't* England.

'I think my gran meant towns like Camborne and Redruth,' Claire mused, as we watched tourists having their photos taken next to the Land's End signpost, which pointed to John O'Groats, 867 miles away. 'Maybe St Keverne and St Just she'd call the "real" Cornwall.'

At first glance, the real Cornwall isn't in great shape, given this is one of the poorest regions in Northern Europe. The rest of Britain often scoffs at the notion of Cornish nationalism, but in an ever-divided country, there's a danger that worsening economic conditions can fuel dangerous nationalist sentiments. It's not so far-fetched. Cornwall has already experienced outlying instances of extremism. In 2017, a shadowy group named the Cornish Liberation Army claimed to have burnt down a Rick Stein restaurant in Porthleven, on the Lizard's west coast (the police said it was an accident) and made headlines after announcing they'd recruited a suicide bomber into their ranks.

The CLA have supposedly joined forces with the Cornish Republican Army – who went around tearing down English flags – and another militant group named after An Gof. They don't seem to care if blood is shed for an independent Cornwall, but their ranks are extremely thin, and mainstream nationalist parties like Mebyon Kernow – which called the groups 'pseudo-terrorists' – have distanced themselves from such organizations. Mebyon Kernow has it right, focusing on democratic means to advance their cause *within* the United Kingdom, rather than trying to break away. My great hope is that Cornwall can create its own space as part of the UK. For that to happen, the rest of the nations that share this island need to respect Cornwall as a land apart from England.

The UK needs to hold itself together, too. In St Keverne, Karen, that most ardent of Cornish nationalists, summed things up when she'd said: 'I'll gladly admit I'm British, at least while Wales and Scotland are still part of Britain. To be British is fine. It means I'm still part of a Great Britain with our Celtic cousins. But what if they go? I'll never say I'm English. I don't dislike the English, but I'm not English.'

Modern Cornwall is a haze of confused identities. Like Britishness, there's no one way to define the Cornish. Some, like Karen, define themselves in opposition to the English; others believe Cornwall's strengths lie in its Celticness, in its fishing fleets or medieval mystery plays, while the popularity of the Tories here in years past, and now the growing influence of Reform, shows that many who live in the Duchy don't want to loosen ties to England.

You'll be lucky to spot the red-billed birds in the wild, but a sign at Land's End explains how the Cornish chough was brought back from the brink of extinction. So, too, has Cornwall's Celtic heritage been saved. Now, it's also evolving, becoming more confident and assertive as it draws on its past and rebels against a present defined by issues like overtourism, second homes and economic disparity.

We left Land's End as the clouds drizzled and took the A30 – the same route marched by An Gof, so many centuries ago – back towards the River Tamar, and then into Devon. Now it was time to visit another of Britain's Celtic nations, to see how history – and the English – have defined Wales's place within the United Kingdom.

3

The Welsh Marches

He passed away like a mist on his own mountains, with his mission unfulfilled.

> T. P. Ellis in *The Story of Two Parishes*, describing the demise of Welsh national hero Owain Glyndŵr

Chepstow

It was a frigid January morning. Thrusting my hands deep into my coat pockets for warmth, I emerged from a bare treeline and on to an ancient earthen mound on the western bank of the River Wye. 'Congratulations, you've made it to the end of your 177-mile walk,' read a mud-spattered sign on the brow of the parapet-like embankment. I felt like an imposter. I hadn't walked 177 miles. Far from it. I'd hiked a meagre three through a residential estate and squelchy fields to Beachley, a small peninsula of English land formed by the meeting of the rivers Wye and Severn outside the Welsh border town of Chepstow.

With sunglasses ambitiously propped atop my woolly hat, I was greeted with a view of the border that would be unrecognizable to Welsh warriors of old attempting to stem the Anglo-Saxon tide arrayed against them. The steel girders and zigzagging suspension cables of the Severn Bridge loomed large through low-hanging clouds. Beyond this, the river widened into the Severn Estuary, where the sail-like spans of the three-mile-long Prince of Wales Bridge connect the muddy banks of England and Wales.

The Welsh bank of the estuary is home to the ever-expanding cities of Newport and Cardiff. On the English side, the faded seaside towns of Portishead, Clevedon and Weston-super-Mare meet the Bristol Channel in a swathe of mudflats and rusting pleasure piers. Britain's longest waterway is named after a mythical Celtic water nymph, Sabrina, who drowned in its turbulent tides, but now the Severn's bridges laugh in the face of the ancient river gods, carrying tens of thousands of vehicles between two nations every day.

A small stone monument, dug deep into grass thick with fallen branches and brambles, informed me in English and Welsh that I'd found the start, or end, of a mammoth, 177-mile-long hiking trail that carves a path through Welsh towns, English villages, mountain ranges and rolling farmland as it follows the rough route of Offa's Dyke, one of Britain's oldest borders.

The Welsh story is much like that of the Cornish. Here, as in Cornwall, relentless Anglo-Saxon expansion had pushed the native Britons westwards after the fall of the Roman Empire. When Bristol fell in the fifth century, a wedge was driven between the lands that became Cornwall and Wales, and Brythonic speakers were forced towards Britain's peripheries. In the eighth century, King Offa built a great earthwork marking the western edge of the Anglo-Saxon kingdom of Mercia, which occupied much of what we now call the Midlands. Dividing the emerging English people from the *'wealhas'* (an Old English word for 'foreigner'), large stretches of Offa's monumental engineering work still define the Anglo-Welsh border today.

The hiking trail, and the dyke, both begin where I was standing, a peninsula where Anglo-Saxon kings met and bargained with Welsh princes. It ends in the Welsh seaside town of Prestatyn, a favoured beach getaway for Liverpudlians, where I planned to finish my own journey along the Anglo-Welsh border. Tradition holds that if you're walking the entirety of Offa's Dyke Path, then you should pick up a pebble here on the banks of the River Severn and throw it into the Irish Sea. I left the pebbles on the ground. Offa's Dyke would be my shadow for the next week, but I wouldn't be hiking much of the path.

Instead, I would road trip (solo, this time, with Claire travelling elsewhere) through a borderland defined by a Mercian king that continues to occupy a murky space between England and Wales. Starting with Chepstow in the south, I'd follow the River Wye north to Monmouth, travel west to Abergavenny, and cross the Black Mountains to Hay-on-Wye. I'd then visit the border towns of Llanymynech and Oswestry, before reaching the Irish Sea.

With a Senedd (Parliament) in Cardiff devolved from Westminster and a resurgent Welsh language, Wales is reasserting its Celtic identity. As the Welsh dragon roars again, I was concerned that ancient divisions along the border might also be resurrected. Among the Iron Age hill forts of Shropshire and the Norman castles of Monmouthshire, I wanted to search out a distinct cross-border identity I thought might exist on an even grander scale than in the Tamar Valley. Now, in a Britain that seemed more divided by the day, perhaps the Anglo-Welsh border could teach a fragmented kingdom how to unite.

My journey had begun earlier that same day when I'd thundered across the Severn Estuary into Chepstow. As the brackish waters of the River Severn flashed below the tarmac of the Severn Bridge, I felt as though I was crossing ancient tribal lines. Driving slowly through Chepstow's medieval streets, I was following in the bloody footsteps of Roman legions and marauding medieval armies, because Chepstow, where a Norman castle on sheer limestone cliffs towers over the River Wye, is the gateway to the southern part of Wales.

As I drove past another Three Tuns pub in search of the castle's car park, I spotted a Welsh dragon flying outside a restaurant advertising the 'Best pizza in Wales'. I made a mental note to verify their claim later, then parked up in the shadow of Chepstow Castle's mighty keep. As the oldest stone castle in Britain – Norman invaders laid the foundations in the eleventh century – the hulking walls of this border fortress strike fear into the heart of any tourist tempted to skip out on their parking ticket.

The scale of Chepstow Castle and its tall walls tell of a borderland that couldn't be tamed. The castle, which was clearly intended for the serious business of war, is cared for by Cadw (an organization looking after Welsh heritage sites), and my English Heritage membership scored me half-price entrance into the grounds. Under massing January clouds, I climbed the stone tower and looked out from the castle's battered ramparts across the River Wye to see a bright Union Jack daubed across limestone cliffs. A statement of unity, perhaps, given the border between England and Wales goes straight down the middle of the river.

The wrought-iron span of the Old Wye Bridge connecting England and Wales was a short stroll from Chepstow Castle. For a border fanatic like me, it's a glorious structure, and I stood in the middle of the bridge with one foot in Wales and the other in England.

Cross the river and you'll be in Gloucestershire. Chepstow is in Monmouthshire; a county only legally incorporated into Wales in 1972. Before this, the 'national status' of Monmouthshire was rather blurry. No one was ever quite sure if the county was in England or Wales. I wanted to know if Chepstow still occupied this hazy liminal space, or if national identities were strengthening here on the border.

In Chepstow Museum – a grand neoclassical building opposite the castle – I climbed creaking wooden stairs to the museum's top floor and knocked on a door labelled 'Anne Rainsbury. Curator'. Maybe it was the rowdy children rampaging through the galleries below, but it felt like I was back at school again, especially when Anne shouted 'Please enter!' from within. I found her surrounded by open books and Post-it notes in an office overflowing with tourist brochures and maps of the Wye Valley, a popular destination north of Chepstow that stole the hearts of Victorian travellers in earlier centuries.

Anne had promised to guide me through the town's past, to understand its borderland identity in twenty-first century Wales. She explained how she was born and raised in the town. For Anne, local history begins with the Normans, who totally disregarded the boundary laid down by Offa, seizing land on either side of the dyke as they pushed on from their conquest of England into Wales. Before this, the Romans had likely built a fort here on the strategic crossroads into the southern part of Wales, but no evidence of it has ever been found.

'I presume you know that *"march"* is an old Norman term for a border?' she asked in an accent more West Country than Welsh, as she explained why the ragged borderlands stretching north from the tidal channels of the Severn Estuary to the windswept shores of the Irish Sea became known as 'the Marches'. The construction of Chepstow Castle began in 1067, intended as a Norman statement of power at the southern end of the Marches, and William the Conqueror appointed 'Marcher lords' to control this porous frontier. The Marcher lords carved out fiefdoms that sprawled across the modern English counties of Gloucestershire, Shropshire and Herefordshire, deep into the Welsh counties of Powys, Monmouthshire and Flintshire. The March became so important that successive English monarchs gave the Marcher lords independent privileges to control unruly borders, and in the thirteenth century, they provided the launch pad for King Edward I's brutal conquest of the surviving Welsh kingdoms. At the same time, the Marcher lords consolidated their own realms, effectively becoming, as Anne put it, 'princes of their own kingdoms'.

The Marcher lords controlled their realms through classic divide-and-rule tactics, with English settlers largely living within the protective walls of border towns like Chepstow and the Welsh relegated to the countryside. Once England had conquered Wales, these quasi-independent kingdoms became less convenient for the monarchy, which no longer needed to stir up trouble and fight proxy wars on the border. In the 1530s and early 1540s, King Henry VIII legally united England with Wales through the Acts of Union (or more accurately, he annexed Wales), and at the same time, abolished the privileges of the Marcher lords.

Monmouthshire clung on to its independent streak, and historically, border towns like Chepstow had occupied a shared space between two countries that blurred further once medieval wars died down and peace ensued. It's a shared space that still exists today.

'You've been to the Old Wye Bridge. You can stand with one foot in one country and the other foot in another country,' said Anne, before pointing out how the town's influence ignores the border to this day. 'For the people who live on the other side of the bridge, in English villages, Chepstow is their town, their social setting. Their kids go to school here, they go shopping in Chepstow's supermarkets, they eat out in its restaurants.'

Chepstow is a quintessential border town. The bulk of it sits on the Welsh bank of the Wye, but pop over the river and you'll immediately find yourself in English satellite suburbs like Sedbury and Beachley. The Welsh town's supermarkets, shops and pizza restaurants attract English villagers and day trippers from Bristol, while Chepstow is proud of its annual Wassail Mari Lwyd, a curious cross-border festival combining the English folk tradition of wassailing (a harvest festival with Pagan roots) with the Welsh tradition of Mari Lwyd (an unusual event which sees a horse's skull paraded through the streets). During the festival, the English wassailers let off a firework, and they're met in the middle of the Old Wye Bridge by the Welsh Mari Lwyd crowd for an exchange of national flags and pleasantries intended to ensure continued peace between the two nations for another year.

The town's cross-border role has never diminished, though Anne said that since the opening of the Senedd in Cardiff in 1999, Chepstow has drawn more prominently on its Welsh culture and history. The preponderance of bilingual signs and Welsh flags throughout Chepstow made a statement that this was Wales, and Anne was happy to increasingly hear Welsh spoken on the streets. Given that school-catchment areas sweep eastwards over the River Wye – giving English students from nearby villages the chance to take Welsh language GCSEs and A levels in Welsh schools – Welsh influence is expanding.

'How would Welsh independence affect Chepstow, if it ever happened?' I asked.

'I hope it would be a minor issue,' she said tactfully, before turning to history for her answer. 'Chepstow's focus was traditionally its interplay with Bristol. For centuries, we've always looked that way, towards the Bristol Channel and across to England. But of course, merchants and traders always had dealings in both camps.'

Anne suggested that Chepstow had historically been caught in the middle. While she loved seeing the Welsh identity flourish – an identity which has lain in the shadow of Englishness for far too long – she didn't want the town's cross-border ties to loosen. I planned to dig deeper into this idea of diminishing cross-border identity at my next stop in Monmouth, a border town claiming to be neither English nor Welsh. After I'd tried out the best pizza in Wales, of course.

Monmouth

The next day, morning mist rolled through the Wye Valley. I took the scenic route north, following the A466's weaving turns through undulating landscapes. From Chepstow, the Anglo-Welsh border follows much the same route as Offa's

Dyke, which utilized the River Wye as a natural frontier. Tarmac and road signs aside, I imagined King Offa himself would recognize this stretch of the border if he were transported to the modern-day Marches.

Trees arched over the roadside, cocooning me for several miles in a dark, forest-like tunnel leading to the crumbling shell of Tintern Abbey, founded by Cistercian monks in 1131 and made famous by William Wordsworth. From the monastery, the road followed the river into Monmouth, where the Wye meets the River Monnow in the middle of a fortified Marcher town.

I parked by Monmouth's fortified medieval bridge – an ugly stone construction, but the last of its kind still standing in Britain – which guarded another traditional gateway into the southern part of Wales. Geographically, Monmouth is in Wales, but long before the Acts of Union imposed English laws on Wales, Monmouthshire was already subject to the rule of English rather than Welsh courts. The county was never quite English though, and traditionally, Acts of Parliament often referred very specifically to 'England, Wales and Monmouthshire' in their wording.

Was Monmouth in England or Wales? That's the 'Monmouth Question', which I wanted answers to. For centuries, it happily sat somewhere in the middle, embracing its distinctly middle identity. Never quite knowing what side of the border it was supposed to be on, the county motto, 'Faithful unto both', announces its unique position with gusto. It wasn't until the 1970s that the Monmouth Question was officially 'resolved' when the county was placed, for good, into Wales.

I spotted signs for Offa's Dyke Path and walked along a

high street busy with morning shoppers, but comprising little else apart from coffee shops, charity shops and chain restaurants. I checked into the King's Head Hotel, a budget Wetherspoons pub and hotel where paintings of kings and battles offered an overdose of medieval English nostalgia for regulars sipping pints of John Smith's at the bar. Outside the hotel, a statue of King Henry V looms over Agincourt Square. Henry V, who took the English crown in 1413, was born and raised in Monmouth Castle, and many of the archers who won the day for him at Agincourt were Welsh. To learn more about Monmouth's curious relationship with both England and Wales, I met local journalist and amateur historian Charles Boase in the Costa Coffee on Monnow Street.

Wearing a flat cap and a smart black blazer, Charles had a clipped English accent far removed from the lyrical Welsh I'd expected to hear in these parts. He's originally Cornish, he told me, with family from Penzance, but having lived most of his life here, he was more than qualified to be chair of the Monmouth History and Field Society. Like many of the local-history enthusiasts I'd meet on my journey, Charles had collected a lifetime's worth of facts rarely known outside the boundaries of the town in question (did I know, he asked, that the Rolls family, who developed the Rolls Royce automobiles, came from Monmouth?). His accent masked his borderland identity, and Charles quickly corrected my Welsh pronunciation, including the 'll' in place names like Llanymynech and Llandudno.

After a quick lesson on the vowels and consonants of the Welsh language, Charles explained over sips of coffee and bites of a Danish pastry how long ago, this area had been part of the Archenfield, a triangle of land between

Ross-on-Wye, Hereford and Monmouth, once part of the lost Welsh kingdom of Ergyng. Mercia occupied the land during its westward expansion in the eighth century, but the native Britons weren't displaced from the countryside and largely retained their customs and language.

'This was always Welsh land,' said Charles, explaining how a two-tiered system separating the Anglo-Saxon town from the Welsh countryside evolved in the Archenfield, a system expanded upon by the Normans. 'The local Welsh population were granted privileges for not causing trouble. Monmouth was always very English, and there were always very few Welsh speakers in the town itself.' It was hardly an apartheid-like system, though. While Welsh may have been spoken in the countryside and English in the towns, the Archenfield, then Monmouthshire, became a blur of identities as nationalities and customs merged.

The Welsh from outside the Archenfield clearly saw the region and its inhabitants as no longer being truly 'Welsh', as Welsh princes devastated the area on multiple occasions. 'Owain Glyndŵr caused terror here. Crops were burnt, people were slaughtered,' said Charles, explaining how Glyndŵr – the last native Prince of Wales – ravaged the borderlands during his decades-long war against England in the early fifteenth century. 'The later populations would have remembered, and they would have been in two minds about the Welsh.'

Despite his extensive knowledge of the history and language, Charles talked as if he wasn't Welsh. He admitted that 'Monmouth is much more English than Abergavenny,' another border town a few miles west. He couldn't quite call himself English either, describing Monmouth as the Welsh town most uneasy with itself, most unsure of its identity. It was something I readily related to myself, given my mixed upbringing across Britain.

In 2011, 63 per cent of Wales voted in favour of increased devolution in a referendum. Monmouthshire was the only area to vote *against* the Welsh Senedd being given full law-making powers independent of Westminster, a result that hints at the county's mixed identity. Unfortunately, the referendum also sparked a nationalist response from the English side of the border. The English Democrats (an English offshoot of the racist British National Party) saw the result as an excuse to call for another referendum asking if Monmouthshire should officially become English. The fringe political party was sadly intent on stirring up old divisions, but as in any borderland, the reality wasn't quite so black and white. Just because Monmouthshire voted against Wales having more devolved powers, didn't mean the county wanted to be in England.

Charles described Monmouth as holding 'a peculiar position between England and Wales'. It has a typical border character, a character neither here nor there. I'd seen this represented in Monmouthshire County Council's coat of arms, visible on public buildings across town, which features an English lion holding a red rose on the left-hand side of a shield and a Welsh dragon grasping a leek on the right. Earlier, on my way to meet Charles, I'd walked down Agincourt Street (named for the battle which the English claim as one of their greatest historical victories against the French) and was surprised to find it led directly on to Glendower Street. Glendower is the Anglicized surname of Owain

Glyndŵr, who terrorized the borderlands in his quest for Welsh independence.

Like Monmouth, Charles didn't want to choose between England and Wales. He dreaded the day he'd be forced to take sides if support for Welsh independence, or English nationalism, picked up steam. Monmouth isn't necessarily representative of its namesake county any more, though. As in Glyndŵr's day, talk of an independent Wales is testing the loyalties of the Marches. Elsewhere in Monmouthshire, the red dragon is unapologetically rousing from its slumber.

I left Charles as he unfurled a copy of the day's *Telegraph*, and spent the afternoon tracing Offa's Dyke Path around Monmouth. After a restless night vainly trying to drown out the noise of Friday night punters who'd descended on Wetherspoons from both sides of the border, the next morning I jumped in the car, bleary-eyed, for a fifteen-mile drive west to Abergavenny.

Abergavenny

The border suddenly swerved westwards, now following the course of the River Monnow, rather than the Wye. Parking in the small village of Llanfoist, which has been all but swallowed by Abergavenny, I could see the Black Mountains draped in clouds, rising like sedimentary titans to divide England from Wales. I walked over a packhorse bridge into the damp fields of Castle Meadow, followed a sodden path along the banks of the River Usk, and – where the town rose above low-lying fields where Herefordshire cattle grazed – I found the broken walls of Abergavenny Castle, built in 1087 by a Norman lord, sullenly soaking up the drizzle.

Weather-beaten information boards dotted among the hollow shell of the once-mighty border castle told a grim tale of medieval atrocities. I was suddenly very aware that I was standing on ground drenched in the blood and treachery of the Marches. On a winter's day in 1175, the baron of Abergavenny invited Welsh princes and nobility to feast with him in the castle's great hall – but this was no parley. The baron ordered the gathered Welshmen to pay homage to the English king. The proud Welshmen refused and were butchered when the baron's soldiers sprang from the shadows. A few years later, Welsh warriors burnt Abergavenny in revenge.

A century or so later, Owain Glyndŵr burnt Abergavenny to the ground when he invaded the borderlands in 1404. For the first time in history, disparate Welsh kingdoms were united by Glyndŵr, who – in a serious nation-building effort – announced that Wales would once more be subject to the ancient Welsh laws codified by tenth-century king Hywel Dda, rather than the English laws imposed since King Edward I's conquest in the thirteenth century. Glyndŵr's vision of an independent Wales attracted tens of thousands of Welsh fighters to his cause, but it ended in failure after fourteen long years of war. Charles had told me in Monmouth that Glyndŵr's war was a rebellion. To the Welsh, it's remembered as a righteous uprising against English rule, and Glyndŵr is revered as a national hero.

Twenty-first century Abergavennians must have forgiven Glyndŵr's ravaging of their town centuries prior, I thought, spotting a sticker supporting Welsh independence as I left the castle. Before leaving for the Marches, I'd been emailing Monmouthshire local Jason Bates, a former soldier representing Yes Cymru, the Welsh independence campaign, in the county. He'd told me how support for an independent Wales was on the rise in Abergavenny, and I'd instantly marked the town on my map as a must-visit. Jason's support for independence arose not just from a sense of patriotism, but from the discrimination he said he'd experienced in the military for being Welsh. Belittlement from the English had led him to nationalism, and now he fought (peacefully) for a country he believed was still oppressed by England.

As I walked along the high street, I saw Welsh flags flying alongside Union Jacks, while a statue of a humble cattle drover in the square remembered the town's agricultural roots. Abergavenny's Welsh identity is indeed on the rise, and in 2016, the town hosted the National Eisteddfod, a cultural festival celebrating all things Welsh.

The National Eisteddfod, an annual celebration of the Welsh language, arts and literature, is rooted in the Welsh bardic traditions of old. The first Eisteddfod was held in the court of a Welsh prince in the twelfth century. It was then revived in the late eighteenth century to revitalize the retreating Welsh language, and the Eisteddfod's modern, festival-like incarnation has since grown from strength to strength. Centred around Welsh-language poets competing for the coveted Bardic Crown and Bardic Chair, I visited the 2024 Eisteddfod in Pontypridd, outside Cardiff, and enjoyed the spectacle of Welsh music, poetry and politics. Pontypridd attracted 186,000 visitors (up from 116,000 the year before), and the event hammered home to me just how vibrant and alive the Welsh language is.

In 2018, a Welsh-language centre opened in Abergavenny's historic Tithe Barn – a building supposedly looted and burnt by Glyndŵr – while the town is also home to one of the few Welsh-medium schools (where subjects are taught in Welsh) in Monmouthshire, a county which traditionally had far fewer Welsh speakers than elsewhere.

Jason was campaigning in Cardiff when I visited, but he'd put me in touch with Melanie Jenkins, a local Welsh-language tutor more than happy to talk about Abergavenny's resurging Welsh loyalties over a cappuccino in the King's Arms pub. Softly spoken but fiercely proud of her native Wales, Melanie was warming her hands by the fireplace within the pink stone walls of the pub when I arrived. Originally from the industrial heartlands of Gwent, she grew up speaking Welsh as her first language in the Valleys. When she moved to Abergavenny as a teenager, Melanie struggled to find her place in what she described as an 'Anglicized border town'.

'I remember my grandparents couldn't speak English well at all when we moved here,' she said. 'I'd been in the Welsh stream in grammar school, where lessons were all in Welsh, so when we left the Valleys, it broke my heart. It felt like we'd landed on another planet.'

Melanie felt ostracized for her Welshness, and she was bullied for her strong Welsh accent at her new school. 'Being English isn't a bad thing, don't get me wrong,' she said, reliving her teenage years in Abergavenny. 'But considering we were supposed to be in our own country, we felt like outsiders. The English here weren't very welcoming to the Welsh. The school didn't teach Welsh at the time. It felt like we were in England. When I left for university in Aberystwyth, I never wanted to come back.'

But she did come back, returning in the 1990s to take up a new Welsh-teaching post at a time when Abergavenny was linguistically changing, a shift she attributes to a 1991 law making it mandatory for Welsh to be taught in Welsh schools. The changes were the result of decades of campaigning beginning in the 1950s when Welsh speakers – including Melanie's parents – embarked on a civil-disobedience campaign that saw monolingual English road signs torn down. Welsh speakers have increased in number across Wales ever since, as part of what Melanie called a Welsh 'reawakening'.

'Demand for Welsh learning is blossoming, and it's really amazing,' she said with pride, adding how devolution in 1999 marked another era of progressive change for Welsh nationalism, with the Senedd passing laws to preserve and promote the Welsh language. 'There are hundreds of courses. Welsh for parents, Welsh for business, Welsh for the community. Anything you want to learn in Welsh, you can do it. I've taught everyone from teenagers who wanted to improve their language skills, to a 93-year-old who wanted to finally pass her Welsh GCSE. We have lots of English people who have moved to the area taking Welsh courses. They want to learn the language. They want to immerse themselves in a different culture.'

Not everyone in Monmouthshire embraces the Welsh language. Despite improved opportunities for Welsh speakers – with regular Welsh-language coffee meets, film screenings and social walks in the town – Melanie pointed out that when you stroll down the street in Abergavenny, it's rare to hear Welsh. Melanie has friends opposed to devolution, and she said there's a minority who don't want Welsh taught in local schools.

For Melanie, it's not a case of learning either English or Welsh. There's no reason the two can't coexist. But resistance to Welsh language learning prompted her interest in politics. She began marching with Yes Cymru in the wake of the Scottish independence referendum in 2014, which, despite its failure, inspired a new wave of independence supporters in Wales.

'I think independence is a realistic concept,' she told me enthusiastically. 'We're a few years behind Scotland; we have a lot of people to win over. But why wouldn't we want independence? It needs to be thought out, but it's definitely attainable.'

Welsh nationalism is gaining support, although it's largely centred on the traditionally Welsh-speaking regions in western and northern Wales, where in 2024, Plaid Cymru had their best-ever election results, taking four Westminster constituencies.

Welsh nationalism has ancient roots, and the dream of an independent Welsh nation has simmered under the surface for hundreds of years. In the nineteenth century, the Welsh language's widespread decline, combined with the growing economic disparity between Wales and England, led to the founding of nationalist movements like Cymru Fydd (which counted future British prime minister David Lloyd George among its founding members) who called for 'home rule', or self-government for the UK's distinct regions.

When small European nations began claiming independence in the wake of the First World War, calls for a Welsh parliament grew stronger, and Plaid Cymru was founded in

1925. As the British Empire dissolved in the 1950s, widespread decolonization movements inspired civil-disobedience campaigns as Welsh speakers fought for equal language rights. Peaceful protests soon turned to anger, stoked in particular by events in Tryweryn, a valley in Gwynedd that held one of the last Welsh-speaking communities in the area, which was flooded to keep the English city of Liverpool supplied with fresh water.

Before the flooding in 1965, Welsh MPs railing against the planned reservoir were outvoted by English MPs in Westminster. Things took a sinister turn, and a militant group named MAC (Army for the Defence of Wales) took matters into their Semtex-laden hands, blowing up pipelines to disrupt what they saw as a colonial project. In 1969, MAC escalated the militant atmosphere when they attempted to attack Prince Charles' controversial investiture ceremony as the Prince of Wales in Caernarfon Castle (a title passed on to the firstborn son of the English monarch since King Edward I's conquest of Wales). The plot failed when two home-made bombs didn't explode. Another bomb exploded prematurely, killing two MAC militants.

Other paramilitary groups like the Free Wales Army formed in the 1960s, with the goal of forcing the creation of an independent Welsh republic, while Welsh nationalists burnt English-owned holiday homes in majority Welsh-speaking areas like Gwynedd. Thankfully, these militant groups disbanded decades ago, and now the Welsh identity is building itself as a force for peace, leading its cultural revolution through events like the Eisteddfod, rather than pipe bombings and arson attacks.

Melanie's support for an independent Wales is deeply

linked to the Welsh culture she loves and the identity she wants to preserve, but it's also driven by what she sees as a rising tide of English nationalism – which, she said, had contributed to Brexit – as England and Wales once again define themselves in opposition to one another. She's become more nationalistic, she told me, because she feels that in the past, people have tried to rip her Welshness away from her.

'Where do you think it all fell apart?' she asked, rather sorrowfully. 'Where did we lose Britain? If Scotland ever voted to leave the UK, I think Wales would need to leave quickly, too. Otherwise, we'd be swallowed up and become West England.'

I asked Melanie what it meant to be Welsh. 'Everything,' she said without hesitation. 'You don't need the language, necessarily. I know people find it difficult, and you don't need it to feel Welsh. But it's about having a different culture. It's about feeling different from the rest of the UK.'

'And I suppose you must feel different from England?' she asked, turning the question back round on me, and making me seriously think about my own British identity for the first time since I'd arrived in Wales. I've never felt Scottish, I realized, because I'd never truly known Scotland other than as a tourist. I also didn't want to be part of an English nation that still othered the Welsh. I felt like I wanted to belong everywhere in Britain, but right now, with the borders closing in, it felt like I belonged nowhere.

'I hope you don't think I'm a Welsh militant!' said Melanie softly, as we wrapped up our conversation on the increasingly bleak-looking future of Britain. 'What I don't like is people bringing the Welsh down. And I'll always speak out against that.'

'Where to next?' Melanie asked more light-heartedly as we said our goodbyes outside the King's Arms, both of us wrapped up in hats and scarves as the January cold began to bite. 'Ah, Hay-on-Wye,' she said, when I told her my plan to follow the border over the Black Mountains. 'They never quite knew if they wanted to be English or Welsh!'

Hay-on-Wye

The windscreen wipers worked furiously as I skirted the eastern edge of the Black Mountains. I'd planned to follow the Old Hereford Road from Abergavenny, up and over the dividing range between England and Wales, but a 'road closed' sign en route to Llanthony Priory – a derelict monastery, built by a Norman lord who'd tired of war in the violent borderlands – stopped me in my tracks. Offa's Dyke Path goes right over the top of the mountains. The highest, Waun Fach, reaches 811 metres, but with dark clouds shrouding the peaks and merciless rain pounding both sides of the border, it wasn't a day for hiking.

This mountainous borderland is difficult to traverse even today, and I was forced to take the long way round, through England's flat plains. After crossing the border back into Wales, I found myself in Hay-on-Wye's monstrously oversized car park, where the pay-and-display machine was stuck on Welsh, causing chaos among English tourists. A sign by the car park entrance announced Hay-on-Wye as the 'World's First Book Town', and everywhere I looked, there were bookshops. Even the Norman castle's moat was home to an 'honesty bookshop', where stacks of second-hand literature were draped in plastic tarpaulins protecting them from the rain. Straddling the border, Hay-on-Wye is home to the largest concentration of second-hand bookshops in the world, and since 1987, the Hay Festival has attracted some 30,000 literature lovers every year for two weeks of talks and debates in the summer (which explained the oversized car park).

I wasn't here to buy books but to trace the story of Richard Booth, an eccentric second-hand bookseller who on 1 April 1977 declared himself 'King of Hay'. Holding a regal sceptre crafted from brass plumbing and wearing a home-made crown, Booth informed a bemused crowd in the square that Hay-on-Wye was seceding from the UK and henceforth was an independent kingdom.

Booth's nation-building project was built on serious satire, but he achieved what Scottish, Welsh and Cornish nationalists have only dreamt of: 'independence'. Things got wacky, very quickly, when his ministers were elected after a few rounds in the pub. He appointed his horse foreign minister, and issued passports and conferred lavish titles upon friends. He even lorded over his growing kingdom from the ageing Norman castle, which he'd purchased with the profits of his expanding second-hand bookshop empire some years earlier.

Booth passed away in 2013, but his largest bookshop – the imaginatively named Richard Booth's Bookshop – is still going strong. His Norman castle on the mound was completely refurbished as a museum in 2022, and after looking through ground-floor exhibits telling tales of medieval border feuds, on the top floor I found a shrine-like room dedicated to the King of Hay himself. There, in a sparklingly clean glass cabinet, were Booth's sceptre and crown. In the gift shop, you could purchase Kingdom of Hay citizenship and peerages, although, sadly, no one knew how I could find the man Booth had appointed as his successor.

I did manage to track down one of Booth's close friends, Dr Reginald Clark (a doctor of Egyptology, although that has nothing to do with Hay's story). He worked as Booth's publicist and served as his 'minister of technology', though he was vague about the specifics of that job. It was Reg who'd fashioned the King of Hay's crown jewels from a copper water tank, and he'd regularly liaised with the press during the heyday of Booth's madcap antics in the 1970s. He's since moved away from Hay-on-Wye, but we later had a phone call where he enthusiastically recounted the strange tale of Booth's self-declared kingdom.

'He initially did it for a laugh. Then realized it had massive financial implications for himself, and for Hay-on-Wye,' Reg, who was ecstatic to be reliving Booth's story even after all these years, told me. 'He was the master of publicity. He was prepared to dress up and make a fool of himself to bring it in.'

Reg described his friend as a 'raconteur', one of the last great British eccentrics, whose booming voice made people stop and listen, no matter what nonsense he was spouting. Together, they sold the Kingdom of Hay to the world, ostensibly to promote the town and its bookstores, but also with a serious political undertone. Booth jokingly retired the Kingdom of Hay from the European Economic Community (the forerunner of the European Union), which Reg said spoke of his desire for sovereignty (and, perhaps, foreshadowed the Brexit referendum decades later). He railed against the 'quangos' he believed ruled Wales, including the

Welsh Tourist Board and (of all things) the Milk Board, which he believed were too bureaucratic, which had in turn contributed to the decline of rural towns.

He styled himself 'Richard, Coeur de Livres', and reporters flocked to meet the crazed king of Hay: the ensuing publicity attracted global tourists to the otherwise sleepy border town. Booth's grand vision turned Hay-on-Wye's economic fortunes around, and the idea of a 'book town' soon spread across the world, revitalizing rural towns everywhere from France to India. On a trip to the Norwegian fjords, I once stumbled across the Fjaerland Book Town (population: 500), where locals told me how Booth's borderland antics had inspired them to establish honesty bookstores in a village surrounded by soaring mountain peaks and covered, for much of the year, in snow and ice.

Hay-on-Wye might revere Booth now, but Reg explained how locals were outraged by his actions at the time. 'He fell out with everyone. The Welsh Tourist Board and the town council had to make statements saying they had nothing to do with Booth's kingdom. Initially there was suspicion and resentment. People in Hay said they didn't need this man telling us what to do. But things have changed over the years. Now he's sorely missed,' said Reg with a sad tone as he remembered his friend. 'He was the mad king who declared independence, but my feeling is that he did a lot for Hay.'

Walking through Hay-on-Wye and seeing not just its bustling book trade, but cafes, antique stores and boutique shops packed with visitors, it's clear that Booth's legacy towers over the town today. His declaration of independence had channelled the energy of independent Marcher lords and rebellious Welsh princes. Booth hadn't given a damn what anyone thought of his mad schemes. He'd carved out his own kingdom in the borderlands, a place that was neither England nor Wales.

Llanymynech

I spent an afternoon lost among the shelves of Hay-on-Wye's second-hand bookshops, and the next morning crossed through Powys, Herefordshire, Shropshire and back into Powys as I followed Offa's Dyke north. Reaching Knighton, a bleak border town of dusty antique shops and muddy tractors that seemed well in need of an eccentric borderland king of its own, the border looped westwards, leaving an English peninsula forlornly poking into Wales.

The heart of this English intrusion – which has spawned villages with names like Newcastle and New Invention – is Clun Castle, a Norman stronghold burnt by Glyndŵr during his war with England. As I drove north, following his ghostly footsteps, country lanes took me through green fields and rolling hills, until later that day I arrived in Llanymynech.

I was here because Llanymynech has taken the concept of a border town to the extreme. It's not just on the border: the dividing line between England and Wales goes right down the high street, a dead straight road lined by fish and chip shops and greasy spoon cafes which don't know, or care, which country they're in. The border even goes through the Dolphin, a pub with bars in both England and Wales, where, locals have it, in decades past Welsh drinkers would step through into the English bar when Sunday drinking was banned in Wales.

My guide would be amateur historian Tony Beardsell, who dismissively told me that living here on the border was exactly like anywhere else he'd lived in Britain. He said he wasn't interested in borders in the slightest. Still, he was happy to humour me. Being a volunteer for the local heritage society, he was keen to show me around, so long as we visited the old lime kilns he'd spent so long restoring.

'We're all getting too old here,' Tony lamented, as he grabbed his walking stick from the boot of his car and set a furious pace into the wooded heritage area on the edge of town. 'We're struggling to find new volunteers to look after everything. Dave died halfway through a canal boat restoration.'

Tony left me traipsing behind as he led the way to limestone cliffs overlooking the town, which Romans and Normans alike had mined and quarried in search of silver. It was easy to see how this was a natural border, and indeed, Tony said we were now walking the route of Wat's Dyke, a forerunner to Offa's Dyke, which was possibly constructed around the seventh century.

Historians aren't quite sure who built Wat's Dyke, or when, or even why. Running for some sixty miles in the northeast, often in parallel to Offa's Dyke but always further east, it's certainly some kind of border. Whether it was built by Romans or Mercians, it shows that by King Offa's day, the border had been pushed deeper and deeper into Wales, closer towards the Cambrian mountains rising sharply to the west.

He may have been several decades older than me, but Tony had far more energy and I trailed behind, his one walking pole working overtime as he guided me off-piste, along a rough track and through spiky bushes that emerged on to a golf course.

'This is the golf course where you can play from England into Wales,' he said, dodging flying balls as I tried to pinpoint the border's exact location with my phone's GPS. 'An international golf course, we like to call it. You can tee off in Wales, play five holes in England, and finish up the game in Wales again!'

Tony was more animated by the border's peculiarities than he liked to let on. He led me out on to the middle of the course (dodging a few more near misses) and proclaimed that we were exactly on the divide between England and Wales.

Llanymynech's border location is the source of the town's unique heritage, which unites both sides of the town over a dividing line that can't keep them apart. Take a walk down the high street and you can cross from one nation to another countless times running simple errands like posting a letter or taking your kids to school. The Village Hall, bowling club, fish and chip shop and (somewhat macabrely) the cemetery are all in England but utilized by everyone in Llanymynech.

The Chinese takeaway, Indian restaurant and Village Pantry Cafe all lie on the Welsh side, but are likewise cross-border institutions. When international rugby or football is on, you can choose which pub you watch the games in and are free to proudly display your support for either England or Wales (or both, so long as they aren't playing each other). Here was the uniting British identity I was looking for, as demonstrated by Llanymynech's last station master, who refused to refer to the different platforms (which were on either side of the border) as either English or Welsh.

'I'm not sure if we're in England or Wales right now, I'm sorry,' Tony said when we'd finished looking at his cavernous red-brick lime kilns and ended up by Montgomery Canal. 'Of course, you know that during Covid, one pub could be open and another over the border had to close when English and Welsh laws were out of kilter.'

I knew all too well about this unfortunate episode in local history. I'd interviewed several pub landlords from my lockdown armchair during the pandemic, asking them about the curious happenings on the border after a group of English golfers were turfed off the 'International Golf Course' by police when they apparently strayed over the border into Wales.

I'd heard stories of police threatening £10,000 fines if landlords in Wales served English punters when pubs were in lockdown in England, but not in Wales. One landlord claimed the police had asked him to check IDs and serve only Welsh residents. With so much media hype – which I probably contributed to myself – it was difficult to separate fact from fiction, but for me, the madness of those days raised uncomfortable questions which locals wanted to push aside by downplaying the border.

It's no stretch to say that Offa's Dyke was resurrected during Covid. Surely something is broken if Britain's internal borders, which we supposedly brought down centuries ago, were raised again, if only for a few months. I hope the chaos in Llanymynech isn't repeated in the future, but I can't help fear it could be a sign of things to come if the United Kingdom's different nations were to go their separate ways.

Oswestry

I said goodbye to Tony in the car park – out of breath after a forced march back along the canal – and followed the A483 as it shot dead north into England. My next stop was Oswestry, some twenty minutes' drive into Shropshire, where my mission was to determine which side of the border (if any) the market town belonged on.

Look at a map, and you'd think Oswestry should be in Wales, but the border takes a wild dive to the west, leaving a huge chunk of Shropshire deep into what should probably be Powys. Oswestry may have been founded by Anglo-Saxons – the name is derived from the Old English for 'Oswald's Place' – but in a borderland fraught with medieval violence, the town changed hands between kings, princes and Marcher lords on countless occasions. English and Welsh lived alongside each other through the chaos, but in 1536, the Acts of Union placed Oswestry in Shropshire as the modern border was formally drawn eight miles west.

Some in Wales see places like Oswestry as part of the 'Lost Lands' (in Welsh: *Lloegr*), regions now on the 'wrong' side of the Anglo-Welsh border. Some even see *Lloegr* as simply the Welsh name for England, encompassing all of the Celtic lands lost to the English. Even the OS Maps I followed unusually labelled both the town's English and Welsh names (Oswestry / Croesoswallt). I wondered if Oswestry didn't belong on either side of the border. Sandwiched between Offa's Dyke and Wat's Dyke, which run to the west and east respectively, this looked like a no man's land on the map, although that phrase does little justice to the thriving cross-border community that's lived here for centuries.

It was market day in town – the traditional meeting place of English and Welsh – and the high street was packed with stalls selling everything from fillets of fish to knock-off football shirts. Perhaps the cross-border raids had never truly ended: a wannabe bank robber in a balaclava caused a huge stir in town as they were apprehended by armed police. Weaving through the excited crowd gathered outside the NatWest, I walked into the town hall, where a grand heraldic tapestry was emblazoned with the simple title: 'Oswestry Borderland'.

Oswestry local Mark Hignett – who's traced his Oswestrian family tree back to the 1620s, and whose grey moustache and floppy grey hair lent him an Einstein-like vibe – was waiting for me inside the Oswestry Museum on the top floor of the town hall. He described himself as 'an ordinary guy who loves history', but he's not just the curator: he founded the museum a decade ago.

Another borderland eccentric, he told me how he'd recently attended a town hall meeting discussing ways to drum up tourism. 'I stood up, and I said, why don't we look to the past,' he said, trying to keep a straight face. 'Let's invade Wales! Like King John did. It'll be a PR coup. Needless to say, my idea wasn't taken up.' Mark had endless energy as he showed me through the museum, which largely consists of exhibits unearthed by Oswestrian locals in their attics and backyards (one lady found a 2,000-year-old arrowhead in her garden), frantically taking me through the town's tumultuous past.

'King John used Oswestry as a base to attack Llywelyn the Great in 1211. Five years later, in 1216, I think, King John burnt the town,' he said, showing me a timeline of the town's history he'd put together himself, which was really just a long list of people attacking the town and burning it. 'Why? Well, my idea is that Oswestry was getting too big for its boots. It was a semi-independent Marcher town, so every now and then, the king had to put us back in our place by burning us down.'

It came as no surprise that Owain Glyndŵr attacked Oswestry during his rebellion. What I hadn't known, though, was that Glyndŵr's ancestral home was Sycharth Castle, just a few miles west of Oswestry, on the Welsh side of the border. Descended from an old family tracing their origins back to the British kingdoms that emerged after Rome's downfall, Glyndŵr was born and raised in the Marches. He spoke French, English and Welsh, and moved with ease through both English and Welsh society. He was a border lad, and maybe that's why he defined himself so vehemently in opposition to the English who tried so hard to impose hard boundaries.

Glyndŵr's rebellion ground to a halt in 1411. He did not die a heroic death on the battlefield, but simply disappeared. As Welsh writer T. P. Ellis so eloquently puts it: 'He passed away like a mist on his own mountains, with his mission unfulfilled.' After the Acts of Union, Sycharth ended up in Wales (perhaps because of its Glyndŵr connections), but many other Welsh villages ended up in Shropshire, leaving the English county with a sizeable Welsh-speaking population that's survived into the modern era.

'Now Welsh is coming back,' said Mark with his characteristic enthusiasm. 'My foster children go to school in Wales, and our eldest is doing quite well in Welsh classes! I don't understand a bloody thing they tell me, though.'

Mark, who lives on what he described as an English farm on a Welsh hilltop, made sure the museum was bilingual, with displays in both Welsh and English. 'You could refer to Oswestry as a Welsh town in England, but the 1536 Act of Union defined Oswestry as English. We were English then Welsh then English,' he said, as I rapidly typed down notes on my phone, trying to keep up with him. 'Technically, Oswestry is now English. But it's not that simple. There are hill forts everywhere here, for example. Stand on the border and you can see them, all along the horizon. It's always been a borderland, ever since the Cornovii tribe built an outpost – right by my home, as it happens. And because we're a border town, we've always traded with or fought the Welsh.'

Oswestry is geographically in England, but with so many boundaries consolidating in this tiny parcel of land, it was easy to see how the town could have a heart and soul straddling a shifting border, rather than being contained by it. Mark recommended popping over to the indoor market opposite the town hall, where I might unravel the other side of the story by visiting Siop Cwlwm, the only Welsh shop in England.

I found Lowri Roberts, Siop Cwlwm's Welsh-speaking owner, serving a steady queue of customers on the second-floor balcony of the Victorian wrought-iron market hall. 'I'm very biased. I'll give you a very Welsh spectrum on Oswestry, but that's only because I know all the Welsh speakers,' she said in a fast but melodic voice when the queue died down and we had a moment to chat. 'I was born in Oswestry, but I live over the border in Powys now.'

She'd established Siop Cwlwm in 2010, knowing there was demand from the increasing number of Welsh speakers living in the area, and from Welsh tourists who see Oswestry as something of a novelty: 'They see it as a Welsh town in England,' as Lowri put it. Lowri sells all things Welsh. I saw signed autobiographies by Welsh rugby stars like Alun Wyn Jones, history books on Llywelyn the Great and Owain Glyndŵr, and dictionaries and reference books, all in Welsh.

'You could say the shop is on the wrong side of the border, but that's our USP. We're a Welsh shop of course, but we do try and keep away from the red dragons,' she said, after turning around a potential customer looking for a Welsh flag. 'First of all, that's because we're in England. And second, there's more to Welsh culture than flags and daffodils. I'd rather sell Welsh children's books.'

Lowri helped establish a Welsh playgroup in Oswestry, and she teaches adult Welsh language classes in the library. 'They're the only classes outside of Wales funded by the Welsh government,' she said in her lilting accent, her broad smile welcoming yet more customers into the store. 'People want to learn because of their heritage, and we have a lot of people here with dual heritage. I've met some who've moved here thinking Oswestry is in Wales!'

For Lowri, it's a welcome resurgence. 'I live in a bilingual world. I could speak Welsh from the moment I wake up until the moment I go to bed, but the person in the cafe who only speaks English doesn't know this world,' she said, pointing out how speaking multiple languages broadens horizons. 'People in Chepstow and Monmouth, they don't know either.'

As Melanie had told me in Abergavenny, Lowri often encounters resistance from people who don't understand the value of Welsh. She tells them she wouldn't have her business if she didn't speak Welsh, and given she spoke Welsh before English, it's an unmovable part of her identity. Lowri simply wanted the English and Welsh to live on equal terms, to learn from and embrace one another's languages, histories and cultures.

'Our differences should bring us together,' she said, adding how she wants us all to open our worlds up to each other just a little bit more. 'There's a lot of fear when we say the word diversity. But language isn't something to divide us. It's something to share. We all speak English, but the Brythonic language was here before English. Its descendants, Cornish and Welsh, they belong to everyone in Britain.'

I had one last question for Lowri before I left her attending a growing stream of customers. 'So, is Oswestry English or Welsh?' I asked. 'Or somewhere in between?'

'There's a spectrum,' she said right away. 'It's the same on any border. I consider myself to be a Welsh Oswestrian. I was born in England, but I don't consider myself English, while there are people here who consider themselves English though they speak Welsh. Likewise, being Welsh isn't about speaking Welsh, because there are so many English-speaking Welsh supporters when the rugby is on! It's what you feel you are. It's not just language.'

As I walked back to the car park, I knew Oswestry didn't belong on either side of the border, but somewhere in the middle. You can choose to be English, Welsh or something else entirely in Oswestry. A shining example of how Britain's borderlands inspire unity.

The Irish Sea

Speeding north along the A5, following the same road laid down by the Romans during their conquest of Britain almost 2,000 years ago, I was nearing the end of the Welsh Marches. The border realigned itself to the east when I reached Chirk – where an oversized Welsh dragon flew from a Marcher lord's castle – before I crossed over the River Ceiriog, back into Wales.

The border swallowed up Anglo-Saxon place names on its deep dive into England, before coming back around to Wrexham after crossing the River Dee. The newest city in Wales, Wrexham has found fame through the Hollywood takeover of its football team by Rob McElhenny and Ryan Reynolds. In my English ignorance, I'd always assumed that Wrexham – the name sounds overly English to me – was in England, but the city was in fact founded by Anglo-Saxons before being absorbed back into Powys.

Further north, the border went right down the middle of Boundary Lane, a residential street separating Cheshire from Wales, before I finally arrived at Prestatyn, where the sea breeze and squawking seagulls reminded me of Exmouth. On the seafront was a small monument. Although Offa's Dyke probably didn't extend this far north – there was no need, given it's all marshland and estuary, as the River Dee empties into the Irish Sea – this is where Offa's Dyke Path symbolically ends on the north coast of Wales.

I wondered what Offa would think of the great border he'd created. Before the disparate English kingdoms had ever united, he would've found it hard to imagine that a United Kingdom, encompassing all of Britain and the north of Ireland, could ever exist. But even the Marches – where blood was shed for centuries – came together, laying the foundations for the cross-border identity I'd found in towns like Chepstow and Monmouth. My journey had also shown that the Welsh dragon was indeed roaring again, and that this cross-border identity is diminishing in the face of increased national pressures from both sides of the border. The Welsh nation is enjoying a long-awaited resurgence, and as I stood on its blustery northern shores, I wondered if I was putting too much faith in the British project.

I recognize the virtues of the British identity and its capacity to unite us, but I now also saw that much of this 'unity' has come from the homogenizing effect of British culture. Chepstow and Monmouth were heavily Anglicized and their border identities lean strongly towards English language and culture, while the Welsh identity is fighting to regain its place in the borderlands. But there's no reason for us to resurrect Offa's Dyke, and in Abergavenny and Oswestry, I'd found a more intriguing path towards national unity. Both towns had shown how English and Welsh could not only coexist but thrive when their diversity is embraced. Rather than putting up walls and asking people to choose if they were English or Welsh, you can indulge elements of both nationalities. Lowri can be a Welsh Oswestrian, and I can be a Scots-born Englishman.

This was the true uniting identity I'd been searching for, yet hadn't adequately envisioned until now. Not an identity overawed by Englishness, but a true 'borderlander' nationality, existing in a liminal place. This, I think, is what the British identity needs to strive towards: to embrace our multicultural nation, indigenous languages and varied histories, and become stronger for it.

Next, I would turn my attention to England, where regional identities are also seeing a resurgence, far from Westminster. To discover how England's modern-day identities evolved from surprisingly multicultural roots, I would follow another lesser-known divide named the Danelaw: a little-known political entity forged by Vikings, which once carved the country in two.

4

The Danelaw

A true born Englishman's a contradiction,
In speech, an irony, in fact, a fiction!

                Daniel Defoe, *The True-Born Englishman*, 1701

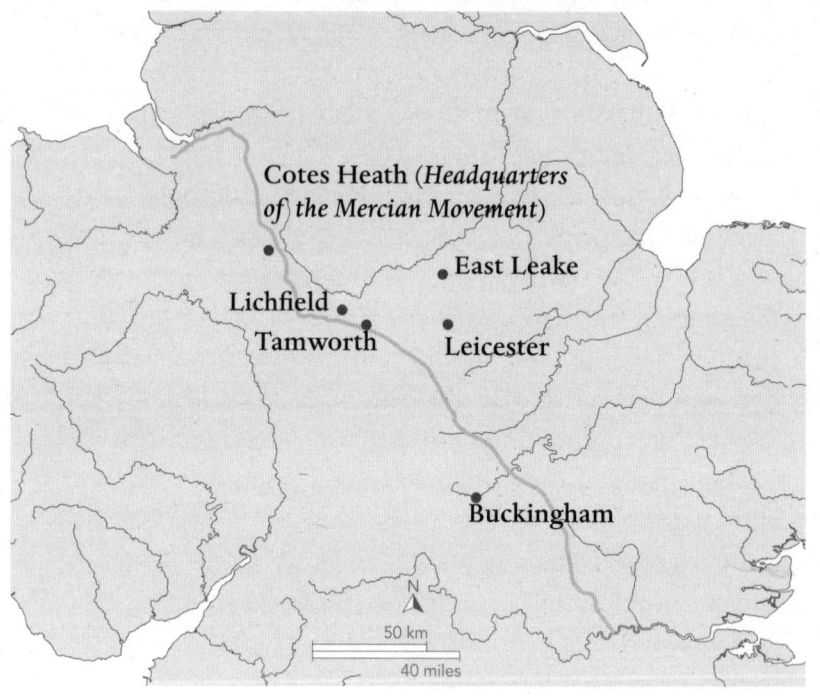

Buckingham

My home town sits on a border, but you wouldn't know it. No ancient dykes scar the landscape, and there are certainly no immigration controls, so I was oblivious to this border during the late childhood and teenage years I spent in Buckingham. But Buckingham – named after the seventh-century Saxon warlord Bucca and now sat in the encroaching orbital path of Milton Keynes – lies in a borderland of old, on a border that still divides England today.

Now I look for it, I see this border on Google Maps. Draw a line from London, northwest to Chester, and you'll trace Watling Street, a Roman road shadowed by the concrete carriageway of the A5. Step back to the ninth century, and the land that became England was divided between petty Anglo-Saxon kingdoms, including Mercia, Wessex, East Anglia and Northumbria. When Scandinavian Vikings invaded these kingdoms and imposed their laws and customs on a vast swathe of territory in the north known as the Danelaw, Watling Street became a political and cultural frontier.

Buckingham sits on the Danelaw's border, a few miles south of the A5. A thousand or so years before, it was home to a timber fortress, a fortified Saxon burh defending the frontier on a strategic bend in the River Great Ouse. Buckingham was a border town – on one side were the Danes; on the other, the Anglo-Saxons – where tributes were paid and treaties made between kings. Slowly, from burhs constructed along the border, the 'English', as they came to call themselves, banded together and reconquered the Danelaw that lay north of Buckingham. Without the existential threat of the Vikings, Anglo-Saxon kingdoms may never have united. Without this border between Anglo-Saxon and Dane, England may never have existed.

My parents were never attached to Buckingham. My mum's from Essex; my dad from rural Oxfordshire. They moved to Buckingham (population: 14,000) because it's in London's commuter belt. There were good schools. House prices – twenty-five years ago, at least – weren't astronomical. An easy place to live. The most exciting events in two decades included the openings of a McDonald's and a Domino's. Buckingham, to me, is the essence of Middle England. A place of flat fields, no discernible geographic features and neutral southern accents. It was my home, but never truly felt like where I was from. I've always craved a deeper sense of identity. I was born in Scotland and have always been envious of the 'real' Scots wearing their tartan kilts to weddings and formal occasions. I spent two years in Oman as a child. I was fascinated by the flowing dishdash outfits and curved khanjar daggers worn by men. English culture, by comparison, seemed to lack this uniqueness: after all, we don't even have a national dress.

With hindsight, I know that's unfair – I'm now guilty of nostalgic trips 'home' to Buckingham, sinking pints with old friends in old haunts, and I know that it's easy to exoticize the unfamiliar, and ignore what's closer to home – but that sense of unbelonging set me on a quest to see the wider world. It started with university. I only moved a hundred miles north to Nottingham, but I crossed an invisible dividing line. The flat farmland changed little, but accents changed. '*Barth*' became '*baff*', bread rolls became cobs and everyone called you 'Duck'. Anything north of Milton Keynes was 'the North' for me, but I soon realized the Midlands was a place in between. A borderland.

Once my sister, my brother and I had all left home, my parents unwittingly crossed the Danelaw, moving an hour north to the Midlands and downsizing to East Leake in Nottinghamshire, a village a few miles outside Loughborough that comprised two long streets and a Co-op, marooned by perpetually muddy fields. They'd moved closer to my sister: she'd started a family with a Midlander who couldn't bear to live elsewhere. Now they have time in their retirement, my parents have made East Leake home.

East Leake was the perfect base for my next journey, along the Danelaw's old southern boundary, where I wanted to discover how England first united, and what now holds England – the United Kingdom's largest and most populous home nation – together. Little remains of this border in the southeast, where London's suburbs long ago subsumed Watling Street, but the divides remain, subtly, in the divergent English identities here in the Midlands and further north. Roughly following the route of Watling Street from Leicester (an old Danish borough a few miles from East Leake) I would road trip northwest to Tamworth, the old Mercian capital. Nations are defined by borders, and I hoped that this ancient borderland, where kingdoms collided and identities clash, could teach me who the English are.

Leicester

My dad dropped me at Loughborough station on a grey morning in late November, and the nine fifty-three East Midlands Railway service whisked me to Leicester in nine minutes. I stepped off the stuffy London-bound train and welcomed the chill autumn air on the platform. Exiting the station, I walked past a statue of Thomas Cook – who in 1841 organized the world's first package tour, from the glitzy heights of Leicester to the even glitzier Loughborough – and saw the first signs of the Christmas season, with wooden market stalls selling mulled wine and bratwursts on Granby Street.

Watling Street, the ancient border I'd be following, runs a few miles south of the city, marking the modern county boundary with Warwickshire, and I was starting here in Leicester, a city with Iron Age roots once ringed by Roman walls, because this was one of the 'Five Boroughs' of the Danelaw. These Danish settlements – the others being Stamford, Derby, Lincoln and Nottingham – were centres of trade and power within Britain's Viking world. Now, they all lie within the East Midlands, but they once formed the heart of the Danelaw.

Linguistic evidence records the extent of Viking settlement in the Danelaw. A remarkable number of Scandinavian-origin words remain in everyday English parlance, including 'law'. Words like slaughter, berserk, skull and ransack are evidence of violent times, while egg, plough and cake point to Danes that farmed and traded. Until the late nineteenth century, English counties were divided into either 'hundreds' (an Anglo-Saxon term found south of

THE DANELAW

Watling Street) or *'wapentakes'* (used in the Danelaw). *Wapentake* is an Old Norse term, roughly meaning to 'brandish weapons', which describes councils of freedmen who were permitted to brandish weapons in meetings. Once you know what to look for, you'll see Danish place names dotting northern England. The suffix '-by' designates a small village or homestead – including places like Kirby and Oadby in Leicestershire – while '-thorpe' – like Scunthorpe in Lincolnshire, or Grimethorpe in Yorkshire – designates a larger settlement. Danish place names stop almost exactly at Watling Street.

I wanted to know if a legacy of the Danelaw survived, beyond place names, in a borderland where English and Danish cultures clashed, so I'd arranged a meeting with a local historian-turned-YouTuber in Leicester's timber-framed, fourteenth-century Guildhall.

Leicester's city centre was lined with fried chicken shops, bubble tea joints and fast-food outlets with names like Chaiiwala and Bombay Bites. A faint cloud of vape smoke lingered around the Clock Tower, where teenagers gathered near a boombox and a man with a warbling voice preached to indifferent shoppers about the end of the world. Leicester's history hides behind damp flagstones and concrete shopping centres. The Romans' granite and sandstone walls were slighted centuries ago during medieval rebellions, the abbeys levelled during the Reformation – but this is a city where English kings are buried under parking lots.

By the old Corn Exchange, I was swept up in the 700-year-old outdoor market's hungry crowds, the cold air thick with the steamy tang of samosas, falafel and biryani.

Among red-and-white awnings, stalls stocked a colourful mass of bright red and green chillies, dragon fruits and tangerines. Market traders wore turbans, women in bright saris haggled over prices and men in flowing dish-dash handed out free Qurans. Leicester (population: 366,000) is the UK's first 'plural city', a city where no single ethnic group forms a majority and where cultures coexist on medieval English streets.

I found the Guildhall's wonky, Tudor facade next to Leicester Cathedral, where it's sat on the ancient Fosse Way connecting Exeter and Lincoln. Jim Butler was waiting in the attached Cafe No:7, where late-morning sunlight streamed through wide glass windows. Jim was born and bred in Leicester. He wore a baggy fleece and walking shoes, his glasses giving him the look of a fun history teacher who loved getting his boots muddy on field trips. He'd spent much of his working life as a museum professional: first in York, the old Viking capital, and now back home in Leicester, where he'd helped entomb Richard III in the cathedral next door, after the king's car-park exhumation in 2012.

I recognized Jim's big grin from his YouTube channel, where I'd first found him online exploring Leicestershire's Danish past on his 'Hidden Histories' show. He puts his enthusiasm to good use leading Hidden History tours of Leicester, too. 'I'm also a freelance driving instructor,' he added, recounting his CV with a chuckle. 'I've got two lessons booked in this afternoon, followed by a lecture on medieval crime and punishment. Variety is the spice of life!'

Jim explained, in his broad Midlands accent, how Leicester's history is one of migration, just as I'd seen in the marketplace. Merchants from across the Roman Empire once plied their trade here, and the settlement is older than York and London. Anglo-Saxons usurped the native Britons, transforming Leicester into a key Mercian stronghold in an expansive kingdom, which at the height of its power in the eighth century (when King Offa built his dyke), stretched from the Welsh border to modern-day East Anglia, swallowing up London and the Midlands. Mercia was continually at odds with its neighbours, including the Welsh kingdoms to the west, its southern rival Wessex and the northern power of Northumbria. It was into this fractured political landscape the Vikings stepped in the late eighth century, ushering in the Viking era with a bloody raid on Lindisfarne's monastery off the Northumbrian coast in 793.

Historians have long debated the term 'Viking'. It's a corruption of the Old Norse term *'Vikingr'*, which means to go raiding. No people called themselves Vikings, and there were certainly no horned helmets. The Anglo-Saxons simply used the catch-all name 'Danes' for these Scandinavian and Norse invaders, who hailed from Norway, Denmark and Sweden. Warmongering yet politically savvy, the Vikings toppled divided Anglo-Saxon kingdoms one by one, and by 874, they'd taken East Anglia, subjugated Northumbria and conquered much of Mercia, including Leicester.

In the south, King Alfred of Wessex fought back. By 886, he had the Danes on the back foot, forcing King Guthrum, who ruled East Anglia, to convert to Christianity and sign a treaty establishing the frontier between Wessex and the Danelaw – those parts of England where Danish law now took precedence – along the line of Watling Street.

Like all borders through history, the Danelaw's boundary was far from impenetrable. Border cities like Leicester became melting points of languages, cultures, customs and laws. Danish traders bargained with their Wessexian counterparts in the markets, and Scandinavian settlers and Mercians intermarried in the countryside. Given the fluidity of medieval alliances, Mercians often revolted against Wessex, and Northumbrians fought with the Danes. In Leicester, a Viking Jarl (Earl) named Orm ('the Serpent') played all sides masterfully for decades, switching allegiances between Danish and English kings whenever necessary to maintain power.

In this liminal borderland, all sides adopted new customs and beliefs. Within a few generations, the pagan invaders were largely Christianized, a transition evident in nearby Repton, now a small Midlands village on the River Trent's flood plain but once a royal Mercian abode the Vikings conquered. There, extensive Viking burial mounds remain in surrounding woodlands. Excavations have revealed fallen warriors buried with Christian crosses, and others with hammers of Thor around their necks. Some had both, which Jim says points to a merging of cultures as Danes settled in for the long haul. 'I reckon they're hedging their bets somewhat rotten for the afterlife!' he said with his characteristic grin. 'The invaders were not just changing England. England was changing them.'

England, though, didn't exist as we know it today. Alfred (who would be the only English king ever given the epithet 'the Great'), still dreamt of driving the invaders out, and uniting the English-speaking peoples under one nation called 'Engla land', the 'Land of the Angles'. He built burhs along the Danelaw's frontier, and with his Mercian allies, began reconquering the Five Boroughs. His successor, Edward, continued

THE DANELAW

his work, and Alfred's grandson Athelstan (the same Athelstan who set the River Tamar as Cornwall's border) would become the first king of what we could call England, after winning a decisive battle against an allied army of Danes, Celts and Scots in 937 at Brunanburh.

The Danelaw was short-lived (it effectively ended in 954, after the final capture of Jorvik from a Viking named Erik Bloodaxe), but the very existence of the Watling Street border united the English-speaking peoples against the Viking invaders (that, perhaps, is their biggest legacy). But Jim believes it was never a case of 'us vs them', English against Dane. Instead, 'England developed a cocktail of cultures,' a cocktail that's continued to be stirred through the centuries.

Danish influence has remained, be it in the place names, the language we speak and even in our very DNA (some 6 per cent of modern Brits have Viking ancestry). 'There's always been a multicultural element to Leicester,' Jim explained, saying we can trace a continual stream of multiculturalism right back to the Danelaw, and even earlier. 'All the way back to the Africans serving in Rome's legions. Geographically we're the middle of Britain, and we've always been a melting pot of people.'

Today, myriad peoples, communities, ethnicities and religions from across the world live their lives in Leicester, perhaps oblivious to the border that runs a few miles to their south, yet still unwittingly defined by the city's borderland mentality.

Jim's grandparents moved here from Ireland and Wales in the 1930s, a time when Leicester's textile industry was begging for workers as it clothed the world. Indian and

Caribbean migrants first arrived in large numbers after the Second World War, and in 1972, around 10,000 Asian Ugandans came to Leicester when the Ugandan dictator, Idi Amin, gave them just ninety days to leave their homes, each carrying one suitcase and no more than £55.

Fearing the arrival of Asian Ugandan exiles (many holding British passports, Uganda being a former colony), Leicester City Council paid for adverts in Ugandan newspapers saying, 'Don't come to Leicester.' 'It backfired spectacularly,' said Jim with a hearty laugh. 'Asian Ugandans had never heard of Leicester until they saw the adverts. After that, they became aware Leicester already had established Asian communities and many decided to settle here.'

Immigration regenerated a city whose traditional industries, including clothing and textiles, were disappearing. Belgrave Road, which Jim said was set to be demolished, was saved when Asian Ugandan émigrés moved into derelict houses and set up shops and businesses. The initial pushback against Asian Ugandan migration dissipated within a generation as Leicester felt the economic benefits of multiculturalism, just as people may have done a thousand years earlier when Danish traders arrived.

Jim grew up in a multicultural Leicester and can't imagine the city any other way. Migrant communities, including Asian Ugandans, Indians, Pakistanis, Somalians and Eastern Europeans all contribute to a city with a majority of minorities, a truly multicultural place, and a representation of the wider character of twenty-first century England.

The history of England is one of migration and change, of a patchwork of regional identities held loosely together by language and shared history, constantly reshaped by outside

THE DANELAW

influences. The Danelaw is the history of England – without it, England may never have come to be – and at the centre of this is Leicester, a borderland holding it all together.

'Leicester is at the heart of England's waves of migration,' Jim said, wrapping up his history lecture with a heartfelt conclusion about the lessons we can learn from his home city's past. 'We're this historical buffer zone, a borderland where people have always lived with change. We can reassure future generations that it's going to be OK. It'll be different, but it'll be all right. Perhaps that's the Danelaw's legacy. We don't fear change because we've always witnessed it.'

That afternoon I wanted to dig deeper into this modern, multicultural identity Jim believes is the legacy of 2,000 years of evolution. I'd recruited two old university friends for the task, who just so happened to be Midlanders. I walked back to the train station and found Joe and Kev in the car park.

Joe grew up in Beaumont Leys, a Leicester suburb. True to his Midland self, he could never leave his roots behind, so chose to attend Nottingham, just thirty miles up the road, for university. Even after scoring high-flying accountancy jobs in London, earning more money than I probably ever will, he returned home to live in the granny annex of his family's home. Kev hails from Rutland, England's smallest county, just east of Leicester and a few miles west of Stamford (which is just over the county border in Lincolnshire), another one of the Danelaw's Five Boroughs. Both are diehard Leicester City fans, and, like Joe, Kev didn't stray from the Midlands either, also attending Nottingham to study economics. Proud of his Midland identity, whenever we chatted about borders he relished telling me the story of how Rutland was forcibly merged with Leicestershire in the 1970s, only to regain its 'independence' in 1997, after what he loved calling a 'Brexit-style referendum' determining the historic county's administrative status.

Joe was acting tour guide for the day. He'd been in hospital just the week before, but no ailment would stop him playing ambassador in the city he loved. We hopped in his car and, ignoring the flashing oil-warning light he said not to worry about, drove around the wide green space of Victoria Park ('the most beautiful park in Leicester,' said Joe), past Leicester City Football Club's King Power Stadium, and over the Union Canal on to Narborough Road, the city's main southwestern thoroughfare.

'Narborough Road?' Joe asked with a laugh as we jumped out for a walk. 'I wonder why anyone wants to go there sometimes. It's a shithole. But officially, it's the most diverse street in Leicester.'

Joe doesn't mince his words. The Leicester he knows, although massively multicultural, has huge areas of deprivation and plenty of low-income council estates like the one he grew up on. Despite his love for the city, he's tough on it, too. Joe described Narborough Road as like an old-fashioned English high street, with small independent shops everywhere. Equally, though, Narborough Road is very *unlike* an old-fashioned English high street. A study by the London School of Economics comparing diversity across English cities recorded shopkeepers and business owners from twenty-two different nations, the highest level of diversity on any road in the country.

We walked past Baltic Stores, the Bucharest Vape Shop and the One Nation Afro-Caribbean cash and carry. There was a Lebanese restaurant, the Turkish restaurant Saray, Global Grocers, Halal Express, a Romanian church, and the Gurdwara, a Sikh place of worship, where, in the Sikh charitable tradition, Joe said, you could get a free meal, any time of the day. 'You get some insanely good food on Narborough Road,' said Joe, his affection for Leicester now shining through. 'Great Turkish restaurants and excellent Asian supermarkets. But let's save ourselves for a curry on the Golden Mile later.'

We hopped back in the car and drove down one of Leicester's long, terraced Victorian roads. Cars parked on either side further narrowed the nineteenth-century lanes of redbrick houses as we passed Polish stores, a Romanian butcher and a Kurdish barber. 'Even in the last ten years, these streets have changed massively,' Joe commented, his tour continuing on to Fosse Way. 'There are so many more Eastern Europeans. I think it's a good thing. It would be empty without all the Eastern European shops. Our high streets aren't dead in Leicester and immigration has a lot to do with that.'

This is how Britain's high streets should be, instead of town centres bloated with charity shops and empty storefronts. Without immigrants, Leicester's suburban shops would lay empty, windows boarded up. Still, Joe warned that Leicester is a long way from being an exemplary model of integration. His experience growing up was of different ethnic groups and communities sticking together. Beaumont Leys, his home area, is predominantly white; St Matthew's is Somalian; Belgrave Road is Hindu; and Spinney Hills Muslim.

'That's human nature,' said Kev from the back seat. 'You have a natural preference to stay within your own groups. A few generations later, you get segregation. Have you heard of Thomas Schelling's model of segregation?'

Kev, who works as a data analyst, explained the theory as we drove out to Abbey Park, where we wandered along the banks of the River Soar, scoping out park benches where Joe once hung out as a teenager. Schelling, an economist, developed a model suggesting that established groups prefer to stay within the boundaries of the familiar, be that ethnicity, religion or nationality. It helps explain why so many waves of migration have occurred in Leicester, with established minority communities providing an attractive sense of familiarity and security for new migrants far from home. The negative side to this, as Kev suggested, was segregation, which can lead to conflict – not just between majority and minority populations, but among minorities, too.

Kev recalled friction between Hindus and Muslims spilling over in August 2022 and there being significant unrest in Leicester, after an Asia Cup cricket match between Pakistan and India ignited underlying tensions between the two communities. 'Protection groups' formed on both sides, and – over the same weekend of Queen Elizabeth II's funeral – Muslims and Hindus clashed on Belgrave Road. The city blamed a spillover of Hindu nationalism from India; Kev blamed sports. 'It happens every time India and Pakistan play. But that was particularly nasty,' said Kev with a shrug. 'It started with cricket and became an excuse to riot.'

The city was left questioning itself. The bishop of Leicester, in an address to the House of Commons, described Leicester as a 'city made by migrants', but the riots showed a greater need for inter-community integration. Immigration has become a defining issue of twenty-first century Britain, but tellingly, it was the Midlands' massive diversity that both Kev and Joe were proud of, because it's moulded Leicester into such a unique place.

The temperature quickly dropped as dusk drew over Leicester's winter skyline. Joe drove us to the Golden Mile, which takes in Belgrave Road and Melton Road. We parked down a dimly lit side street and walked on to Leicester's most famous thoroughfare, so called for the extensive concentration of Asian-owned gold dealers. Leicester hosts the largest Diwali celebrations in England, with 30,000 people turning out for the Hindu festival of lights in late autumn, and the remnants of 'Happy Diwali' banners were still strung between lamp posts, Christmas lights and wreaths slowly replacing them.

Joe took us to the Indian Queen, a Leicester establishment known as a 'Desi Pub'. I'd never been anywhere quite like it. There wasn't much to look at on the outside, and if not for the queue of lads in flannel shirts, I'd never have known it was there. They were waiting to be buzzed into the long, narrow pub which, with its 1970s decor and shuttered windows, felt like a late-night lock-in.

Football commentary buzzed from TV screens. A man pulled pints of San Miguel, Kingfisher and Cobra as the flannel shirt lads crowded the bar. Turbaned Sikhs drank Madri at round tables, and an old man in a flat cap sipped ale in the corner. The smell of lager mixed with the aroma of paneer and masala, and we sat down at the back of the cash-only pub and looked at faded A5 menus printed in wonky fonts.

'In Leicester, a lot of old boozers and working men's clubs are now Desi Pubs,' Joe explained, as we ordered fish pakora, samosas and poppadoms. 'Lots of pubs that were struggling, not bringing in the punters any more, they'd palm their kitchens off to an Indian restaurant so people could have food with their drinks.'

The first Desi Pub in Leicester might have been the Durham Ox, opened by Sohan Singh in 1962. Sporting names like the Woolpack or Paddy's, Desi Pubs combine two of Britain's greatest pastimes: drinking beer and eating curry. They're a cracking example of different cultures bouncing positively off one another.

We followed up the starters with prawn masala, cheesy naan and biryani, the menu a tantalizing feast of Anglo-Indian cuisine. Now an immovable element of British culture, the first Indian restaurant in the UK was the Hindoostane Coffee House in London, opened by Sake Dean Mahomed in 1810. The Balti was first cooked up in Birmingham kitchens, and a Pakistani chef, Ali Ahmed Aslam, is credited with inventing the chicken tikka masala in Glasgow's Shish Mahal restaurant in the 1970s.

As we sank Kingfisher beers, Joe said he sees the Midlands as traditionally English, yet hugely multicultural. Kev described the Midlands as dead, flat farmland, a place defined by its agricultural and industrial past. They had their canals, coal mines and potteries, while folk songs told tales of poachers and farmyard antics. 'Forget the Cumberland sausage,' said Kev, who was somehow still thinking about food, despite the curry on the table. 'The Lincolnshire sausage is clearly the greatest!'

Kev also felt that as a Midlander, there was no room for them in the north–south divide, and that their identity, that's neither northern nor southern, gets lost. The Midlands is a place in between, one of many regional identities comprising the wider English, and in turn, British identities. The Midlands identity, at least here in Leicester, also represents the changing face of Englishness, quite literally. Leicester is no utopia, and integration, segregation and deprivation are all serious issues, but the city takes clichéd ideas of what Englishness means – stereotypes based on class, race, tea drinking, beefeaters and what have you – and turns them on its head.

Leicester's motto is *'Semper eadem'*, Latin for 'always the same'. It's a contradiction and a truth, because Leicester never sits still. It's never the same from one generation to the next, but at its core, it *is* the same. The English nation that united for the first time under Athelstan over a thousand years ago also comprised myriad peoples from both home and abroad, and in that respect, little is different. Leicester is the England that has always been.

Tamworth

As Tamworth Castle cast long shadows in the dying sunlight, screams, shouts, jeers and chants echoed across the ancient Mercian capital. This was no heathen army of Danish warriors marching on Tamworth, but an equally heathen army of two hundred right-wing nationalists rioting outside the Holiday Inn in August 2024.

Riot police formed a shield wall in front of the high-rise hotel. The mob tore up bricks from the car park, and hurled them through windows. Molotov cocktails sailed through the air, fireworks bounced off pavements and the smell of burning petrol tainted the evening's summer breeze. The Holiday Inn almost went up in flames, the asylum seekers trapped inside fearing for their lives. As arrests were made and rioters charged, Tamworth, an ordinarily quiet Staffordshire market town, was left asking, 'Why?'

I arrived in Tamworth (population: 80,000) on a cold day in late November. Overlooking the confluence of the rivers Tame and Anker, twenty miles or so west of Leicester, Tamworth Castle sits atop a grassy motte surrounded by pleasant Victorian gardens.

From the castle's turret, where cold gusts of wind snapped a large Union Jack taut, I saw the bright green letters spelling out 'Holiday Inn' on the white front of the hotel across the river. I traced the line of Watling Street, the Danelaw's old border, through the town's southern suburbs, and to the north, where red-brick buildings and council flats spilt into Staffordshire's rolling countryside.

King Offa held court and built a royal palace in Tamworth. On my way into the castle – hewn in sandstone by the Normans – I'd found a statue of Lady Aethelfled of Mercia, King Alfred the Great's eldest child, at the base of the mound. From Tamworth, Lady Aethelfled orchestrated the fight against the Danes, leading her troops into battle, recapturing Derby, forcing Jarl Orm to surrender Leicester and paving the way for Alfred's son and grandson to reconquer the Danelaw. The men took the glory, but it was really Aethelfled, a warrior heroine to rival Boudicca, who had made it possible.

I wondered if the rioters in the Holiday Inn car park believed they were defending England when they tried to burn the asylum seekers' refuge. They weren't. There are very few times I've been ashamed to be English, but in the summer of 2024, I was. There were twenty-nine 'anti-immigration' rallies, demonstrations and riots in towns and cities across England and Northern Ireland – including Tamworth – in the wake of the tragic deaths of three young girls after a stabbing at a Taylor Swift-themed dance class in Southport, Liverpool, on 29 July 2024. Right-wing rioters attacked mosques, detention centres and hotels, incited by a misinformation campaign blaming the stabbing on a migrant, when the perpetrator was born in Cardiff to Rwandan parents and raised in Lancashire. The Southport murders were atrocious, but the right-wing reaction to it was also shameful.

Leicester is less than an hour's drive away, but Tamworth, which is 94 per cent white, couldn't be more different. In the same borderland where England was born, the riots spoke of a nation grappling with its identity, as seismic demographic shifts reveal the darkest depths of English nationalism. Shivering in the cold wind atop the castle's tower, I feared petrol bombs and racism would be the future of England, but hoped Tamworth, King Offa's Mercian capital, would prove me wrong.

I followed an uneven stone staircase down from the tower, stopping in the gallery below to look at finds from the Staffordshire Hoard, the largest cache of Anglo-Saxon gold, silver and bronze found anywhere in England. An exasperated teacher shepherded a party of rowdy schoolkids through displays of Viking swords and shields, and above a fireplace hung the yellow cross and royal-blue field of the Mercian flag, the first inkling that this old Anglo-Saxon identity is still remembered.

I crossed through the castle's gate and along the mossy Herringbone Wall into the Castle Grounds. A faint mist hung low over the River Anker, seeping into green bushes on either bank. I could almost picture Danish warbands emerging like wraiths in the night from the longboats they had sailed up Mercia's wide waterways. Inside the old burh, still the commercial centre of Tamworth, market-stall traders stamped their cold feet on medieval pavements.

I looked up at Tamworth's town hall, where in 1834, Sir Robert Peel read the nation's first political manifesto from the balcony, then I strolled past a craft beer taproom and greasy spoon cafes selling full English breakfasts. Tamworth is the sort of town where you can still buy a jacket potato with three fillings for a fiver, and indeed, one of Tamworth's most famous sons is 'Spud Man', a TikToker drawing large crowds to his jacket potato van in the square. A rare town where locals say 'Hi' to strangers on the high street, among mobility-scooter shops and Turkish barbers, this seemed like an unlikely setting for a far-right riot.

I was looking for 'Offa House', the headquarters of Tamworth Community Together, a non-profit organization running homelessness-prevention schemes, youth programmes and – key to my stop in Tamworth – providing support to asylum seekers. In the wake of the riots, I hoped that Chief Operating Officer Lee Bates could reveal the real character of Tamworth. I found him inside the Helping Hands Cafe below the social enterprise's office, where the warm hiss of a barista machine welcomed me in from the cold.

Lee works tirelessly to bring his town together. Wearing casual clothes with a lanyard draped around his neck, he knew everyone and happily greeted all the regulars walking through the community cafe's doors by name. 'Tamworth's a lovely place. There's a great community spirit. Everyone knows everyone,' he said, as we sat down with big mugs of coffee by steamed-up windows. 'Despite the riots, it's a wonderful community.'

Middle-aged, with a gentle tone and distinctive Midlands accent – he said *grass*, not *grarse* – Lee's worked in the community for decades: first on Staffordshire County Council, and now on projects like Tamworth Community Together. His contributions to Tamworth were recognized when he was granted the honorary role of deputy lieutenant of Staffordshire, a role, he said, which comes with a fantastically archaic ceremonial costume.

'So, I suppose we could be Vikings,' he said with a humorous glint in his eye as I told him about my journey into the Danelaw so far. 'And, obviously, we're very proud of our history as the capital of Mercia. This is Offa House. We've got a lot of history, but the town is changing. It's predominantly white, but we've had a big escalation in terms of different cultures, from Ukraine, Spain and the Middle East.'

Lee had just finished leading his team's morning meeting. Twelve refugees had been temporarily homed in the Holiday Inn that week, where the social enterprise provided SIM cards, translation services and mental-health support for what he described as a 'voiceless community'. The Holiday Inn was the only hotel in Staffordshire providing asylum seekers with temporary accommodation when rioting broke out across England, which is why, Lee said, it had become a far-right target. The riots were a blight on Tamworth, he added, but he's proud that the community, by and large, has since come out in support of asylum seekers.

'We had a welfare meeting with asylum seekers last week, now they've recommissioned the hotel,' he explained. 'New arrivals were desperately in need of clothes, shoes and adapters. Within two hours, we galvanized thirty bags of clothing. That's the power of Tamworth's community network. It's a large town, but it's a small town really. Everyone knows each other and that helps get things done.'

Lee also recognizes that a large cohort of locals were arrested and charged following the riots. 'We have to own the fact that our own residents were motivated to go and try and set fire to a hotel,' he said, adding how he wants to understand why some local people felt so aggrieved by the presence of asylum seekers. 'It's important we understand what people's motivations were. Was it the cost of living? You know, "I'm struggling, and these people are coming here and getting free things." Is it genuine racism?'

The biggest factor, theorized Lee, wasn't necessarily racism, but disillusionment. Protestors were striking out against the frustrations of living in a country with plummeting services and a shrinking economy. It's easier for the government and media to blame immigration and asylum seekers than to battle underlying causes. To counter this, Tamworth Community Together holds community meetings and publishes FAQs on asylum seekers to combat disinformation campaigns. They source volunteer placements for asylum seekers, providing them with an opportunity to give back, to show themselves in a positive light. 'We're a nation that doesn't like unfairness,' he said. 'The perception is that asylum seekers are getting X, Y and Z above everybody else, which people hate. But that's not the reality.'

Asylum seekers don't simply waltz over the border into a five-star hotel, a new iPhone in their pocket and their wallet stuffed full of benefit payments. In fact, they're always at the back of the queue for NHS services (GPs visit the Holiday Inn out of hours, Lee said, so as not to interfere with their normal practice schedules); the Home Office approval process keeps people in limbo for years; and they can't work while they are waiting for approval, so are forced to live off £8 a week. The word 'hotel', though, conjures notions of luxury, which angers locals feeling hard done by themselves.

'I think it's ridiculous,' said Lee, his fiery side bursting through an otherwise gentle demeanour. 'We've got an economy that's struggling, and we've got people here who want to work but the government say they can't. So many skills wasted. Doctors, surgeons, construction workers, plumbers and electricians. All the things we need. There wouldn't be this us versus them situation if people could see asylum seekers working and paying taxes. There wouldn't be so much animosity.'

Lee's angry that we gave up, through Brexit, agreements with European countries, ensuring that asylum seekers need to be housed in hotels as backlogs increase. He passionately explained how asylum seekers aren't here for free things, but because they might be thrown in prison for their sexual orientation, or persecuted for their faith. People make perilous journeys here because of what Britain stands for. We are the Britain we project to the world, and the moment we turn people away, we surely become as bad as the regimes that asylum seekers are often fleeing.

Part of my quest is to discover what it means to be English and British. While protesters firebombing a hotel full of immigrants think they're defending some warped ideal of England, or Britain, they're wrong. The Britain I want to exist is one full of people like Lee, people who don't have some distorted sense of patriotism, but own up to their nation's shortcomings, admit what's wrong and try to find solutions.

I asked Lee what he thinks modern Britain stands for. 'We are a multicultural society. That much is evident,' he said after a pause. 'Britain should be respectful, tolerant. We need to be nice to each other. We all want to be part of a society, to be loved, connected, and that transcends your skin colour or religion. It's the basics really. It's not how many flags you have, or how loud you sing the national anthem.'

Lee should know what it means to be British. He runs British citizenship ceremonies in his honorary role for Staffordshire, a role in which he directly represents the king. He said he loves seeing new Brits dressed up in their finest for the ceremonies; their excitement and appreciation for their adopted home country is infectious. We should rightly celebrate Britishness: we should be excited about being British if we want to be. But we don't need to set hotels on fire. That, I think, is particularly un-British.

After our chat, Lee took me to see St Editha's Church. Built in the fourteenth century, it stands in the centre of the old burh, on the same hallowed ground where the Danes destroyed an earlier church in 874AD. Inside the church, home to a rare double-helix staircase, there was a buzz of activity among the wooden pews, war memorials and stained-glass windows depicting Saxon warrior saints.

English lessons occupied one corner of the church, where a Japanese couple and two ladies in hijabs practised with volunteer teachers, and a heritage group was meeting in the cafe. A smiley church volunteer named Charles happily showed us into what he called a 'secret' crypt, packed with Anglo-Saxon relics unearthed beneath St Editha's. Charles said Tamworth was proud of its Mercian heroes, heroes like Aethelfled and Athelstan (Athelstan was raised here by Aethelfled, before becoming king of England).

When I said I was exploring Britain's borders, he excitedly exclaimed how the county border between Staffordshire and Warwickshire once cut through the middle of town, too, before it was moved south. There were once two town halls, two councils, two of everything. 'This is a border town,' Charles said. 'We're proud of that past.'

Identities clash on borders. By looking to this ancient borderland – where Anglo-Saxons and Danes once battled – I'd seen a darker side of English nationalism, one of racism and rioting. But through this dark undercurrent, Tamworth's community spirit offered hope. That's the true character of Englishness.

Lichfield

The next day, I picked up the route of the A5 from Tamworth, following the old Roman road for five miles before shooting north into Lichfield. The Staffordshire city (population: 35,000), home to an unusual three-spired cathedral and the birthplace of Samuel Johnson, the eighteenth-century essayist who compiled the first comprehensive dictionary of the English language, is Tamworth's posh neighbour. There were no spud vans, but a high street lined with fashionable outlets selling Le Creuset sets, Hunter wellies and Barbour coats. Gourmet bistros offered fine-dining set menus at excruciating prices, antiques shops sported names like 'Quercus of Quonians' and the medieval centre retained an abundance of black-and-white timber frame buildings, including a wonky-looking coffee shop dating to 1740.

I was intrigued by the Mercian flag I'd seen in Tamworth Castle. Lichfield Cathedral, one of King Offa's favoured haunts and the ecclesiastical centre of Mercia, seemed like an excellent place to investigate the existence (or not) of this Mercian identity. The cathedral's three spires rose above bare trees by Minster Pool, fallen leaves crunched underfoot, and I walked past a sign warning, 'No wagons or carts or cattle allowed in Cathedral Close.' Sunshine cut through dull clouds, saturating the cathedral's magnificent facade of saintly effigies, gargoyles and royal statues with a bright golden light.

I stepped through heavy wooden doors into the cathedral's dim interior, where rows of wooden pews sat under a cavernous, pitched roof. Hidden crypts lay beneath my winter hiking boots, and centuries of renovations and extensions were evident in layers of Anglo-Saxon, Norman and Victorian masonry. I met Patricia, the cathedral's resident historian, by the entrance. 'Let me show you what we can't see,' she said rather cryptically, before giving me the grand tour. Patricia lives and breathes Mercian history, quite literally, given she's a resident on Cathedral Close. Wearing heavy winter clothes to combat the cathedral's chilly interior, her accent was suitably RP, but she was well grounded by her Black Country roots.

'I understand you're writing about borderlands,' she added in a quiet yet clear voice, honed by years spent working in the cathedral's peaceful environs. 'This was a borderland. We are standing in what was the Danelaw. But I'm afraid there's not much left in the way of Watling Street's legacy. As we go around the cathedral, I'll say, "we think" and "possibly" quite a lot, because we're just not certain of the past.'

The first church was founded here in 700AD (we think). Inside a gloomy side vault, Patricia showed me the Lichfield Angel, a thick slab of cracked limestone masonry depicting the carved likeness of the archangel Gabriel, unearthed beneath the cathedral during renovations in 2003. Dated to the eighth century, the slab was (possibly) part of a shrine containing the relics of St Chad, a seventh-century Northumbrian monk who converted pagan Mercia to Christianity. The Lichfield Angel is a rare fusion of Anglo-Saxon and Roman elements, the religious artwork of a recently converted people. By King Offa's time, Mercia was proudly Christian. Testament to his kingdom's power, Lichfield was made the centre of a new archbishopric. The highest division of religious power in the land, Lichfield became the third archbishopric in England after Canterbury and York. After Offa's death in 795, Canterbury rescinded this archbishopric, and soon after, pagan Danes were knocking on Mercia's door.

Archaeologists found the Lichfield Angel buried facedown beneath the cathedral. The nature of its burial suggests panicked monks hurriedly concealed the limestone slab before Viking raiders ransacked Lichfield. Patricia showed me the Lichfield Gospels, a velum tome compiled here (again, possibly) in the eighth century. They ended up in Wales, as evidenced by medieval Welsh scrawled in the margins, where they may have been sent for safekeeping as the Viking onslaught swept into Mercia. The gospels found their way home, and today, bishops, deans and canons still take oaths upon the beautiful book. 'It's amazing when you see this going past in the cathedral,' Patricia said excitedly. 'It's 1,200 years of continuous worship and history.'

As Patricia had said, what we can't see is often as telling as what we can. What else was destroyed in raids or carted off to Denmark or Norway, lost in North Sea storms or buried beneath ransacked churches? We'll never know. Similarly, Patricia said, there's much we'll never know about the people of Mercia, who lived and died in these turbulent times. The one constant is that Mercia was always a borderland, a fact Patricia said gives us some clue as to the endemic violence, clashing identities and fluid allegiances that pervaded the land.

It's a history and identity echoed in the very name 'Mercia', which comes from the Old English *'merce'* – meaning the same as 'march', denoting a border or frontier. Mercia loosely means 'people of the border'. The Midlands has readopted this borderland identity in recent years. There's West Mercia Police, the Mercian Trust in Walsall, the Mercian Academy in Derbyshire and, if you have a quick google, you'll find businesses like Mercian Skip Hire and Mercian Windows listed across the Midlands. 'When you have a wider area and you need a name for it, somewhere that's not either Staffordshire or Warwickshire,' said Patricia, 'then Mercia is always a good bet.'

By the gift shop, there's a memorial chapel to the Mercian Regiment, a name adopted when Midlands army regiments were downsized in the twentieth century. There was a Mercian flag, too, although Patricia believes this to be a recent creation. 'Aethelfled would never have flown that,' she said dismissively.

As we stepped outside to admire the cathedral's facade, I asked Patricia if there's been a reawakening of this Mercian identity. 'Ask your average person working here in the cathedral and they'll not know what the Mercian flag is,' said Patricia indifferently. 'I don't imagine the border folk of Mercia will rise up for independence any time soon. Where would you even draw the border? Mercia's time has come and gone, I think.'

Given the rising tide of nationalism I'd found on my earlier journeys through Cornwall and Wales, I'd expected to find a growing desire for increased regional autonomy along the Danelaw's border. Although Patricia suggested otherwise, there was, however, at least one man who believes in Mercian independence. I left the triple spires of Lichfield Cathedral behind, driving north into the heart of Mercia to meet Jeff Kent, co-founder of the Mercian Movement and Convener of the Acting Witan.

Independent Mercia

A forty-five-minute drive northwest of Lichfield, I found myself in Cotes Heath, a few miles south of Stoke-on-Trent's congested ring road. It was no more than a hamlet, surrounded by the rolling farmland I'd come to expect in Staffordshire. A solitary main road branched off into Cotes Heath's lonely new-build housing estates. Jeff's house – labelled on Google Maps as 'The Mercia Movement: Political

Party Office' – was a picture of Middle England, a classic suburban abode with space for two cars in the driveway and a cherry tree on the front lawn.

But Jeff, who gave me a light handshake and asked me to leave my shoes at the door, is hardly your average Middle Englander. A willowy figure, now in retirement, his long grey hair reached past his shoulders, his bushy beard a throwback to his younger days when he released environmental concept albums and animal-rights protest songs as part of a band named the Witan, released under his own label, Witan Records. With his black T-shirt tucked into jeans, Jeff looked like he would've torn up Woodstock back in the day, but his rounded glasses gave him a slightly scholarly appearance. He'd studied international relations, taught history and founded a small publishing house named (you guessed it) Witan Publishing. An activist at heart, Jeff resolutely believed Middle England's problems – be it the environment, housing or the economy – could be solved by looking to a golden past, to a time when Mercia was independent.

Jeff is keeping ancient Mercia's hearths warm. He believes the United Kingdom is illegally occupying Mercia, and in 1993, co-founded the Mercia Movement to campaign for this Anglo-Saxon region's independence. Jeff's 'Independent Mercia' would encompass twenty English counties, including parts of what is now London and Buckinghamshire (which I wasn't too happy about, I'll admit, given we don't see ourselves as Midlanders). He wants to reinstate 'the Witan', the ancient council of elders and noblemen who once ruled Mercia, and although it sounds nostalgic (it is), at its core lies a desire for regional devolution.

I looked around at neat rows of CDs, vinyl records,

videos, DVDs, books and family photos as we sat down with cups of tea. Jeff's living room hardly looked like that of a Mercian separatist. There were no Mercian flags hanging above the fireplace, and aside from printed copies of the Mercian Manifesto and Constitution placed delicately on the coffee table, it was homely, not revolutionary. Then again, what had I expected?

Jeff was born up the road in Stoke-on-Trent. It's a 'strange city of six towns', as he described it, known for its potteries and oatcakes, where each town – Burslem, Fenton, Hanley, Longton, Stoke and Tunstall – clings on to a sense of independence. Stoke-on-Trent defies centralization, a formative experience defining Jeff's belief in regionalism. This belief was cemented by the world in which the Mercian Movement was born in the early nineties, when the collapse of the Soviet Union – almost overnight – redrew international borders.

'Who gets to draw the borders that define us?' asked Jeff, who has long been fascinated by the idea of nation states and sovereignty. He sees the United Kingdom as a remnant of the British Empire. Save for isolated territories like Gibraltar and the Falklands, everywhere else has broken away. The next step, according to Jeff, is for the UK's home regions to break away, too. But his true inspiration comes from the England of old, where he believes Anglo-Saxons lived freely and independently in their kingdoms. Had William the Conqueror not arrived in 1066, forcing the English into serfdom, he believes England would have a fairer, more egalitarian system of governance. Jeff was describing the 'Norman yoke' theory, a yoke he believes still shackles us today.

Jeff pointed out how the class system that traces its roots

to Norman feudalism still pervades England. Former public schoolboys shape policy in Westminster. As little as one per cent of the population own 70 per cent of England's land, with many landed families tracing their lineage back to the Norman land-grabs. Inequality, in a word, is the legacy of this Norman yoke, and thanks to centuries of propaganda, we rarely question things. 'It's ingrained in us. The idea of a hereditary monarchy keeps us tied into the United Kingdom,' he said with a look of disgust. 'Yet in this day and age, that shouldn't be happening. People living in these mansions, they're descended from Norman conquerors!'

The Mercian Movement's manifesto describes itself as a blueprint for the future, inspired by the past. The three core principles of an independent Mercia are 'ecological balance' (living in harmony with natural surroundings); 'cooperative community' (working together for the good of all); and 'organic democracy' (bottom-up democracy in which everyone can participate). Jeff would reintroduce the Mercian system of democracy, which he said starts at the bottom with 'regular folk', which are small meetings of locals in, say, villages or towns. These small councils would feed upwards into increasingly larger administrative divisions and regions, named the Leet, Hundreds and Shires. They're all overseen by the Witan, whose job is to guide democracy rather than hold absolute power.

Jeff said it's a peaceful movement, only seeking change through democracy, and the Acting Witan he's convened regularly writes letters informing 'agents of political control' – the monarchy, the prime minister, etc. – that they're illegally occupying Mercia. In 2003, Jeff and his fellow Mercian separatists issued a Declaration of Mercian Independence in

Birmingham's city centre; in 2010, they claimed the Staffordshire Hoard was the rightful property of Mercia's citizens; and at the time of 2014's Scottish independence referendum, they campaigned for independence votes in England's regions, too.

Jeff, who wants to reinstate old Mercian laws he says were forcibly removed by conquest, is clearly looking to a highly romanticized past. Jeff once wrote a song called 'Saxon Dream', but he conveniently overlooks how the Anglo-Saxons took what he considers 'Mercian' land from the original British inhabitants through force and colonization, and shows that too often, we only recall the history we want to remember. His message has resonated in some circles, though, and the Mercian Movement has amassed 2,600 like-minded members in its three decades of existence. Many who join have an affinity with the Mercian or Midlands identities, and while numbers are small, they hint at a growing sense of regionalism across England.

This desire for regional devolution is stronger in the north than the south. Government figures suggest 90 per cent of the north is already covered by some form of devolution, including mayoral systems in places like Manchester and the East Midlands (compared to 46 per cent of the south, including mayoral systems in London and Bristol). But regionalist parties calling for further devolution or outright independence are slowly gaining traction. The Yorkshire Party, North East Party and the Northern Independence Party have all stood in local and national elections.

As Westminster increasingly offers devolution to the Celtic nations, so too are parts of England slowly realizing they're not best served by current political boundaries, and several English regions are seeking devolution deals with the government, too: Devon and Torbay signed such a deal in January 2025, and there are ongoing consultations for devolution agreements in Greater Essex and Hampshire and Solent.

Jeff's wider vision is a confederation of independent English and, perhaps, even Celtic regions. The Mercia Movement has allied with Independent Northumbria – another fringe political group campaigning for independence, based on the historic Anglo-Saxon Kingdom of Northumbria – under the moniker 'Independent England'. Other fringe groups like the Wessex Regionalists also believe they can find a sense of modern identity by looking to the past.

But even Jeff can't imagine an independent Mercia in his lifetime (although he did point out how the SNP were considered a joke party a few decades ago), and his desire to effectively return us to the Middle Ages shows the dangers of misremembering the past. Aside from the Anglo-Saxons stealing land through conquest, it could hardly be said your average Mercian had much in the way of democracy, given the Witan was composed of lords and nobles. However, the Mercian Movement and other regionalist groups do point to a deeper crisis of identity within England, the same crisis that played out violently in Tamworth.

The desire for an independent Mercia is really an outcry against a country Jeff believes is failing its people, particularly – for the environmentalist in him – when it comes to climate change, which he called the biggest global threat in human history. 'It comes down to this. If the UK now, despite what happened in history, was benign,

THE DANELAW

communitarian and had an organic democracy that was working towards ecological balance,' he said passionately. 'Then we wouldn't need independence. We wouldn't be here having this conversation.'

I left Jeff's house in the waning light, my journey along the Danelaw's southern frontier complete. Modern England is hard to place, I thought, stuck in Stoke-on-Trent's evening traffic on the drive back to my parents' house in East Leake. History, myth and stories weave together, creating the England we think we know. We fill in blank spaces, we look to history for inspiration and reimagine eras we can't comprehend. I don't think we can look to the past to forge the future. Rather, we need to accept the present.

England is having an identity crisis. That's clear from the riots in both Tamworth and Leicester. It's a result of shifting demographics, strengthening regional identities and decline. Broken industries, empty promises, long NHS waiting lists, Brexit and a shrinking economy. As Britain changes, as the Celtic nations find their sense of self, so too will the English need to define their identity, something I feel we've never really had to do before.

But what does it even mean to be English, I wondered? Is it the rolling countryside of the home counties? The cross of St George (which is based on crusader symbols, evoking a Roman soldier from Cappadocia)? A stiff upper lip? *Downton Abbey*? Noël Coward's image of mad dogs and Englishmen in the midday sun, Heinz baked beans, cream teas or queuing? These are all 'English' things, but who can say why one person is more English than another?

England has the right to an identity. The danger, though,

is in trying to save a past that never existed, something which English nationalism excels at. As my journey along Watling Street had shown, England has always been changing, and it's always been a diverse and multicultural nation. Ultimately, therein lies Englishness. In his book *The English*, Jeremy Paxman (that most quintessential Englishman) describes us as a mongrel nation, one defined by Celts, Romans, Anglo-Saxons, Danes, Normans and the numerous peoples coming here from across the globe in the wake of an empire that once ruled the world.

England was never a concrete idea, more of an ideal, simply aiming to unite English-speaking peoples. It's an ideal that can evolve with the times, and with the people that come here to call this land home. I'd found two extremes of modern Englishness in the Danelaw. One a multicultural future, no utopia of course. The other looking to the past, inspiring English nationalism in its darkest form. The truth sits somewhere in the middle.

5

The Anglo-Scottish Border

England was a menace to Scotland because Scotland was, by its separate existence, a constant anxiety to England.

George MacDonald Fraser, *The Steel Bonnets: The Story of the Anglo-Scottish Border Reivers*

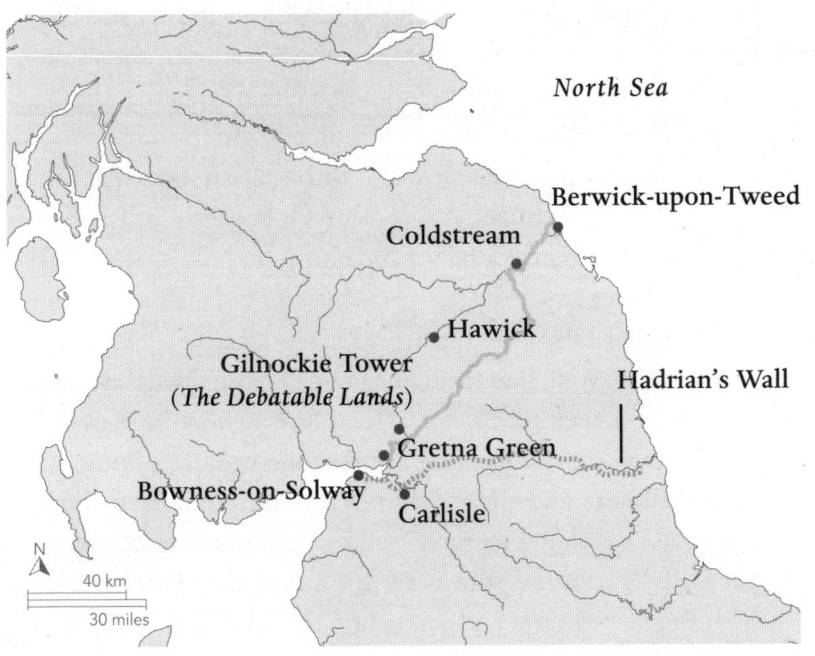

Carlisle

It was mid-March when I drove north from Devon, but spring was nowhere to be seen. Snow had fallen on Exmoor, and early-morning fog wrapped the M5 in its cold embrace as I flew past the Welsh Marches. By late afternoon – once I'd passed Manchester's sprawling␣Lancashire suburbs and the Lake District's mist-strewn fells – the Cumbrian sunshine punched through lingering clouds and illuminated the Anglo-Scottish borderlands in a haze of golden light.

I was heading to Carlisle, a city with Roman roots that lies eight miles south of the Anglo-Scottish border. Carlisle has sat amid a raw borderland for millennia, and it was the ideal launch pad for my next journey, which would take me along the length of England's border with Scotland.

Hadrian's Wall, that most ancient of British divides, starts, or ends, fourteen miles to the west in Bowness-on-Solway, a coastal village overlooking flood-prone mudflats home to oystercatchers and the ruins of Roman marching camps. Today, it's a tranquil scene of rolling hills and church spires, but for centuries the Solway Firth – a tidal inlet that merges with the storm-wracked waters of the Irish Sea – was the domain of smugglers and border raiders.

Memories linger along the ninety-six miles of the Anglo-Scottish border, which was first formally defined by the Treaty of York in 1237. Raiding was endemic, and even in the early seventeenth century (when England and Scotland shared the same monarch), the Scots crossed the Solway Firth and stole Bowness-on-Solway's church bells, only to lose them in the mudflats on their way home. In retaliation, the English stole church bells from the Scots. Visit St Michael's Church in Bowness-on-Solway, and you can see the same heavy bells hanging in the belfry. Every year, the minister of Middlebie, a parish over the Solway, still asks the English to return the bells.

Follow the Solway Firth east and in spring you'll see haaf netters wading into dangerous tides to catch salmon in large nets, just as their Norse ancestors once did. Tractors spew manure, and Lycra-clad cyclists speed along dead-straight Roman roads to Carlisle, roughly following the route of Hadrian's Wall. On its journey east to the North Sea, though, the modern border always lies north of Hadrian's Wall, separating Cumbria and Northumbria on the English side from Dumfries and Galloway, and the Scottish Borders.

After dividing the Solway Firth, the border skirts around Gretna Green (where English couples famously elope) before thrusting eastwards into the Debatable Lands, an ambiguous realm carved out by violent 'Border Reivers' who raided, pillaged and plundered England and Scotland alike. The border defines the northern edge of Northumberland National Park, then veers abruptly north to meet the River Tweed, leaving a large chunk of northwestern England jutting unnaturally into what was once Scotland. It ends at Marshall Meadows on the North Sea, a couple of miles outside Berwick-upon-Tweed, a border town that's never quite known if it's English or Scottish.

This was the rough route I planned to travel, road tripping through a countryside blighted by windblown peel towers and boggy battlefields, where kings met untimely ends in battle. I wanted to know what this ancient middle land between England and Scotland could teach us about co-operation in a new age of separatism. By looking to the past, I hoped to uncover the bloody history of a border that forged the foundations of Britain's eventual union in 1707, and which could hold the key to the Union's survival in the twenty-first century.

Sodden green-brown dales were replaced by red bricks and mortar when I entered the post-industrial outskirts of Carlisle. The city's struggling football team had lost again that weekend, and despondent Carlisle United fans spilt on to Botchergate's pavements from the Border Rambler and William Rufus pubs as I walked into the dilapidated County Hotel, after six hours on the road. The northwest of England lived up to its boozy reputation. Paper-thin walls did little to muffle the wild karaoke renditions of Celine Dion and Oasis punters belted out in the hotel bar below. The next morning, bleary-eyed, I crunched my way over broken Smirnoff bottles and discarded vapes as I set off in the rain to find Carlisle Castle.

English Street led me directly on to Scotch Street, and folk did morning shopping rounds as unfortunate council workers cleaned up last night's debris by the Market Cross. A short stroll through Carlisle Cathedral's green grounds brought me to a noisy dual carriageway. Over the road, a grassy moat soaked in morning dew protected sandstone towers. Guarding a strategic bend in the River Eden a few miles south of the border, Carlisle Castle was built on the foundations of a Roman fort. The roughly hewn walls of

Cumbrian sandstone were never intended to be pretty, and they've endured countless savage sieges since the Normans raised them in the twelfth century. A Union Jack flew from the ramparts, an iron portcullis hung from the gateway and inside, the modern Border Regiment's barrack blocks – carrying names of famous battles like Alma and Arnhem – spoke of the continued military legacy of a borderland first fortified by the Roman Legions who built Hadrian's Wall two thousand years ago.

Colin would be my guide to the 'Great Border City'. He was waiting for me next to a chalkboard displaying the English Heritage cafe's daily specials in the castle's courtyard. Well-prepared in a waxy, olive-green jacket that looked like it could repel borderland drizzle and Scottish raiders alike, he brushed rain droplets off his notes as I introduced myself. I wanted to understand the role that Carlisle, the largest city in Cumbria, has played in England and Scotland's history. Colin was the perfect candidate for the job. A born and bred local, he'd worked on the city council for twenty-five years, rising to the lofty rank of council leader before retiring from local politics the year before. Now he wanted to show off his beloved Carlisle, and I'd agreed to be his guinea pig on a trial walk before his first tourist season began.

'You know, someone once asked me why we built a castle next to such a busy road!' Colin said with a laugh, raising his voice as traffic flew along the dual carriageway. In a calm, clear Cumbrian accent honed by years of local political debates, Colin explained how the castle was built on a defensible position on Britain's north–south and east–west junctions, taking its sandstone shape when William Rufus (whose legacy lives on in the name of the local Wetherspoons), son of William the Conqueror, wrested control of Carlisle from the Scots.

The Scots – who had begun to coalesce as a distinct people in the ninth century, when Gaelic-speaking settlers from Ireland united with the native Picts under King Kenneth MacAlpin – had themselves taken Carlisle from the Kingdom of Strathclyde, which formed after the Roman departure from Britain. A Cumbric-speaking people (Cumbric is a form of Old Welsh), Strathclyde's borders reached far above Hadrian's Wall, beyond Glasgow to the Trossachs, where you can still find the *Clach nam Breatann* (the 'Stone of Britain') marking what was their northern boundary with the Picts.

'The Scots weren't best pleased with the Normans,' Colin said as we made our way towards the towering steeple of Carlisle Cathedral, which was built in 1133 to solidify the Norman presence in the north. 'The Norman conquest was the start of Carlisle becoming a solid English city. Whoever controlled Carlisle controlled a huge chunk of northern England and the borderlands. That's why the Scots and English would fight over it for so many years.'

The most besieged city in England, Carlisle changed hands many times. King David I of Scotland built his palace here after retaking the city in 1136, and King Edward I of England – who was nicknamed the Hammer of the Scots, for his brutal victories over Scottish armies – was laid in state in the cathedral after he died on the banks of the Solway in 1307, while preparing to invade Scotland one final time. His son Edward II was proclaimed king of England in Carlisle; Mary Queen of Scots was imprisoned in the castle's tower in 1568; and even after the Union of the Crowns in 1603 brought England and Scotland together under one monarch, Carlisle was besieged again during the English Civil War and Jacobite Risings.

'Look up at the clock tower,' Colin directed me, after we'd wandered back to English Street, past an antiquarian bookshop brimming with books about border history, and a butcher selling Cumberland sausages by the kilo. 'Did you notice one clock is missing?'

As we stood beneath the tower protruding above the light pink facade of the Old Town Hall, it struck me. There were clocks on three sides, but the fourth did indeed lie bare.

'The empty face looks north to Scotland. As the story goes, the mayor of Carlisle refused to have a fourth clock installed,' Colin said with a chuckle, showing how the fierce rivalry that developed between England and Scotland is still remembered today. 'He literally didn't want to give the Scots the time of day!'

Now he's retired, Colin is consumed by Carlisle's history, but his long council service (he initially signed up for one year, not thinking he'd even be elected) left him with a lasting concern for the city he calls home, including its declining economic fortunes. Next to St Cuthbert's Church, where fourteenth-century stained-glass windows depict the life and exploits of the Northumbrian saint, we looked out across Carlisle's industrial sprawl.

The barren skyline was punctuated by a tall chimney that once spat out the fumes of the textile industry that made Victorian Carlisle rich. All that remains of Carlisle's industrial economy is the McVitie's biscuit factory.

Here in the Anglo-Scottish borderlands, much of the 'rivalry' between England and Scotland is now historical posturing. Common challenges – including the loss of textiles and manufacturing industries – have instead fostered a sense of comradeship across the border. 'Unless England are playing Scotland in football or rugby, we don't really think about the border,' Colin said, as the wind whipped across the old Roman walls. 'We all go backwards and forwards over it for work. If it wasn't for the England and Scotland signs, you'd never notice the border was there.'

I was surprised when Colin told me how the Scottish referendum in 2014 strengthened ties in the borderlands. I'd presumed the threat of a hard border would have driven communities apart, but rather than sitting back and waiting for events to unfold in distant capitals, the Anglo-Scottish borders united.

'We wanted to secure the economic future of the borderlands, regardless of what happened in the vote,' Colin said, explaining how he'd worked on the Borderlands Growth Deal, a cross-border and cross-party project that scored £450 million in funding from Edinburgh and Westminster for regional developments on both sides of the border. 'We didn't want to suddenly wake up and find there was an international border closing us off. We wanted to make sure we could continue working together regardless of what happened. Think of all the barriers that came with Ireland and the EU after Brexit. Where's the Irish border now? Is it in the sea? On land? We don't really know.'

The deal was born from the frustrations arising from the Scottish independence campaign, when neither side really knew what would happen in the borderlands if the yes vote won. Colin was surprised how well people of political and national persuasions – Labour, Conservative and the SNP – worked together to prioritize the region over their political allegiances. Five separate councils in England and Scotland came together, developing an ongoing economic plan for the borderlands and kick-starting regeneration projects to attract younger, working-aged people to the region, which in Carlisle included a revamped railway station and a new university campus. The success of the project shows that if Scotland does one day claim its independence, the borderlands could find ways to come closer together, rather than drift apart.

As we took a seat in the rain-soaked gardens of Tullie House, a Jacobean mansion turned art gallery and museum, it was only then that Colin informed me with a grimace of pain how he'd undergone a hip replacement a few weeks before. As he rested his new hip after our two-hour walk through two thousand years of history, I asked him what the future held for his Carlisle.

'Every day, I meet people who are intensely proud of their city, and that never stops them criticizing when things go wrong! Whatever is thrown at the city, we'll deal with it like we always have,' he said in a positively determined tone. 'Whether it comes from the Romans, Normans, England, Cromwell, the Jacobites, Conservatives or SNP; whoever. In the borders we get along with things. I only wish our football team was doing better!'

The next morning, I met John Stevenson, then MP for Carlisle, who couldn't sing Colin's praises high enough. That was a surprise, because I'd assumed that John, as a Conservative, would be diametrically opposed to his Labour opponent.

'Sure, we'd never vote for one another, but we have a shared love for Carlisle,' John told me, as we sat down to chat in a Costa outside Carlisle station. 'I have great respect for the work he achieved on the council, particularly in the Borderlands Growth Deal.'

John – who was wearing one of those smart, dark suits favoured by politicians – is a Scottish lawyer first elected to parliament in his adopted Carlisle in 2010. Like me, John is originally from Aberdeen, only he had the accent to prove it.

'Carlisle's citadel is a fabulous piece of history,' he said, as he pointed out the sandstone citadel built by King Henry VIII to fortify the medieval city's gateway, which we could see through the coffee-shop window. 'Carlisle is a hidden gem. Come out of the station, you see the citadel, then it's a fifteen-minute walk to the cathedral and castle. You've got all these amazing hikes along Hadrian's Wall, and yet I find it extraordinary that we've never been able to sell Carlisle as a major tourist destination.'

I completely agreed with John. Despite the city's boozy evenings – my fault really, for booking the cheapest hotel on the street with the most pubs in Carlisle – the city had grown on me already. The history in Carlisle is palpable. Celts, Romans, Anglo-Saxons and Normans reach out to grab you from the past. Break ground anywhere in the city, and you might dig up Roman wine jars from a long-forgotten night out, or find coins minted by English or Scottish kings. The cricket club even unearthed a Roman bathhouse during pitch repairs. History is everywhere, but John explained how the city not only struggles to attract tourists, but new business, too, causing younger generations to leave and go north or south in search of work.

'The fact is, we could do with some youngsters to come

and live here. There's an exodus of youth,' he said grimly. 'I mean, our population hasn't really changed in years. The rest of the country complains about huge amounts of immigration, but nobody wants to come and live in this part of the world.'

John's vision was to turn Carlisle into a northern powerhouse (his political slogan was 'A stronger north equals a stronger Britain'). 'Scots come to Carlisle for their nights out, to go shopping and for work,' he said, telling me how he sees Carlisle as the de facto capital of the Anglo-Scottish borderlands. 'People in the borders look to us more than Edinburgh.'

By working together, John believes the borderlands could create more economic opportunities for each other. That's why, like Colin, he was so proud of the Borderland Growth Deal, which was now seeing fruition – as the mass of scaffolding covering the front of Carlisle station showed – years after the Scottish referendum had inspired it. 'It was an interesting study of the potential for cooperation across the United Kingdom because it should never have worked,' he told me, hinting at his initial scepticism of the plan. 'You had Labour, SNP, Conservatives, but everyone realized it was beneficial to the region to work together. I give credit to Colin for his efforts over the years. It's a good example of what can be achieved when the UK works together, rather than talking about separating.'

John is a firm unionist (as a Scotsman living in England, he saw himself as British first), but he'd also forced himself to envisage a best-case scenario where Carlisle benefitted from an independent Scotland. Given the lower tax rates here (different levels of income tax mean that if you live in

Scotland and work in Carlisle, you're taxed more than if you live and work in Carlisle, for example), Carlisle could boom if businesses in the Scottish Borders moved south to capitalize on that.

'But we would diminish ourselves in the eyes of the rest of the world. The richness of British society is that we're a mixture of people,' he said, telling me how he believes the effects of Scottish independence would be hugely negative across all the home nations. 'I think, when all is said and done, the Scots will realize that actually, the Union benefits them as well.'

I'd imagined John's take on modern Carlisle would be totally opposed to Colin, who was staunchly Labour. I couldn't have been more wrong. They both shared a real love for their city that trumped their political parties' ideals, calling for more cross-border and cross-party cooperation to transform Carlisle into the 'Great Border City' it deserved to be. John had to hurry off to catch a train, and I left Carlisle later that day knowing I'd found an example of unity across political and national boundaries that the rest of the UK would do well to learn from.

Gretna Green

'So, what brings you to Gretna Green?' James asked in an accent somewhere between Scottish and Geordie, after I'd tramped up a faded red carpet into Gretna Hall Hotel, a grand old building with the date 1710 emblazoned above its entrance. 'You're not getting married, are you?' he asked with a quizzical look after seeing my muddy hiking boots and the battered duffel bag I'd dumped in front of reception.

THE ANGLO-SCOTTISH BORDER

'I'm writing a book about Britain's borders,' I said a little too loudly, just so the couple filling out paperwork in their wedding finest didn't think I'd been jilted. 'Ah, well,' said James, handing me a card for an oversized family suite on the ground floor. 'We're *definitely* on the border, so you've come to the right place! Enjoy your stay.'

James wasn't wrong. After driving the twelve miles north from Carlisle, I'd crossed the River Esk and turned off the M6 into Scotland. Gretna Green shows how love bridges boundaries, and I was excited to discover a section of border that might bring unity, rather than division. As I drove through Gretna – a planned town with a mammoth retail outlet park and granite suburbs sprawling into the quainter, neighbouring village of Gretna Green – I'd passed battered roadside signage announcing how the First Inn had hosted 10,000 weddings in two centuries. The first stop in Scotland on the old north road connecting London and Edinburgh, Gretna and Gretna Green were awash with marriage halls and hotels, all offering wedding packages and vow renewals.

England and Scotland have two distinct legal systems, and there are wide-ranging differences in areas as diverse as property law and drink-driving limits. Nowhere exemplifies those differences so much as Gretna Green. English couples have taken advantage of comparatively lax Scottish marriage laws in Gretna Green since 1754, when the Clandestine Marriages Act prohibited couples under the age of twenty-one from marrying without their parents' consent in England.

The Act didn't apply to Scotland, where simple marriage ceremonies could be performed with just a witness ratifying proceedings. Rebellious English couples – often pursued by angry parents, and sometimes involving dramatic, high-speed horse-and-carriage chases, as lords and earls tried to stop their heirs marrying the wrong sort – raced over the border to be wed in Scotland. Gretna Green's locals were happy to cash in and perform rustic marriage ceremonies, and for almost three centuries, local businesses have boomed off the back of elopements.

'Gretna is such an interesting place to live,' Susan, the co-owner and co-director of the Gretna Green Company, said the next day, after I'd made the short walk to meet her in the lobby of the nearby Smiths Hotel, a huge, more modern hotel with space for hundreds of couples. 'Everyone's always in a good mood because everyone's getting married.'

Susan's family business owns several of the 'marriage hotels' in town, including Smiths Hotel and Gretna Hall Hotel. They also own the Gretna Green Experience – a marriage museum set around the old forge, where, legend has it, a fire would burn through the night, guiding English couples across the border to be wed over an anvil by the blacksmith.

The Forge – a fully licensed wedding venue – retains its traditional black-and-white wooden timbers and famous anvil, but the surrounding farmyard has been transformed into a sprawling commercial border hub home to a canteen serving haggis and a 'Courtship Maze' adorned with love-heart-shaped hedgerows. A smartly dressed couple were organizing a same-day vow-renewal service when I'd popped in earlier for a look, while a coach load of Americans enthusiastically bought up clan tartan and whisky in the Wee Big Shop. I'd always imagined Gretna Green was a tacky, touristy place, a leftover from a bygone era, but although it was heavily commercialized, the history and romance clearly still resonated with couples and visitors from all over the world.

Susan told me more about this enduring allure. Her great-grandfather had moved here in 1886, buying a farm which just happened to have the blacksmith's forge on its land. He hadn't realized the significance until he found tourists peering through dusty windows for a look at the famous anvil, and decided he could make a good living off the attraction. Three thousand marriages a year now take place in Susan's hotels and wedding venues alone, but the business of marriage on the border has gone through its ups and downs. Scottish marriage laws were toughened up after church disapproval of easy elopements in the nineteenth century, and at one point, it became illegal for anyone who wasn't a resident in Gretna Green for at least three weeks to be married, a move which inadvertently spawned the town's hotel industry.

'You know, you see headlines these days saying that marriages are on the decline,' she said in her soft Scottish accent, as couples checked into the hotel. 'But not here. We're on the increase.'

Susan put Gretna Green's popularity down to its history. The night before, I'd had a pint of Gretna Ale (of course they brew their own beer, too) at the Gretna Hall Hotel's bar, where I'd felt rightly out of place, as a wedding party held a raucous dinner in the restaurant area. As men in smart kilts and ladies in lavish wedding hats ordered rounds of beer and bottles of wine, I read up on tales of past elopement displayed on the walls all around the hotel, accompanied by drawings of eighteenth-century cavalry officers and photographs of Victorian couples who'd wed in Gretna Hall Hotel. The stories were suitably dramatic, and romantic. In 1845, for example, Lieutenant Colonel Charles Ibbetson had boarded a train from London to Carlisle with his love, Lady Adela Villiers, the daughter of the Earl of Jersey. From there they hired a horse and carriage and raced to Gretna Green, where they wed against the earl's wishes at Gretna Hall.

'We had a couple recently. One of them was diagnosed with cancer. They decided to take the plunge and elope to Gretna Green to get married quickly,' she said, telling me one of the many heartfelt stories she hears. 'We get older couples and second timers, and for them, it's more about themselves, rather than other people. Most people who get married here are English. I think they love that rebellious feeling of running away over the border to Scotland to get married.'

The business of marriage is a firm part of local history, not to mention the economy, and when Susan also added that she's proudly Scottish, I asked how Scottish independence would affect Gretna Green. 'It was a strange time,' she said of the referendum, held over a decade ago. 'It stirred up bad feelings and behaviour. We're passionately Scottish, but we're also very much a British company and I can't see how Scotland would survive financially on its own.'

The next morning, the smell of haggis and tattie scones drifted through Gretna Hall Hotel from the buffet, where a suitably hungover crowd – some still wearing wedding regalia from the night before – stoically dug into plates piled high with sausages and hash browns. As I chucked my duffel bag in the back of the car after breakfast, I thought it refreshing to have found a place in Britain's borderlands – where all too often the story revolved around battlefields and blood feuds – that promoted love.

Gretna Green's marriage industry might be built on the legal distinctions between England and Scotland, but it shows how differences can bring people together in unexpected ways and places. I left with a smile, but I also knew the next stage of my journey along the Anglo-Scottish border would bring me back to a harsher history of cross-border conflict that, thankfully, Britain left behind long ago.

Hawick

The sound of galloping horses echoed off pavements as shouting soldiers woke Hawick's high street with a cacophony of morning noise. Sabre-wielding riders trotted past butchers selling borderland game and handmade haggis, pubs advertised Tennent's and Belhaven beer, and polished pikes gleamed in the sun as musketeers in red jackets and white breeches marched off from the Bodrum Kebab House.

'Stand and deliver, Englishmen!' schoolchildren dressed in makeshift medieval garb gleefully screamed at bystanders as the parade moved under the shadow of Hawick's baronial clock tower. 'Hear ye, hear ye! Greetings from the ancient town of Hawick to Tanzania!' shouted the tartan-clad town crier who jumped on a spectator's international video call. 'May you bring the sunshine here!' The sunshine had indeed been brought, and there was even enough of it to put a grin on the faces of the two volunteers who'd drawn the short straw and followed the horses around with shovels and wheelbarrows. This was the start of the annual Hawick Reivers Festival, a three-day commemoration of the Scottish border town's marauding past, now in its twenty-first year.

This year, the theme was 'Feud and Alliance', which the programme described in rather heroic terms as 'the code our ancestors lived and died by'.

From the thirteenth to the sixteenth century, Reivers were the scourge of the Anglo-Scottish borderlands. Little concerned with national allegiances, these bandits and thieves raided both sides of a lawless border ravaged by endemic medieval warfare. Border historian George MacDonald Fraser, whose book *The Steel Bonnets* is a seminal history on the Reivers, described them as

> aggressive, ruthless, violent people, notoriously quick on the draw, ready and occasionally eager to kill in action, when life or property or honour were at stake. They were a brave people and risked their lives readily enough. When they had to die, they appear to have done so without undue dramatics or bogus defiance.

Their origins can be traced to the death of King Alexander III of Scotland, whose untimely fall from a horse in 1286 unleashed centuries of conflict between England and Scotland, as rival claimants battled for the Scottish crown. The Reivers – a name derived from an old Scots word meaning 'to raid or plunder' – stole cattle, gold, silver, crops and anything else they could put on the back of their skinny Hobbler ponies for a quick getaway. They handed us down such common words as 'blackmail' (protection money they forced people to pay them) and 'bereaved' (to have been the victim of Reivers), and the legacy of powerful Reiver families like the Armstrongs, Elliots and Irvings lingers on in common surnames found across the English-speaking world to this day.

THE ANGLO-SCOTTISH BORDER

Hawick (pronounced *'Hoyk'*, as I'd soon learn) is in the heart of reiver country, an hour's drive east from Gretna Green. There, granite buildings lie in the shadow of run-down textile mills that once produced the finest tweed in Britain. I was curious to see if Hawick revered or reviled its ancestors, and to discover what mark the Reivers had left on the modern identity of the Scottish Borders today.

The parade soon crossed over Slitrig Water, a narrow tributary of the River Teviot that runs through the town. The malty smell of a riverside brewery drifted across the water, where innovative locals are repurposing former textile mills. Indeed, I was fascinated to later discover that Hawick's Victorian textile industry gave the world tweed, despite the town's location being miles from the namesake river. A clerk in Victorian London misread the word *'tweel'* – a Scots word for the woven patterns we now associate with tweed – on a shipment of goods from Hawick, and the name 'tweed' has stuck ever since.

I followed the parade as it moved uphill through what was once the town's medieval gate, a piper at the head playing a marching tune. The crowd was soon distracted by the Reivers market, where stalls did a brisk trade in mac and cheese and Scotch pies, before wardens in hi-vis jackets marshalled the parade to a halt by Hawick Motte, a grassy hilltop mound built by the Normans.

'In a minute, you'll see galloping horses, sword fighting and hear really bad accents!' shouted an excited soldier with bushy grey hair, dressed in Scottish tartan and waving a claymore in the air, as ten or so riders formed up on a playing field already churned by horses' hooves. 'And here they come! A victorious army arrives in glory. They've just robbed this chest from the English. It's heavy, it's beautiful and it's full of English gold!'

After witnessing the first clashes between England and Scotland, I made my way back through the market to the Heritage Hub beside St Mary's and Old Parish Church, where John Barton, a local Reiver enthusiast, was giving a talk on his Reiving ancestry to the archaeological society.

Dressed in practical hiking trousers and a merino fleece – perfect gear for a borderland hike – John had an accent somewhere between Scottish and northern English. His humble attire hid a colourful creative side, and I flicked through an illustrated copy of his book, *There's Blood in the War Saddle*, which was packed with poetry inspired by the exploits of Reivers. John was fascinated by these cross-border raiders and by looking to the past, he hoped to find some understanding of the forces that shaped the borderland he lived in today.

'When I started tracing my family,' he said during his talk, explaining how he'd heard snippets of history growing up on the Scottish bank of the Solway Firth, 'I discovered I was related to both the Irvings and Carruthers, two fearsome Reiver families.'

The search for his ancestors took him to Solway Moss, where the Irving side of his family had fought with the Scots in 1542. It was a disastrous battle that left hundreds of Scots dead – most of them drowned when retreating over the River Esk. The Carruthers side of his family became powerful, land-owning elite off the back of Reiving, and they could raise hundreds if not thousands of men in times of war.

John's interest in the Reivers took him deep into the Debatable Lands, a ten-square-mile area of lawless valleys and barren fells that neither England nor Scotland could control. Marked by the rivers Esk and Sark in the west and the River Teviot in the east, I'd driven through the Debatable Lands on my way from Gretna Green to Hawick. I still can't shake the sense of desolation as I swept past the abandoned peel towers – stone strongholds where entire families could shelter with their livestock – in a bleak borderland that was somehow beautiful in its ruggedness.

'It was a no-go zone,' John said, explaining to a riveted audience how the Reivers plundered farms and villages in England and Scotland, forcing poor smallholders to pay up protection money to avoid the same fate. 'The Debatable Lands were so wild they had their own ruler, the Keeper of Liddesdale, who holed up in Hermitage Castle, a place which has been called the guardhouse of the bloodiest valley in Britain.'

The Debatable Lands existed as a truly liminal space, and in times of war, Reivers happily mobilized to fight for either England or Scotland, seeking battlefield booty as their fast-moving horses made them indispensable in border wars. They were unpredictable, though, and at the Battle of Flodden in 1513, a troop of 'English' Reivers plundered the English baggage train even as the Scots were driven from the battlefield.

By the sixteenth century, as England and Scotland's monarchies became increasingly entwined during the build-up to eventual Union of the Crowns in 1603, the Reivers became a liability. In one telling episode in 1525, the bishop of Glasgow, Gavin Dunbar, was so infuriated by the Reivers' antics in the lawless borders that (from the safety of his pulpit) he cursed absolutely *everything* about them:

I curse their head and all the hairs of their head; I curse their face, their eyes, their mouth, their nose, their tongue, their teeth, their neck, their shoulders, their breast, their heart, their stomach, their back, their womb, their arms, their legs, their hands, their feet, and every part of their body from the top of their head to the soles of their feet.

The Reivers' legacy echoes through the ages. I'd seen the same curse immortalized on a stone in the underpass beneath the dual carriageway leading to Carlisle Castle. The stone was inscribed as part of 2000's millennium celebrations, but a few years later, the city council debated its removal when they considered whether the curse had caused massive floods and an outbreak of foot-and-mouth disease.

The bishop of Glasgow's outspoken tirade had been a sign of changing times, and the Debatable Lands could no longer be allowed to exist. Allegedly, a Frenchman was brought in to arbitrate and divided the Debatable Lands in two with the construction of Scots Dyke, which was completed in 1552. You can find its overgrown, shallow remnants in a field off the B6357, if you search hard enough through the scrub.

Successive English and Scottish monarchs tried to stamp the Reivers out. After his talk, John told me of an infamous incident when the Reiver Johnnie Armstrong – who had his base at Gilnockie Tower, which still stands above a lonely valley in the area – was invited to parley by Scotland's King David V. The Armstrongs were tricked. Johnnie and some thirty of his followers were hanged for treason, which only served to antagonize Reiving clans who saw nothing but treachery in the king's actions.

A code of honour had developed among the thieves, who would hold truce days and were subject to a border law allowing them to reclaim stolen cattle and seek vengeance. For this reason, the exploits of the Reivers have often been romanticized – the tale John told me is immortalized in 'The Ballad of Johnnie Armstrong' – with later writers, including Sir Walter Scott, reflecting almost fondly on the heroic savagery of people forced into banditry by the endless border wars ravaging their lands.

Despite his own family connections to the Reivers, John wasn't having any of that. 'I don't carry a romantic view of the Reivers at all,' he told me bluntly. 'Not when you know what they did. The Reivers were gangs. They basically ran protection rackets. They were the medieval mafia.'

After the death of Queen Elizabeth I, the Reivers went wild, raiding and plundering across northern England in what became known as the 'Ill Week'. But James VI and I, the first king of both Scotland and England, wasn't having any of it either. 'The Irvings were a really nasty border Reiving family,' John said, explaining how the king set about systematically dismantling the Reivers and their tradition of blood feuds and blackmail. 'Many were hung when James VI got sick of it. He got rid of the Marches and created the Middle Shires.'

King James dreamt of a borderless Britain. The borderlands were to be tamed and transformed into a 'Middleland'. Hundreds of Reivers were hanged without trial, many meeting their fate at Jedburgh, a town just down the road from Hawick, leading to summary executions becoming bitterly known as 'Jeddart justice'. Many more were transported overseas, creating a huge Reiver diaspora. Neil Armstrong, the first man on the moon, is descended from an exiled Reiver family, and he was granted the Freedom of the Burgh of Langholm, the town in the Debatable Lands his ancestors hailed from, in honour of his achievement.

Descendants are fascinated by their Reiver roots. The Armstrong Clan, a charitable trust, turned Gilnockie Tower in the Debatable Lands into a museum. The Carruthers Clan has thousands of members on its Facebook page and hosts an annual gathering attended by clan members from all over the world. One of the school groups in the parade that day had travelled over from Northern Ireland, where countless Reivers were exiled by King James.

John was angry that many of the Reivers who deserved Jeddart justice got away with it. The most powerful Reiving families sided with King James to protect their own backs and property, turning on other Reivers when they realized which way the wind was blowing. 'The Duke of Buccleuch was the biggest Reiver of them all, but he got in with the king and got away with it,' said John, with a sense of betrayal never forgotten in the Scottish Borders. 'The Buccleuchs are still the biggest landowners in the Borders today.'

Whether good or bad (mostly bad, was my conclusion), the Reivers are remembered to this day. Their fierce sense of independence in a borderland distant from national capitals is greatly revered. That evening, I saw this admiration firsthand, when I joined a torchlit procession through Hawick Park, a huge, grassy common on the banks of the River Teviot.

Several hundred people had gathered in the Common

Haw car park, where sparklers were sold out of the back of a van and wardens in hi-vis jackets set flaming torches alight. The smell of burning kerosene filled the chill evening air, and – frantically snuffing out embers that threatened to set my walking trousers alight – I followed the march to a great bonfire in the centre of the park.

The torches lighting up the dark, moonless March night symbolized the 'Hot Trod' of old. During the Reiving times, if your livestock were stolen you had the right, by Reiver custom, to reclaim your property in a retaliatory raid. The clan would set off with flaming chunks of turf held aloft on the ends of pikes to let people they met en route know they were invoking this right. Anyone they met on the way had to join them on the Hot Trod or were against them. When the last of the torches had been thrown on to the fire to the tune of bagpipes, fireworks dazzled the spectators and the crowd dispersed into the cold night.

Hawick is staunchly proud of its enduring traditions, and as impressive as the Reivers Festival is, I was told it pales in comparison to the Common Ridings. Every August, horse riders ceremonially mark the boundaries of Hawick's common lands, ensuring they aren't encroached upon by local lairds and landowners (like the Duke of Buccleuch). The Common Ridings have been held since 1703, and a memorial board in the town centre has space to record the names of future Cornets – the riders who hold aloft the flag, symbolizing the capture of an English flag in a raid long ago – until 2100.

The town's history is its modern identity, but I found few people willing to answer my questions about when Hawick became Scottish, and how Scottish the town is today. A wariness hung in the air whenever I mentioned Scottish independence. Back in my Airbnb, the next morning I read the latest 'news' pamphlet from local Conservative MP John Lamont, which had clearly been posted through letter boxes all over town. In 'the Border News', he railed against the head of the SNP, writing: 'I'll keep campaigning for the people that want to keep this country together rather than tear Scotland apart.' I needed to learn how people viewed Scottish independence in the Scottish Borders, so I organized a meeting with the local SNP councillor, Annette Smart.

I wasn't expecting Annette to be English. 'I'm from Nuneaton originally,' she said with a smile as we met for coffee and a political chat in the Heart of Hawick cafe. 'But I've lived everywhere from Kathmandu to Malawi, and now here in Hawick.'

Smiley, with short, cropped hair and a well-travelled vibe about her, Annette's accent blended Midland and Scottish tones. She'd originally moved to Scotland in the 2000s to work as an outdoor instructor in Fort William, but, surprisingly, her interest in Scottish independence was sparked when she later lived in Nepal.

'My Nepali friends knew I'd been living in Scotland, and at the time of the referendum in 2014, they kept asking why Scottish people were voting to stay in England,' she said, explaining how the distance helped her question Britain's political structures from afar. 'They said it was like Nepal choosing to join India. That's where my interest in Scottish independence began, because the Nepalese have their own troubles with larger neighbours like China and India. The notion of small countries caught between larger countries fascinated me.'

THE ANGLO-SCOTTISH BORDER

Annette's story, like my own, is born from a love of travel, but here in Hawick, she'd finally found somewhere to call home. 'I really love it here. It's an area of contrasts,' she said, telling me how she moved here permanently in 2020 and now runs an art studio on the high street. 'You have people interested in independence, and people who are staunch unionists.'

I'd always thought that after the referendum in 2014 (the Scottish Borders voted 66:33 to stay in the Union, as opposed to the wider 55:45 split across Scotland), talk of independence would drift away like a crumpled political pamphlet caught in the breeze. That never happened, and the SNP – which won its first seat in Westminster in the 1960s and slowly grew from strength to strength – instead took control of Holyrood and held most of the Scottish seats in Westminster until 2024's election defeats.

'If you can find somewhere that feels like home, you'd fight for the same things,' she said, explaining how she sees Scottish independence as a solution to Hawick's economic problems. 'Hawick is one of the most deprived areas in the Scottish Borders, if not Scotland. It's the biggest town in the Borders, it's a strong town, with a strong identity and strong traditions, and it deserves better than Westminster can offer.'

Hawick suffers from a lack of jobs, investment and housing, and has one of the worst levels of child poverty (meaning children are growing up without, or with limited access, to basic necessities) in Scotland, a disgraceful state of affairs due in large part to the town's industrial decline through the twentieth century. Annette believes an independent Scotland could solve these problems, but I wanted to know why the people of Hawick – with their mixed ancestry, which Annette recognized when she noted that people from Hawick are 'not necessarily English or Scottish, but often have family on both sides of the border' – should get behind it.

'Well, Scotland is far better than England. The people are far less miserable for a start!' she said jokingly. 'But seriously, I could never go back to England now. My daughter pays no fees to go to art school, everyone gets a baby box when they're born, there's the right to roam and free university tuition. There are a lot of differences, simple but good differences.'

Annette isn't wrong, and I'd always been peeved that I had to pay tuition fees in England when Scottish residents get their university for free over the border. Living in Devon, where the issue of land access on Dartmoor has been a key battle in recent years, I love Scotland's liberal approach to the right to roam, while the proportional representation system used in local Scottish elections – a much fairer system, in my opinion – is something I think we need on a national level. England has much it can learn from Scotland. If we absorbed ideas from up north in the south, we could become better for it. But the question is: do the English want to listen, or will we drift further apart?

'We still get vetoed by Westminster. The main reason I want to see Scotland as an independent country is because I'm sick of living in an undemocratic system,' she said passionately. She thinks the British system has failed us all, and one of the key reasons she wants Scotland to break away is for democratic reform. 'We cannot have an unelected House of Lords. We need more devolved power, so we have the power to make more of our own laws to suit Scottish needs.'

Annette seemed driven as much by the failings of the British state as by a sense of patriotism for her adopted home country, and I wondered what it would take for her to change her mind on Scottish independence. What would it take to save the United Kingdom?

'For me, it would take the abolition of the House of Lords for us to bring Scotland and England back together,' she said without hesitation. 'But why shouldn't Scotland be an independent country? Iceland has four hundred thousand people, and they get on just fine. I think it's an inevitability, but how long it takes is another question. Of course, there would be problems with the border. There's the question of identity, too. People in Hawick are Scottish, but they often see themselves as borderers first and Scottish second. And they love their traditions here. "Why break what we have?" That's the most common reason I hear for wanting to stay in the Union.'

We wrapped up our political chat as the cafe closed for the day. I took a last walk through the park – past the ashen embers of last night's bonfire and along the banks of the Teviot, where wildflowers were beginning to bloom – before I headed east the next morning. A plaque on a bench dedicated to Brian Riddell, a Hawick local who died in 2011, said simply: 'The borderlands, the borderlands, the borderlands, my love.'

Berwick-upon-Tweed

It was a dreich (miserable) afternoon when I arrived in Berwick-upon-Tweed after a dreary fifty-mile drive from Hawick. The route east had taken me through Scottish border towns like Jedburgh, where so many Reivers met their fates in a noose, and Coldstream, where the border meets the River Tweed after taking a giant leap north. Each year, the Scots in Coldstream play a football match against the neighbouring English village to decide who owns the Ba Green on the south bank of the Tweed.

Clouds hung low over the River Tweed as it neared the North Sea a few miles south of the border. Fortified Elizabethan walls loomed large through the rain, and the wide spans of the Royal Border Bridge – which carries LNER trains into Scotland – loomed larger still on my left-hand side. To my right, as I drove over Berwick Bridge, the weary stone arches of the Old Bridge were a mess of scaffolding as its centuries-old supports underwent desperately needed repairs.

The Old Bridge was commissioned in 1603 by King James on his journey south to be crowned King James I of England in London. The king was cowed by the flimsy wooden structure spanning the Tweed, and his first act on English soil was to order the construction of a solid stone bridge connecting his two realms. A long-standing symbol of the Union of the Crowns, I couldn't help but think how its current sorry state spoke volumes about England's creaking relationship with Scotland.

The only English town on the River Tweed's northern banks, Berwick-upon-Tweed is a curious anomaly. Its namesake county, Berwickshire, is in Scotland, and while the town is officially in England, its football team plays in the Scottish league system; the King's Own Scottish Borderers had its regimental headquarters here for centuries; and in 2010, an SNP MP even called for the town to be returned to Scotland. But Berwick-upon-Tweed isn't Scottish. Nor is it quite English. Historically, the town's changed hands so many times it doesn't know where it belongs. Berwick-upon-Tweed has carved its own borders on to the map, a space between England and Scotland, and I wanted to uncover the 'third' national identity – one that's not English or Scottish – the town claims to have.

I left the car in a waterlogged moat doubling as an overflow car park. My raincoat was soaked through before I'd made it on to the high street, where I spotted the *Scotsman* newspaper and the *Northumbrian* magazine standing side by side in a shop window. A sign on the adjacent hairdresser informed customers that they operated from a second salon over the border in the Scottish town of Kelso on Mondays and Wednesdays (and here in England the rest of the week), while the temptation to seek shelter in a cafe serving Cullen skink, a creamy Scottish seafood soup, was strong.

I marched on up the hill to meet Alexander, a local writer and history buff who's better known in Berwick-upon-Tweed as the 'Rambling Historian'. I found him outside the Victorian train station, which was built on the site of the now largely demolished medieval castle. Alexander has spent years working on a mammoth tome of Mediterranean history, his speciality, but he keeps getting distracted by history in the borders he now calls home. His desire to share Berwick-upon-Tweed's fascinating past inspired him to establish a series of walking tours around town, including the 'Rampart Ramble' I'd signed up for.

'Officially, Berwick town, or its castle, changed hands

thirteen times,' said Alexander, as we scrambled down a steep embankment to the Tweed, where heavy rain pelted a riverbank lined with crumbling stone walls. 'Sometimes the town was taken or sacked, sometimes the castle, sometimes both. And there were many more sieges that failed.'

Berwick-upon-Tweed has Northumbrian rather than Scottish roots, but guarding the mouth of the River Tweed, the town controlled the last natural border before Edinburgh. In the shadow of the Royal Border Bridge, Alexander explained how Berwick-upon-Tweed was in Scottish hands by the eleventh century, but in the twelfth century, King Edward I (the Hammer of the Scots) sacked the town, massacring almost the entire population of seven thousand Scots in a violent episode that we might today call an act of genocide. One of William Wallace's severed arms was displayed here after his grizzly execution during the Scottish Wars of Independence, but the Scots weren't deterred, capturing Berwick repeatedly until 1482, when the English recaptured the town for the final time.

We stoically marched through worsening rain – all the while Alexander enthusiastically regaling me with stories of medieval battles fought in the nearby borders – and on to the Elizabethan Walls, where the furious North Sea wind almost ripped off my hat. Brave dog walkers tramped along the grass-topped stone ramparts, and a foghorn sounded through the grey haze obscuring the Tweed. Built to defend against a Scottish invasion that never came, the walls cocooning Berwick-upon-Tweed's Old Town were the most expensive military project the Tudors ever undertook.

Alexander raised a shivering arm and pointed south, where on sunny days you can see Lindisfarne. Lindisfarne is the reason why Alexander moved to Northumbria from his native Wiltshire, after he scored a historian's dream job on the 'Holy Island' with English Heritage. 'I never learnt much Scottish history until I moved up north to Berwick,' he said, explaining how the job on Lindisfarne fuelled his desire to learn more about the history of the Anglo-Scottish borders. 'I've recently moved over the border to Kelso, and I'll have to admit I've switched allegiances. I work for Historic Environment Scotland at Melrose Abbey when I'm not leading tours in Berwick.'

As we walked to Wallace Green, where a Scottish kirk stands next to an English church outside the King's Own Scottish Borderers Regimental Museum, Alexander explained how Berwick-upon-Tweed forged an identity crossing England and Scotland's boundaries. Historically, legal documents referred to 'England, Wales and Berwick-upon-Tweed', as if it were a country. This spawned the colourful urban myth that Berwick-upon-Tweed declared war on Russia during the Crimean conflict. As the story goes, Berwick-upon-Tweed wasn't mentioned in the subsequent peace treaty in 1856. It remained 'at war' with Russia until the town's mayor signed a separate peace treaty with a Soviet official in 1966. It's untrue, given an Act of Parliament legally incorporated the town into England in the 1740s, but it's fun to imagine.

'I love seeing so many elements of England and Scotland side by side,' said Alexander, as we finished the tour outside the Visitor Centre, where English, Scottish, British and Northumbrian flags all flew in a line. 'But is it English or Scottish? Based on its history, it's neither. It's in England but not of England. It's a place of its own.'

★

Georgina, a local councillor I met the following drab morning, agreed with Alexander. 'We even have our own weather system here,' she jokingly said in an accent that mixed Scottish and Northumbrian. We were warming up inside the Maltings, a community space and cafe where all of Berwick-upon-Tweed seemed to be sheltering from the rain. The menu was suitably cross-border, featuring pork and haggis Scotch eggs, more Cullen skink and grilled Indian-style chicken with a mango salad. 'We feel we're a separate place, and that's got a lot to do with our history. I notice people down south in the county feel Northumbrian, but we don't. We all have Scottish connections, but we're not quite Scottish either.'

Georgina has endured a career in local politics. She used to work for the local Conservative MP but stood as an independent councillor after becoming disillusioned with their policies. She knew people living in mouldy council houses, bemoaned the lack of infrastructure connecting Berwick to Edinburgh, Newcastle and London (despite the northeastern train line stopping in town), complained that the town lacks investment and felt Westminster was uninterested in helping with local issues.

'We're the real north,' she said, lightly thumping the table and explaining how England's 'true' north isn't understood by policymakers down south. 'The government will say they've invested in the "north", but really, they've invested in Leeds or Manchester.'

She said Berwick-upon-Tweed feels isolated from the rest of England. With increasing divisions across the border, it was almost as if the town was marooned between two competing nations. She sees Berwick-upon-Tweed as a place that's neither English nor Scottish, and because of this, her view is that we need to preserve the Union.

'I've got mixed Scottish and English ancestry,' she said. 'I support Scotland in rugby and England in football, but people feel that we're not English or Scottish. It's hard to explain, but we have that separate identity, that independent spirit. When I'm down south, I feel more Scottish because of my accent, but when I'm in Scotland I don't necessarily fit in. The real Berwickers have a stronger identity as a *Berwicker* than any other nationality. If someone asks, I say I'm from the UK, and I'm from Berwick, the most northerly town in England. But I don't say I'm from England or Scotland.'

As we finished our coffees, Georgina said she thought it strange how the Scottish National Party wanted an independent Scotland to rejoin the European Union, but didn't want to remain in the three-hundred-year-old Union. Independence supporters in Scotland clearly believe this latter union has failed them, though, and as someone who wanted us to remain in Europe, I can see how the EU offered more hope, more chance for investment, democratic reform and a better-connected continent than an outdated Union governed from London does.

It's a mindset I believe we'll see more of across Europe, as smaller regions like Catalonia or the Basque Country seek independence from their respective capitals, and would likely push to join the EU. Scotland knows it would struggle outside of the UK, but the hope of rejoining the EU is an appealing counter-argument. It's a positive that would tempt even me, a unionist, to get behind Scottish independence, assuming I'd be eligible for a Scottish passport. Ultimately, though, neither I, Georgina nor the people of Berwick-upon-Tweed will have much say in the matter. We, the people and places in between, must largely sit back and watch with rapt curiosity as Scotland decides which path to pursue.

As I said farewell in the foyer, the sun suddenly streamed through the Maltings' glass windows. I had one more trip to make before I headed home, and the tides and sun aligned for a final, sunny sightseeing tour on the Tweed.

'It wasn't much of a morning,' said the captain of the garishly yellow *Border Belle* over a loudspeaker, once the six or so passengers had boarded the ship from the cobbled harbour beneath the high Elizabethan walls. 'A bit dreich. I'm not sure how much we'll see today, but we'll head upriver and find calmer waters. We might see some canny ducks if we're lucky!'

As soon as the tour boat moved under the scaffolding of the Old Bridge, a seal burst above the water's surface, a pink salmon clamped in its jaws. Salmon season on the Tweed was about to begin: a thousand-year-old tradition that sees fishers using old fashioned 'nets and cobbles' to land wild salmon. Seagulls and oystercatchers flew over the muddy banks and a heron glided low over the water. The captain pointed out Simpsons Malt on the southern bank, the largest employer in Berwick-upon-Tweed, which Scots might be outraged to discover provides increasingly large quantities of English malt for Scotch whisky producers.

The captain pointed out Castle Hills House on the northern bank, a grand country home that was once converted into Berwick-upon-Tweed's maternity hospital. 'Tens of thousands of us were born there,' he said nostalgically. 'But the new maternity hospital in town is only open on weekdays. If you're having a baby outside of opening hours, you have to travel over the border to Edinburgh or Melrose!'

As the *Border Belle* drifted back down river, seeing the sheer scale of the gargantuan stone walls from the water helped me fully appreciate why Berwick-upon-Tweed was coveted throughout British history by kings, queens and politicians on either side of the Anglo-Scottish border. Now, Berwick's murderous walls are peaceful. Daffodils and wild garlic line their grassy ramparts, and rusted cannons stand idle among allotments. Built in the shadow of the great rivalry between England and Scotland, here, in the borderlands, Berwick-upon-Tweed has defied both sides to create its own place in Britain.

Berwick shows another way, a third 'nationality' that's neither English nor Scottish, a place where identities merge and flourish. I felt right at home here, and I lapped up the idea that it's places like this where Britishness, whose ideals lie in a united national identity transcending its older borders, was really born. Berwick-upon-Tweed doesn't want to choose between England or Scotland, but sadly, it's hard to imagine that its unique, third identity could continue to exist in a Britain broken into its constituent states. My fear, though, is that the forces of nationalism have already marched too far in a Union failing to satisfy its home nations.

'Welcome back to Berwick,' the captain said, snapping me out of my geopolitical pondering as we docked in the harbour. 'And look, the canny ducks are finally making their appearance!'

On the long drive home to Devon, I had plenty of time to contemplate the borderland I'd travelled through. While most I'd met in the borders, in both England and Scotland, wanted to preserve the United Kingdom, it felt like they were preparing in hushed whispers for what they feared was an eventual inevitability: Scottish independence.

I've always wondered what I'd do if Scotland did become independent. Would I try to get a Scottish passport? Would it be hypocritical of me? Although I firmly believe the British project, in some shape, can continue to unite the islands I call home, I also agree with many Scottish policies, and I believe England could learn a lot from our northern neighbour.

However, I fear independence would push Scotland further away. While it's uncertain if there would ever be a hard border – it's a remote possibility – it's unlikely that the 'Middleland' of the Anglo-Scottish border would survive intact. Local, regional identities would suffer as people would be forced to choose between England and Scotland when really, they've always stood somewhere in between.

I understand, though, why many Scots do want independence. Scotland was an independent nation long before the United Kingdom was ever created, and that independence was hard fought for. The UK needs to change if it's to satisfy everyone within the Union, be it through increased devolution or even, as Annette had suggested in Hawick, complete democratic reform.

I'd be back soon, venturing north to explore the Highland–Lowland divide, and to discover the legacy of a Norse past on Britain's most northerly frontier. For now, I was left with the feeling that the Anglo-Scottish border was preparing for change, and that I needed to ready myself for great upheavals to come, too.

6
The Highland–Lowland Divide

My heart's in the Highlands, wherever I go.

Robert Burns

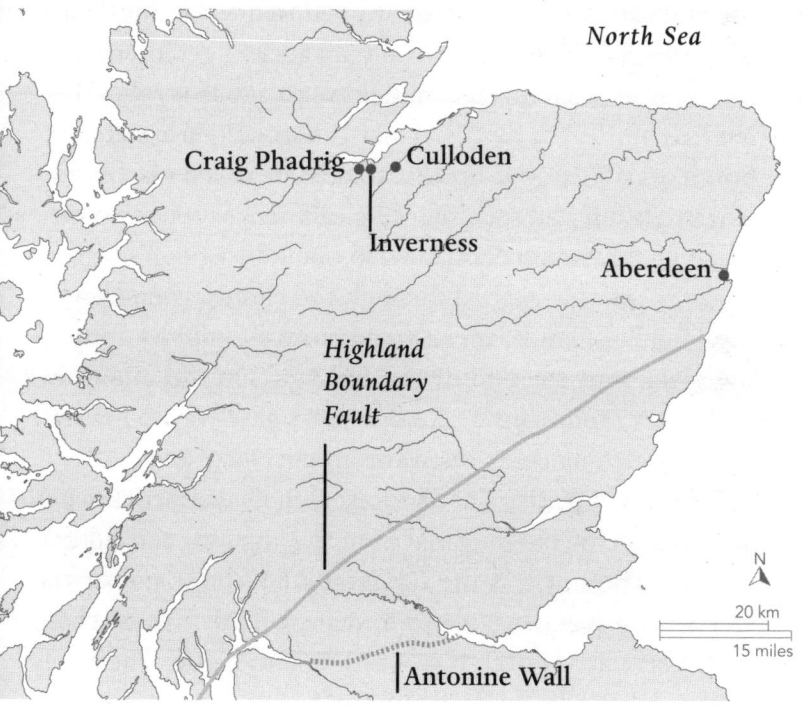

'*Fàilte gu Cathair Inbhir Nis.*' The unfamiliar consonants of the Gaelic language announced in Celtic tones that I'd landed in Inverness, Britain's most northerly city. It was a late afternoon in mid-March, and the sun left a fiery trail across Highland skies before dipping over distant Munros.

The next stage of my journey would begin in Inverness, the Highland capital, where I wanted to uncover the legacy of the Highland Boundary Fault, an ancient geological scar rent in stone cold fury 450 million years ago that splits Scotland's mainland in two. Extending diagonally from Helensburgh, near Glasgow, northeast to Stonehaven Harbour in Aberdeenshire, I'd seen the stark differences on either side when I'd flown over Scotland. On one side, Britain's highest peaks rose snow-capped through the clouds, overshadowing Highland landscapes carved from granite by retreating glaciers at the end of the Ice Age. On the other, the Grampian Mountains' Dalradian rocks gave way to lowland plains stretching easily eastwards to the North Sea.

This great geological division, with its distinct climates and ecosystems, has nurtured enduring linguistic and cultural divides. The north is the *Gàidhealtachd* (the 'Land of the Gaels'), a sparse place suited to rearing hardy cattle, where bagpipers paced tartan-clad warriors into battle. The Gaels call the other side the *Galltachd* (the 'Land of the foreigners'), a gentler place where Lowlanders farmed fertile fields and spoke dialects of Old English and Scots. Hidden away by the lochs and glens beloved by millions of visitors each year, this ancient divide shaped a darker history of Highland Clearances that drove the Gaelic language to the brink of extinction. But Highland culture survived, and by visiting Inverness and the bloody moors of Culloden, I wanted to know how, in a remarkable turnaround, tartan, kilts and bagpipes came to be adopted across Scotland. I would then cross the Highland fault line east to Aberdeen, where, among granite buildings on blustery North Sea shores, I'd finally revisit my Scottish 'homeland'.

Inverness

I plotted the journey ahead on my mobile map as a Scotrail train whisked me from the airport to Inverness station. In its chilly interior, I waited on a cold bench for an arrival from England. Twenty minutes later, my dad sauntered through the open barriers, trailing a small wheelie suitcase behind him. He was wrapped in a down jacket, a woolly hat on his head and his nose bright red from the cold blast of Highland air that greeted him on the platform.

My dad had been quick to sign up for the Inverness trip. He'd lived here in the 1980s, commuting by helicopter to oil rigs in the North Sea, before moving across the Highland Boundary Fault to the Lowlands of Aberdeenshire, where my sister and I were born a few years later. For him, this was a sort of homecoming, and there was many an old haunt he planned to revisit. His favourite Indian, Sam's, was somehow still there, and the next morning, shaking off the groggy haze of a few too many drams, our stomachs heavy from Madras, biryani and beer, he took me on a nostalgic walk into

Inverness, where I hoped to trace the history of Scotland's earliest inhabitants: the Picts.

Taking its name from the shallow, fast-flowing River Ness, which stretches from Loch Ness north to Beauly Firth, the city is overlooked by the crenellated sandstone towers of Inverness Castle, where Macbeth murdered King Duncan. We crossed a wobbling suspension bridge and walked along a high street paved with Caithness flagstones quarried from the Highlands. I knew Inverness drew heavily on its tourism industry but I was bemused by the sheer number of gift shops selling tartan, shortbread and cuddly Loch Ness Monsters. 'Tartan tat,' my dad said dismissively, before stopping abruptly outside a ragged-looking pub claiming to be the oldest in Inverness. 'The Gellions!' he proclaimed, as we peered through a smeared window to see morning punters already ordering pints at the bar. 'We'll pop in later for a drink.' We failed to find the jewellers where my dad had bought my mum's engagement ring, but we did find a crudely out-of-scale map at the tourist office. '*Craig Phadrig*,' my dad announced, after pulling out a pen and tracing a rough line to a hilltop above the River Ness. 'That's where the story starts.'

The story of Inverness begins not with the Gaels, but the Picts: indigenous Celts who lived in the fog-shrouded land known to the Romans as Caledonia. If we're to believe the Roman sources, the Picts fought naked in battle, their bodies daubed in swirling blue tattoos. In the year 142, the Romans marched north from the safety of Hadrian's Wall to subdue them but were forced to halt by the impenetrable Highland Boundary Fault. Between the firths of Forth and Clyde, Emperor Antonius Pius ordered the construction of a line of earthen ramparts and wooden forts, the most northerly extent of the Roman Empire in Britain. The Antonine Wall was short-lived, however. Picts ravaged the frontier garrisons, and just forty years later, it was abandoned.

In Inverness, a Pictish kingdom left behind a ruined hill fort at Craig Phadrig. Its palisade was possibly built in the fourth or fifth century, and it's said that a Pictish king who resided here welcomed St Columba – the Irish monk who spread Christianity across Scotland and allegedly fought the Loch Ness monster – to his court. My dad knew the way, and we hiked along the River Ness to Carnac Point, a flat headland next to the one-kilometre-long Kessock Bridge. The cable-stayed bridge stretches across Beauly Firth to the Black Isle. Beyond lay Sutherland, where wrathful capes, rocky cliffs and white-sand beaches lead to John o'Groats, the most northerly point in mainland Britain. My dad's attention was drawn to the harbour, where seagulls circled a marine support vessel. In more recent times, the North Sea oil and gas boom transformed Inverness into one of Europe's fastest-growing cities. My dad moved here during those heady days, spending weeks at a time on shaky offshore platforms surrounded by nothing but white-tipped waves, as the rigs drilled deep into the earth's crust.

We continued west towards Craig Phadrig, crossing the Union Canal and crunching over fallen pine cones as tall trees darkened the afternoon sunlight. A trail looped gently around the hill, and at the top, we hopped over rocks and across jagged granite outcroppings, emerging on a flattened brow that had clearly been shaped into earthen ramparts by human hands.

In the fifth century, Old Gaelic-speaking warriors from

Ireland, known in Latin as the *Scotti*, began colonizing Scotland's west coast. Their language spread across the Highlands and into the Lowlands. In the ninth century, the Gaelic kingdom of Dál Riada absorbed the Picts, and the two peoples came together as the Kingdom of Alba (*Alba* is the Gaelic name for Scotland). In the early medieval period, as Norse raiders made their home along lonely coastlines in the far north, Gaels, Picts, Welsh-speaking Cumbrians and English-speaking Northumbrians began coalescing into a semi-recognizable Scottish nation in the south. I'll never truly understand the complex movement of peoples and cultures marking Scotland's diverse beginnings, but standing on the blustery ramparts, I felt the country's story etched into the earth beneath my feet.

We left the ruins to the ravages of the Highland winds and hiked back to Inverness, where pro-Palestine protestors massed by the Mercat Cross. We jumped into Dad's old pub, the Gellions, to be greeted by loud roars from a solid wall of blue shirts and tartan kilts. England were playing Scotland in the rugby – the age-old national rivalry now fought on the sporting field. The Scots were leading. It was an appropriate warm-up for the next day, when we were set to visit a Highland moor where the fate of Britain was decided in bloody battle, and with bloodier retribution.

Culloden

Six miles east of Inverness lies a moody moor where the early-morning mist lingers like a ghostly spectre, a desolate place where thistles crunch underfoot and boots sink into soggy bogs. In the early hours of 16 April 1746, Culloden

Moor was the scene of the last pitched battle fought on British soil. After the final Jacobite Rising came to its bloody conclusion, the British government stripped the Highlands of its people and culture. The Battle of Culloden marked a turning point in Britain's history, and I wanted to know how its cruel legacy is seen today.

In 1707, the Act of Union formally united England and Scotland, not long after the last Stuart king, James II, was unceremoniously turfed out in 1689. In Scotland, deepening economic woes made the union an attractive option, but not everyone was happy to surrender Scotland's sovereignty to London. Riots broke out when the Act was signed in Edinburgh, and as the Scottish parliament dissolved, church bells in Edinburgh's St Giles Cathedral famously played the tune of 'Why Should I Be So Sad on My Wedding Day?'

The exiled Stuarts and their supporters – known as Jacobites, after the Latin name for 'James' – launched unsuccessful uprisings against the new British government in 1715 and 1719. Then, in 1746, the dashing young Bonnie Prince Charlie tried again to take the throne back for the Stuarts. A Catholic of Scottish descent, Charles found support among the rebellious, Gaelic-speaking Highland clans. He landed in the Western Isles, raising an ever-growing army on his rapid march deep into England, but was turned around at Derby. British forces chased the ill-fated rebels into the Scottish Highlands, where they made a last stand at Culloden. Tartan-clad Highlanders led the fight, but orderly lines of British redcoats decimated the Jacobite ranks. For many Scottish nationalists, the Highlanders' final charge has become an enduring symbol of Scotland's lost independence.

It was bitingly cold when we hopped off the bus that

morning. In the distance, the Caledonian Sleeper train trundled along the Culloden Viaduct on its morning run into Inverness. Fluttering eerily in the wind, blue and red flags arrayed across the battlefield marked the dispositions of the Jacobite and British forces on that fateful day in 1746. Granite stones inscribed with clan names like Fraser and MacDonald lined a well-trodden pathway heavy with frost, and in the centre of the field, a rocky cairn piled high to the heavens remembered a generation of lost Highlanders buried beneath the cold moor.

The Visitor Centre's polished timber frame and perfect cuts of Caithness stone seemed somewhat out of place on the edge of the otherwise bleak moor. 'It's a bit Baltic today,' Gavin Wilkie said in an easy-going Inverness accent as he shook my frozen hand by the ticket desk. Fast-talking and enthusiastic, young Gavin was an Inverness local with the vague job title of 'Experience Provider', which meant leading battlefield tours and answering silly questions from tourists like me who had only a loose understanding of Culloden.

Gavin described himself as a 'serious history buff'. He loved leading tours dressed as either a musket-wielding redcoat or a plaid-wearing clansman, but in the interest of neutrality, today he was sporting his bland National Trust for Scotland uniform. 'People imagine this as a war between England and Scotland,' he said, slowing his pace down for emphasis after giving us a passionate spiel about the Jacobite Risings. 'But the traditional narrative is not how it was. Jacobites weren't just Highlanders. They were drawn from all over Britain. Plenty of Englishmen fought and died for Bonnie Prince Charles at Culloden. There were English, Scots, Welsh and Irish on both sides of the conflict.'

In the centuries since, the meaning of Culloden and who the Jacobites were has been twisted for political or cultural gain. Because Highlanders led the charge at Culloden, writers like Sir Walter Scott – who hailed from the Scottish Borders and did much to inspire the rest of the world's view of Scotland through his idealistic nineteenth-century poetry and writings – mythologized them, portraying them as heroic romantics doomed to fight for Scotland's lost cause. The Victorians embellished the idea that this was the last stand of Scotland against England, an idea that Gavin said is seized upon by anti-unionists today. 'It's not true, though,' said Gavin with a shake of his head. 'This was a British Civil War. It's so important because this is the last challenge to what Britain would become. Without the Jacobite rebellion, Britain as we know it wouldn't exist.'

On the battlefield, Gavin brought the battle to brutal, frightening life, giving us a blow-by-blow account as we marched across the frost-laden field where puddles melted into quagmires of mud. Four hundred British soldiers and two thousand Jacobites became casualties in a battle that lasted just forty minutes. Bonnie Prince Charles fled as his army collapsed, eventually escaping to France where he lived out his days in exile, but there was no mercy for those left on the field. The duke of Cumberland, commander of British forces, ordered his soldiers to shoot or bayonet the wounded where they lay on the moor. Today, the Highlands remember Cumberland as 'the Butcher'.

As we stood by the cairn, Gavin described the Jacobites' last stand at Culloden as a cultural and political turning point for the Highlands. The Highlands, with its distinct clan systems and rebellious people, had always been viewed as a savage, backward place by Lowlanders. Ancient prejudices came to the fore, and the British government blamed the Gaelic-speaking Highlanders for the uprising. For ten years after Culloden, occupying British troops scourged the Highlands, forcibly breaking up the clans. They classified bagpipes as weapons of war, outlawed tartan and plaid and banned Gaelic in churches. The oppression of the communal clan systems led to the later Highland Clearances, when some 70,000 people were forcibly removed from their ancestral lands in the eighteenth and nineteenth centuries. This retribution echoes in the silence of mountain glens and lochs. With a population of just 100,000 people, the Highlands remain one of Britain's most sparsely populated places. 'It was devastating,' Gavin said simply. 'You could argue it was an early case of ethnic cleansing.'

It's no surprise Highlanders would want to reclaim what was taken from them, but I'm always surprised it's the culture of those Highlanders, who were feared and derided by Lowlanders, that's now an integral part of Scotland's national identity. Gavin explained how later generations seized upon the 'myth of the Highland warrior'. Highlanders were later mobilized in their tens of thousands to fight overseas in crack 'Highland Regiments' raised from the clans, spurring a process of rehabilitation cemented when Sir Walter Scott (who else?) orchestrated the visit of King George IV to Edinburgh in 1822. He dressed the monarch in the romanticized style of the Highlanders he'd portrayed in novels like *Waverley*, and the lavish public spectacle kick-started a tartan revolution.

To this day, the world's enduring vision of Scotland is one of soaring mountain peaks, clan tartan and bagpipes – the vision of Highland Scotland expounded by Scott, who was himself descended from Border Reivers, rather than the clans. Perhaps that's because this version of Scottish history is more distinct than the shared history he knew from the borders, which for many in Scotland is too intertwined with that of northern England.

Lowlanders may have felt some guilt for their role in Culloden's aftermath, but the Highland elements of Scottish culture have no doubt become an easy way for Scotland to distinguish itself from its southern neighbour and rally a national identity. However, despite the trappings of Highland identity surviving, much can never be reclaimed, and as we stood on the battlefield, the wind relentlessly battering the Highland Cairn, I felt a keen sadness at the Highlanders' brutal oppression.

Culloden united a young nation, instilling a growing sense of Britishness across the new country. This was a bloody but defining moment. The Jacobites would never rise again, the Union was cemented and England and Scotland, their borders secure, would go on to build an empire over which the sun never set. The cost of this nation-building battle was extortionate, though, and there's a darkness to Britain's violent birth that sits uncomfortably in our history. 'Culloden is like a rock being dropped in the puddle,' Gavin said, as he wrapped up his battlefield tour. 'From here, it ripples out across the world. This was a battle for what Britain would become.'

The Inverness Gaelic Society

We left the rain-soaked moor in the growing mist behind us and hopped on the bus back to Inverness. The language divide was once the starkest difference between the Highlands and Lowlands. Once spoken across almost all of what's now Scotland, Gaelic dwindled in the Lowlands as early as the thirteenth century, when towns became dominated by dialects of medieval English and Scots (itself a distinct language, which evolved independently of English, though from the same Germanic roots). Lowlanders saw Gaelic as a barbaric language, and after Culloden, its days seemed numbered. Speakers had their native language literally beaten out of them in the classroom, and, now only one per cent of Scots speak Gaelic.

My dad pointed out how Gaelic had become more visible on signs and in businesses across the city in the decades since he'd lived here. He didn't recall ever hearing or seeing Gaelic when he first moved to Scotland, but the last census showed the number of speakers has risen modestly from 57,000 in 2011 to 69,000 in 2021. To find out how the Gaelic language is being reclaimed, I'd arranged a meeting with the Inverness Gaelic Society. My dad went off to explore more of his old haunts, and I went to find Margaret Mulholland and Andrew Ferguson at the Inverness Creative Academy.

The Inverness Gaelic Society had just raised some £50,000 to buy an old kirk which once hosted Gaelic-speaking congregations. They were transforming it into a Cultarlann, the city's first dedicated Gaelic-language centre. They had grand plans for Gaelic immersion classes, a Gaelic-speaking cafe and a host of Gaelic music and storytelling events. They wanted to strengthen cultural connections and build a stronger Gaelic community, away from the stereotypical tartan tat.

Margaret, who was born and raised in Inverness, would've loved such a project when she was a youngster, when it felt like Gaelic was dying out. 'My granny and grandad had no English when they went to school,' said Margaret, who had a grandmotherly look about her as she sipped on tea, her light-blue knitted jumper perfectly suited to the chilly Highland weather. 'But there was psychological abuse. Gaelic speakers were given the stick and beaten. It was cultural destruction, leading to a loss of confidence among native speakers. Now, we want to bring that confidence back.'

Margaret's accent was smooth, her Scottish tones light. I'd wondered why the Inverness accent was so clear, almost neutral, with little of the slang you find in places like Glasgow. Margaret explained how the accent is itself a product of Gaelic's oppression. From the nineteenth century onwards, Gaelic speakers were taught what we'd now call the 'Queen's English'. The English and Scots spoken in the Scottish Lowlands, however, developed their dialects and nuances over centuries.

Andrew's thicker Glaswegian accent was a stark contrast to Margaret's. He told me of the great sadness he felt for the generations who lost their language. The loss of Gaelic is one of the enduring tragedies of the Highlands, but things are changing. Andrew, who moved here some thirty years ago, happily explained how Gaelic is spreading across Scotland again (ten per cent of all Gaelic speakers now live in Glasgow), as a language once relegated to the islands and remote Highland communities now reaches into urban areas.

'Worldwide, people are looking for their roots,' he said, explaining how people like himself are turning to Gaelic in search of a stronger sense of connection and identity. 'Modern society produces an alienation; people feel disconnected from their communities. Gaelic provides a richer identity that allows you to connect with the past.'

Margaret agreed, telling me she sees a desire among Scots to reconnect with a stronger sense of place and identity, a trend I'd also seen meeting language learners in Cornwall and Wales. 'At the root of it all,' she said, 'it's about community. It's about connection, a continuity with the past.'

Gaelic's reach is international. There are around two thousand native Gaelic speakers in Canada, for example, another legacy of the Highland Clearances. Demand for a Gaelic centre comes not only from locals, but also from a diaspora visiting Inverness in search of their Highland heritage. Modern tech is helping people worldwide connect with Gaelic, too: Duolingo claims a staggering 1.8 million learners on its app.

I was making this journey across Britain in search of the British identity at the core of my own roots and heritage, but Margaret and Andrew were so keen to reconnect with Gaelicness because of a diminishing sense of their own Britishness. 'I don't know what it means to be British any more,' Margaret said sadly. 'The idea of a British identity doesn't have positive connotations for me. I link it to Culloden, to empire, and I don't like it. Older generations used to link the identity to the Queen, particularly the war generations, but that's gone now.'

Andrew had the same sentiment. 'I wouldn't identify myself as British,' he said unashamedly. 'I never have. Labour helped link the idea of Britishness to a welfare state, which was celebrated, but that's all in decline. The rise of the SNP wasn't just linked to identity, it was economic, that sense of losing welfare and industries.'

'The nationalist feeling here is driven by distance. London is so far away,' Margaret added, as our linguistic chat turned political. 'Decisions being made in London aren't relevant here. It's the same, whether you're in Scotland or Wales or the north of England. People don't want power to be centralized. Scotland's historical independence means that we have more power to make that change happen than elsewhere in Britain.'

'Make York the capital!' Andrew said with a hearty laugh, suggesting that a federal structure might benefit the United Kingdom. This was something I'd heard already in Britain's borderlands. On a research trip to Wales, for example, I'd spoken with a Plaid Cymru MP who, despite advocating for Welsh independence, also believed that a federal Britain might be the more practical answer to soaring nationalist sentiment.

He blamed the overcentralization of government and the dominance of London as a political, economic and cultural force for increasing desires for Scottish, Welsh and even English devolution. Indeed, it's England that's perhaps worst served by the current constitutional settlement in Britain. Given the English have no parliament of their own, this leads to the rather curious system in which England's parliament is the UK Parliament, allowing devolved nations like Wales and Scotland to vote on what happens in England, but not the other way around. Implementing a federal structure – similar to that of the USA or Germany, with a defined constitution – might be a way to appease desires for increased self-governance and avoid the United Kingdom fragmenting into its constituent nations.

A federal structure, or even outright independence, would be unlikely to increase the number of Gaelic speakers, however. Scotland already has the power to make laws regarding education, and while Scottish schools have the option of providing Gaelic classes, it's not compulsory. Doing so would likely cause division in the Lowlands, where English and Scots have long been the dominant languages. But surely if we want to preserve true British culture, we need to start with indigenous languages like Gaelic.

My phone pinged. My dad was in the Highlander bar. With the cafe closing in the late afternoon, I said my goodbyes and strolled down the steep Market Brae Steps on to Church Street, where Gaelic tunes thumped out across the dimly lit pub. My dad had a seat on a tartan bar stool, whisky in hand. On the menu, I noticed curious dishes like 'Irn-Bru sausages', while inscribed in golden paint on the pub's walls were the words of Scotland's most renowned bard, a certain Robert Burns:

> *Chasing the wild-deer, and following the roe,*
> *My heart's in the Highlands, wherever I go.*

It's easy to view the Highlands through rose-tinted glasses, as Burns, a Scots-speaking Lowlander, surely did when he was writing in 1789, the memory of Culloden still fresh. Pubs like the Highlander promote this misty-eyed vision of the Highlands' past and present, but this is just one version of history. As difficult as it might be, Britain should never forget the awful human and cultural costs paid by our ancestors on both sides of the Highland divide to build the country we live in today.

Aberdeen

We needed to cross the Highland Boundary Fault for another homecoming of sorts in Aberdeen – and in preparation for yet another journey, even further north – so the next morning, we hopped on a Scotrail train east to the 'Granite City'.

As snow-capped Munros peter out into the Lowlands, the coastal town of Nairn, fifteen miles east of Inverness, marks the start of Scotland's linguistic divide. Here, Old English replaced Gaelic long ago, and a unique dialect known as Doric, or the *Mither Tongue*, evolved, which can still be heard spoken on fishing boats and farms between Nairn and Aberdeen.

After the ticket inspector had done the rounds, my dad told me he'd lived on a croft (a traditional Highland farm) in the Nairn Valley during his time in Scotland, where he'd been a tenant of none other than Baron Campbell of Croy. Campbell, who won a Military Cross during the Second World War, was the Conservative MP for Moray and Nairn between 1959 and 1974. As secretary of state for Scotland from 1970 to 1974 – the highest position north of the border before the Scottish Parliament reopened in 1999 – he sent North Sea oil and gas revenues south to Westminster, to the great dismay of Scottish nationalists.

His decision proved divisive, and in 1974, Campbell lost his seat to Winnie Ewing, one of the first SNP politicians elected to Parliament. Money from oil and gas was central to the SNP manifesto, an assertion of the potential for an economically independent Scotland. Regardless of where the taxes went, northern Scotland experienced an economic boom when oil flowed into Scottish ports.

As the train swept into Aberdeen's suburbs, I had my first glimpse for over two decades of the Granite City where I was born. The oil boom transformed Aberdeen. In the 1960s,

39 per cent of families in Aberdeen had no access to a private toilet; many lived in abject squalor. By 2012, Aberdeen had the highest number of multimillionaires per 100,000 people in the country (more than London at the time). Aberdeen's wealth hides under perpetually leaden skies and grey buildings. But when the sun breaks through, it shimmers off minerals embedded in the granite, giving some indication of the sparkle of riches beneath its industrial mask.

From the station, we walked to the harbour, where petroleum mingled with the salty air. Machinery cranked as garishly painted marine support vessels loaded up supplies and oil tankers pumped their crude cargo into vast dockside containers. 'I did survival training in this port,' Dad said, as we walked the streets. 'The look of the water gives me the chills. A helicopter I was supposed to be on crashed in the North Sea. There weren't many survivors.'

Offshore work was well paid, but risky. In 1988 – a few weeks before my older sister was born here in Aberdeen – the industry was struck by the Piper Alpha disaster in which an oil rig exploded, killing 165 people. Dad still shuddered at the fierce North Sea winds that could bring down helicopters. Not long after I was born, he gave up the work and moved us south to England, where my brother was born in Luton. The oil industry still had a hold on us, though, and we soon moved to the Middle East where we spent two years in the hot, dusty city of Muscat before moving to Buckinghamshire.

I never spent much time in Aberdeen, but I felt an indelible link to a homeland I'd never really known. If my mum and dad had decided to stay rather than move south, would life have been different? Scotland is still ingrained in my life, literally stamped into my passport, and I felt at home on rugged shores that were just as windblown as the sandstone cliffs I'd found in my new home in Devon. This link to Scotland is why I felt so attached to Britain, rather than just England. If that link was severed, if Britain was lost to the tides of history, then some small but important part of me would feel lost forever.

We were killing time waiting for Mum and Claire to arrive. They were joining us on the next journey to Shetland, the most northerly isles in the United Kingdom, and we walked back to the station when their train was due. 'Welcome to Scotland!' I said, as they strolled through the barriers. 'I need a drink after that journey!' my mum exclaimed. Not for the first or last time on this trip, I found myself in that most British of institutions, the pub.

As we lazed around in the Archibald Simpson on Castle Street, a grand old bank that's now a Wetherspoons, my mum said she'd never been to Scotland until she moved north to live with my dad. 'I loved the ceilidhs up here,' she said, reminiscing with my dad about the dances they'd attend when I was a bairn. 'It's a shame we don't learn how to dance in England.'

'Hogmanay was always the best,' Dad added, as the drinks arrived. 'You won't remember, but in Stonehaven they'd roll flaming fireballs down on to the beach!'

Claire had never been to Scotland. She had no idea what we were talking about. 'I was the same when we first moved here,' my mum said, remembering her apprehension about fitting in as a Romford girl in Aberdeen. 'My first job, they always used to take the mick out of my accent. They said I was posh! And you know what, they'd always ask "Ye ken?" I didn't figure out who "Ken" was for months! But I never felt unwelcome.'

Outside of Scotland, the UK's northern nation often seems so confident, so sure of itself. It was this robust sense of identity – which I see in its ceilidhs, in its distinct dialects and even among the lochs and mountain peaks – that I'd always been envious of, growing up in England. However, after travelling from the Highlands and back down to the coastal Lowlands where I was born, I also knew that Scotland hid its darker history behind a mask of tartan and plaid, a history defined by the immovable Highland Boundary Fault, but not constrained by it.

As Scotland asserts its national identity through a Highland culture once demonized and so nearly lost, it's easy to forget that the nation remains a patchwork of regional identities. This is a country with three official languages (English, Scots and Gaelic), whose boundaries sweep up the Pictish past of Inverness, the Reivers of the Scottish Borders, the sectarian rivalries of Glasgow and the North Sea riches of Aberdeen. In this sense, Scotland couldn't be more British. It's a place where multiple languages, histories, peoples, cultures and ideals of nationhood can coexist (and also compete, as the rise of Scottish nationalism has proven). This, I realized – and not the tartan and dancing and whisky – is why I felt at home here.

We headed down to the harbour as the sun set over the Granite City. Blinking red and green lights flashed across dark waters. Past the breakwaters, I could hear crashing waves on the open sea as we boarded the MV *Hrossey*, a NorthLink Ferries vessel with a horned Viking emblazoned on its white hull. We walked out on to the slippery deck and watched the mainland disappear under darkening skies. The next time we saw daylight, we'd be in Shetland, the final piece of Scotland's puzzle.

7
Shetland

Dear to the seabird is her rocky ledge, dear to the Islesman is the World's Edge.

Vagaland

Viking red. Severe gale warnings. Rough seas. Squally rains. I vainly interpreted the Shipping Forecast as the MV *Hrossey* pitched around like a drunken sailor. Not knowing precisely what 'rough seas' entailed in the high latitudes we were cruising towards, we stumbled back inside, grasping on to brass balustrades on our retreat to the relative sanctuary of the canteen.

'This is your captain speaking,' a calm voice announced over the loudspeaker as the boat's stabilizers worked overtime. 'We're going to experience weather-related delays on board tonight. We should have a comfortable ride up to Orkney. Beyond this we're expecting a lot of movement, so please be careful.'

Scotland isn't solely defined by its Highland–Lowland rift. In Shetland, boundaries, histories and identities are as hazy as the North Sea mists that sweep across the United Kingdom's most northerly frontier. In this distant archipelago, where Nordic winds whip across cliffs populated by lonely puffins and screeching seabirds, I wanted to see how Norse culture and history is being revived in the face of the mainland's ever strengthening Scottish self.

Claire had brought along a stash of seasickness pills for the stomach-churning fourteen-and-a-half-hour journey to Lerwick, Shetland's largest town, which we happily popped as the ship shook around. 'Oh, I don't need them, I did my lifeboat training in worse,' my dad said with unbridled confidence, my mum looking unimpressed. We fumbled our way down the grand staircase to the cabin deck. Passengers and crew stumbled around the corridors, swaying like drunks after a long day at the pub. 'Hadn't the captain said this was the easy part?' I thought ominously, before crashing into my bunk.

The seasickness pills did a number on me. I woke with a start at 6 a.m. as an annoyingly chirpy voice on the PA system announced the canteen was open. 'How's your cruise going?' Claire asked in a strained tone from the bottom bunk. She didn't know if we were abandoning ship or going for breakfast. 'It was wild at 4 a.m. The boat wouldn't stop rocking. I barely slept, even with the drowsy pills.'

We found Mum in the canteen, but Dad was nowhere to be seen. 'I've no idea how he survived the oil rigs,' she said, calmly tucking into a bacon bap, even as the boat pitched starboard without warning. 'He spent all night in the toilet. He couldn't get up off the floor!'

The sun was rising when we staggered on to the open foredeck. The cold North Sea air hit me like a block of ice, seabirds squawked in the morning glow and I had my first look at Britain's most northerly frontier, where sheer cliffs rose dauntingly high above white-tipped waves. The merciless seas calmed as we rounded Sumburgh Head, Shetland's most southerly headland, where a lighthouse stood close to the excavated remains of Jarlshof, a 4,000-year-old Neolithic settlement once occupied by Pictish kings and Norse chieftains.

I could see the long, spindly peninsulas of Shetland's Mainland (its principal island) grasping out into the North Sea at irregular angles. Clinging desperately to its tenuous hold in the remote ocean, over one hundred miles north of

Scotland, it looked like Norse gods had sheared the rugged, volcanic coastline. Treeless hills spoke of fierce gales, while brown, peat-covered landscapes obscured the hardy history of a seemingly barren archipelago of around one hundred islands on the edge of Britain. Every now and then, guano-covered clifftops gave way to stunning white sand beaches, and if it wasn't for the chill winds and six-degree temperature, the turquoise waters would be well at home in the Caribbean.

As the sun rose higher, MV *Hrossey* entered Bressay Bay, where Lerwick shelters from the worst of the northern climes. The brightly coloured red and blue houses in Lerwick's suburbs had a supremely Scandi look to them. I'd seen the same architecture in Oslo and Bergen, and indeed, Oslo is closer than Edinburgh. For Norse raiders and settlers, Shetland was a convenient stopover on their way to plunder and colonize British and Irish coastlines. The islands – alongside their cousins Orkney to the south – became the domain of Scandinavian earls, then later, a possession of the Norwegian crown. In 1492, Shetland was given to the king of Scotland as part of a marriage dowry, but even into the nineteenth century, a distinct language named Norn, a descendant of Old Norse, was spoken here.

I'd soon discover that Shetland is both familiar and foreign. There aren't Munros here as there are in the Highlands, but 'Marylins'. The haar (the North Sea mist) obscures Shetland in a sea of clouds when it sweeps in from the high reaches of the Atlantic Ocean, and in winter, the Mirrie Dancers (Northern Lights) illuminate dark night skies. We found my dad in MV *Hrossey*'s reception, his face pale as a white sheet. 'Why did we come to Shetland in March!' he exclaimed, as we disembarked and set off to find our Airbnb on King Harald Street. Bleary-eyed from the rough crossing, we settled in for a day's rest, and the next morning, drove west to Scalloway.

Scalloway

I wanted to unravel Shetland's distinct identity, one that's neither Highland nor Lowland, but born of Norse, Scottish and British influences in this northern borderland. To kick things off, I'd organized a meeting with a fellow travel writer, Laurie Goodlad, a Shetland native who has produced a library's worth of guidebooks about her home. She's also the museum curator in her home town Scalloway, an old fishing port advertising itself on the tourism board's website as the 'Ancient Capital of Shetland'.

Scalloway sits on Shetland's west coast, a twenty-minute drive over Mainland's hilly, peat-covered spine. We picked up a small hatchback from Bolts, a local company which seemed to have a monopoly on Shetland's hire cars, and turned right at the end of King Harald Street. As we joined the A907 – the island's only major A road – I felt a strange mix of isolation and excitement as we passed lonely red phone boxes and battered bus shelters in the middle of what felt like nowhere.

The sense of remoteness dissipated as the haar swept out into the Atlantic Ocean. Scalloway revealed itself at the end of narrow roads leading further westwards. Scattered across a sheltered bay, small yachts and fishing boats were battened down behind the harbour's stout stone walls. Along a blustery seafront lined with colourful granite cottages we found a war memorial, the base decked with windblown poppy wreaths. Norwegian and British names mixed on the stone, a tribute to those killed running the 'Shetland Bus', a resistance operation based in Scalloway during the Second World War, which transferred supplies and commandos into Nazi-occupied Norway. Further along, a more timeless memorial immortalized the women who wait for their men to return from sea.

Scalloway Castle's baronial-style towers stood eerily on a lonely headland overlooking the East Voe, a narrow inlet lined by bright red and navy-blue cottages. Scalloway served as Shetland's capital until the 1700s. That honour then moved to Lerwick, where the larger harbour served ever larger ships. Scalloway Castle's cracked facade stood in stark contrast to the modern timber-and-steel exterior of Scalloway Museum, where a Norwegian flag rattled wildly about in the wind next to Shetland's flag.

The Shetland flag – a white Nordic cross over a blue background – was clearly influenced by the Norwegian flag, a fact which Laurie, her light ginger hair also flying around in the wind, confirmed when she arrived and let us inside the museum. In her strong Shetland accent, she explained how the flag was designed in 1969 to commemorate – or for some, commiserate – five hundred years since the end of Norse rule. The president of Norway had opened the museum in 2012, and inside, many displays – particularly those about the Shetland Bus – had parallel texts in Norwegian and English.

I was fascinated by these Norwegian ties. To me, Norway feels like it's on the edge of Europe, and so Shetland had felt just as distant. But Laurie said my perception of Shetland as a frontier was just one possible interpretation, a southern interpretation. Laurie, who was born and raised here in

Scalloway (she's only spent four years away, when she was at university in Dundee), sees things differently. Historically, Shetland – which separates the open Atlantic Ocean from the North Sea – was always well connected. Shetland is the North Sea's crossroads, sitting at the centre of a world which once enjoyed a roaring trade among Hanseatic merchants, Baltic Sea ports and Scandinavian cities.

Shetland's unique sense of place is nurtured by the islands' close-knit communities, which Laurie said help to remove any sense of isolation. While most people tend to leave when they're younger, she said Shetlanders are almost always drawn back home, eventually. Laurie, who works as a tour guide when she's not writing guidebooks or helping at the museum, wants tourists to understand that in Shetland, they're not arriving in some distant land at the end of Britain, but visiting a distinct place, with its own history, culture and identity.

The northerly climes, the weather systems and Shetland's unique bird and sea life are unlike anywhere else in the United Kingdom. Scalloway's history stretches back some 3,500 years, to the Picts that built ancient brochs, and the Norse settlers and seafarers that arrived later. After Shetland was ceded to Norway, Scottish lords were distant rulers. It was Shetland women who spun the wool and worked the fields (work which locals named, rather ominously, as 'harrowing'), and Shetland men who braved icy seas to fish or work on merchant ships, all forging a sense of identity from the hard ground and frozen waters.

'I do love Scotland, but the history of Scotland doesn't feel like our history,' Laurie said, as we paused to look at a swede-harvesting machine invented by a Scalloway local. 'We only have two castles, but we have plenty more longhouses and Viking history. Cruise ships dock here, and American tourists are wearing their kilts thinking they'll fit in. We say, aye, thanks, but you should'na bothered! We never had kilts or bagpipes here!'

It's that Viking history that really sets Shetland apart from much of Scotland. She said there's even a longing, among many Shetlanders, for what they see as a Golden Age of Shetland history. 'There's a fondness in Shetland for this better time, a time before the Scots arrived,' Laurie said, as we looked at 'Viking-style' costumes worn during Scalloway's annual Norse-inspired Up Helly Aa fire festival. 'There was an unhappy integration into Scotland. Landowners like Earl Patrick, who built the castle outside, tested the Shetlanders in awful ways, seizing land and oppressing the language. A lot of it is nostalgia, of course, for a history that never really existed, but the bonds have remained with the Norse countries. If we hadn't been given away to Scotland in the 1500s, things would be very different. We'd be speaking Norse languages. We'd fly to Denmark or Norway for hospital treatments rather than Aberdeen.'

It might be rooted in nostalgia, but Shetlanders I spoke to over the next few days also had a fondness for the Scandinavian ethos and way of life, one built on egalitarianism and public-wealth funds that puts people, rather than profits, first. Norway has an economic model Shetlanders aspire to, and a focus on sustainable energy Shetland is attempting to emulate. The autonomous Faroe Islands – of a comparable size and climate to Shetland – have a higher GDP and many more powers to decide their own fate away from the Danish parliament. Shetlanders are looking north, and asking, 'Why can't we do the same?'

All this has combined to erode any sense of a British identity Laurie had. 'I don't think anyone sees themselves as British here any more,' she said with a pained look, not longing for a lost national identity, but because she was telling me what she thought I didn't want to hear. 'First off, I'll always say I'm a Shetlander. Then maybe that I'm Scottish, and British as a last resort. But London is so far away. So is Edinburgh. It feels like neither of them can make decisions for us.'

I wasn't expecting Laurie to then say she'd voted in favour of Scottish independence. 'I'd like to see more autonomy here,' she said, explaining her reasoning. 'And I think Shetland would be able to have more autonomy within an independent Scotland than it does now. Ye ken?'

At this stage of my journey through Britain's borderlands, I did understand. Her reasoning was representative of a practicality born on these islands, a practicality instilled in the Shetland identity, rather than a national attachment to Scotland. It was the same story I'd heard in Cornwall and the Scottish Borders. London and Edinburgh are too engrossed in their own politics to enact change. People in the borderlands want to decide their own fates, regardless of their national allegiance.

Urdale Farm

I'd seen Shetland's liminality in its flag, mixed heritage and Laurie's pragmatic politics. I'd also heard it in her lilting Shetland accent, and she'd explained how she still hears those old Norse connections in the place names all around her, including the 'Voe', the inlet where Scalloway's fishing fleet harbours. Gaelic was never spoken here, and few traces of the Pictish language ever survived. Until the nineteenth century, Shetlanders spoke Norn, a North Germanic language derived from Old Norse. The language withered as Scots became dominant, but it's thought to have held out until around 1850.

Norn lives on in Shaetlan, the distinct local 'language' spoken today. Linguists traditionally considered Shaetlan to be a variant of Scots with a high number of Norn loan words thrown into the mix, but in my pre-trip research, I'd come across Viveka Velupillai, a linguistics professor at the University of the Highlands and Islands who had successfully campaigned for Shaetlan to be recognized as a language, rather than a dialect. She happened to live on a sheep farm down the Voe from Scalloway, and she'd invited us over for a good old yarn about Shaetlan that afternoon.

I tried to provide a snapshot of Shaetlan from the 'I Hear Dee' website – an online resource for Shaetlan speakers that Viveka helped establish – for the others as we set off to find Viveka's farmhouse.

> *Shaetlan . . . pre-daets English apø da isles an isna mutually intelligible wi English. . . . Hits main ancestor languages is Norn (extinct) an Scots, wi a lok o Dutch an Low German bits in aboot it.*

In English:

Shaetlan . . . pre-dates English on the islands and is not mutually intelligible with English. Its main ancestor languages are Norn (extinct) and Scots, with a lot of Dutch and Low German influence.

As I attempted to speak Shaetlan, and with the East Voe wracked by gales on our right-hand side, we followed Viveka's precise directions and turned inland at a standing stone. My dad drove slowly along the potholed gravel road, extra careful not to scratch our little red hire car. As peaty hills rose slowly above Atlantic shores, it felt like we'd returned to the middle of nowhere. Shetland's confined landscapes are glorious in their sense of remoteness, but it's often an illusion crafted by sparse settlement and dark skies: in reality, it was only a half-hour drive to the Tesco in Lerwick.

'Keep your outdoor clothes on,' Viveka commanded in a firm tone when we met on the driveway outside her farmhouse. 'We'll see the sheep come in now.'

Viveka is a distinguished academic, but she looked the part of a Shetland farmer with her agile frame, thick wellies and hand-spun woollen hat, scarf and gloves. Her accent wasn't local; she'd moved here from Sweden over a decade ago to research North Germanic languages.

'That's right,' said a square-shouldered man with a clipped moustache and a smiley, rotund face who came out of the farmhouse a few moments later. 'I'm Ronnie,' he added, wiping raindrops off his glasses. 'And I found some sheep for youse this morning!'

I thought we'd be discussing Shaetlan around a cosy fireplace, but before we could ask any questions, Ronnie strode off into the damp field by the farmhouse, his long waxy jacket reaching down to his wellies. Over by the pen, we watched Ronnie's sheepdog round up six scraggy, bleating sheep, their thick woollen coats a patchwork of colours, from whites and greys to blacks and browns.

'These are what we call Northern short-tailed sheep,'

Ronnie proudly said from inside the pen. 'This is the closest you can get to a Neolithic sheep!'

Ronnie's Neolithic sheep are the most ancient breed of sheep left in Europe. Although they've disappeared elsewhere, these small, agile sheep with thick double coats lingered on in Shetland, where farmers needed hardier stock to survive colder climes. Shouting over the wind and rain, Ronnie – who's been a farmer his entire life – explained how his sheep look after themselves, roaming the hills from here to Scalloway, and he often finds them nibbling on seaweed by the Voe. Their inner coating is particularly fine, and once sheared, Ronnie has this spun into a yarn that's prized by knitters for its softness, insulation and water resistance.

We soon sought shelter inside the farmhouse, where every shelf was stacked high with colour-coded balls of yarn that Viveka and Ronnie ship all over the world. Knitted jumpers were hanging on railings, woollen hats lay in big piles and the yarn was so raw you could still smell the sheep on it. There was method in the yarn madness, and as Viveka passed around Tunnock's Tea Cakes, she explained how knitting helped to preserve Shetland's distinct language. Long after Scots became dominant, knitters continued using Norn terminology when they spun wool from sheep like Ronnie's. Similarly, superstitious fishers continued speaking Norn at sea, helping many Norn words survive in Shaetlan.

'Ronnie thinks he's descended from the last Norn speaker,' Viveka added, when he burst through the door after letting the sheep out of the pen to roam. A native Shaetlan speaker, Ronnie gave us an example of how the language is intricately intertwined with the landscapes and culture around them.

'The Mirrie Dancers,' said Ronnie. 'To *mir* is to shiver. So, the Northern Lights are the "Shivering Dancers".'

The widespread use of English, or more specifically Scots (Viveka, who had studied languages her entire academic life, reminded me that Scots and English both evolved separately from the same Old English roots, and are themselves different languages) put Norn into decline. Shaetlan evolved out of this extinction, but it's not simply English or Scots with Norn thrown in.

'If you analyze the data, you see that Shaetlan is more different from Scots than Norwegian is from Swedish,' she said, pouring tea and explaining how Shaetlan's grammar is largely Scandinavian in origin. 'Both of those are considered languages, but Shaetlan isn't. Scientifically, it makes no sense.'

Out of a population of 23,000, she estimates anywhere from 30 to 50 per cent of Shetlanders speak Shaetlan. Hard figures are difficult to arrive at because the census has never listed Shaetlan as an option. The language has had little formal recognition until recently, and historically, Shaetlan speakers were demeaned and told it wasn't 'proper' English – to the point where many Shetlanders don't even recognize their own language as a language.

Later, another native Shaetlan speaker I spoke to, who helps Viveka conduct interviews, described how the language is a huge part of Shetland's identity. To lose the language would be to lose a sense of Shetland itself. 'Shetlanders don't identify as being Scots or even British,' he'd told me. 'We have our own unique identity here. It's not because we don't like Scottish culture, we just don't identify with it. We don't have tartan, we don't wear kilts and we don't eat shortbread.

We do have our language, though, and I don't want to see a Shetland without the language.'

Too often in Britain, the homogenization of our culture leads us monolinguals to believe that everyone should speak English. But cultures become fragmented when they lose their language. Ultimately, they lose their identity. Claire, Mum and I listened intently to Viveka's explanations of Shaetlan while in the corner of the cosy, yarn-draped living room, Dad and Ronnie were getting on like a croft on fire, chatting away merrily about the types of beef Ronnie reared, and the feasibility of salmon farming in Shetland.

Dad had been a regular visitor to Shetland when he was working out of Inverness and Aberdeen. He'd fly into Sumburgh Airport, staying in what he loved calling the 'Sumburgh Hilton' – really a collection of damp Portakabins – then head deeper into the North Sea by helicopter. But he never learnt much about the history of Shetland until this trip.

'Shetlanders are quite shy and reserved,' said Ronnie, who seemed nothing of the sort as he loudly talked away. 'So, people probably nae bothered to tell you much about the history. The struggle we have now is deciding which history is important, which is worth talking about. I feel sorry for all the cruise-ship passengers seeing the same six Shetland ponies from the bus. The Shetland pony is just an ornament; they used to have a function, but no longer!'

Ronnie wants visitors to look beyond such superficial tropes about Shetland. 'We're a gateway here, we're at the centre of the Norse world,' he said enthusiastically. 'And I think that, genuinely, people really want to learn about things like peat restoration, geology, salmon farming, wind turbines and the oil industry when they visit places like Shetland. Ye ken they're even launching rockets up in Unst?'

That's why Ronnie and Viveka host tours on Urdale Farm, demonstrating sustainable farming methods and telling the intertwined stories of Neolithic sheep, yarn and Shaetlan. It's all these things colliding that have created a distinct Shetland identity, an identity rooted in the archipelago's geography, climate, wildlife and history. At the heart of that is the connection to the Norse world, still heard in its language, which in late 2025 finally received the recognition it deserves when Shaetlan was internationally recognized as a distinct language, receiving an ISO code in SIL Global's *Ethnologue* database.

We'd been talking for over an hour and were now on our third or fourth round of teacakes. Before we left, my mum, a keen knitter and crocheter in her retirement, bought a bag of yarn to knit into hats. Then, with the afternoon sun dipping over the Voe, we drove back to Lerwick.

Lerwick

The next morning, I braved a raging hoolie and walked downhill into Lerwick's town centre. Overlooked by the rusting artillery of Fort Charlotte, among granite buildings topped with slate, I found a confusing single-stop department store selling everything from Viking swords to frying pans; a dusty sports shop with Shetland football shirts (bearing the logo of their sponsor, NorthLink Ferries) in the window; and a Chinese takeaway named Kung Fu Cuisine, run by a family from Hong Kong, advertising a multicultural feast of cheesy chips and ramen. The high street was a throwback to the 1970s, but it was the Oxford Street of Shetland: despite the aged facades and prolific seagulls, you could acquire anything you needed for island living.

The others were off tracing filming locations of the detective drama *Shetland* around Lerwick. I was more intrigued to see if the islanders' proud sense of identity stretched as far as a desire for either Scottish independence, or even, dare I say it, Shetland independence. To find out more, I'd scheduled a meeting with Alex Armitage, a paediatrician and Shetland's first Green Party councillor, who's campaigning for sustainable energy *and* Scottish independence.

I met Alex at Scandi-inspired cafe Fjarå – (*fjarå* means 'shore' in Old Norse) – overlooking Berwick Bay's tumultuous waves. A twenty-minute walk from Lerwick's high street, I'd almost been blown off Da Sletts, a stretch of windy coastline leading to the Tesco superstore, caught off-guard by a fierce gust. Shetland's winds are the strongest in the United Kingdom (the most powerful ever recorded was a staggering 197 miles per hour), and there are often reports of tourists being blown over cliffs. I hadn't been added to the statistics, yet, but I had appreciated the harsh weather-beaten reality of Shetland life as I teetered on the edge. I'd rushed into the shelter of Fjarå, and as waves crashed into the cafe's panoramic windows, it felt like we were meeting at the end of the world.

Alex, who looked like a true Shetlander in a big cable-knit jumper that would be right at home on a North Sea fishing vessel, told me his story as we settled down with mugs of coffee. Originally from London, like many of Shetland's incomers, he'd returned to his ancestral roots as he searched for a sense of self away from the big city. Now he'd decided to stay, he wanted to help campaign for a greener future as North Sea oil and gas dries up.

He explained how renewables were going to be huge here. After my experience on the cliffs, I completely agreed, but the energy sector's future here is still up for debate. While the Viking Wind Turbine Project is aiming to harness Shetland's wind power, not all Shetlanders want to see turbines on the hills. Some want to keep drilling in the North Sea, particularly given how Shetland was transformed and enriched by the oil and gas boom.

'We need to oppose new oilfields. It's Britain's opportunity to say to the world that we need to keep oil and gas underground, rather than burning it,' he said, his London accent mixing with twangs of Shaetlan he'd picked up. 'It's a windy place, you can make twice as much energy from a single turbine here than in Scotland. Shetlanders need a share of the profits; they need control of production. "Green capitalism", I call it. That's the big political fight, where does the energy and the profit go? With more devolved power, Shetland can fight for that.'

The Scottish Greens support an independent Scotland. Alex, though, described the idea of Scottishness in Shetland as loose, which seemed at odds with his chosen political party's manifesto. For Alex, the Shetland identity isn't Scottish, but one born of the rough, windswept environment Shetlanders call home, moulded by a history of disenfranchisement and bondage that has created a language, culture and economy far removed from Scotland.

It's an identity he's come to identify with through his heritage, which he traces back to the time of the Highland Clearances, when his great-great grandfather was thrown off Shetland's land by Scottish lairds. Part of that identity is a practicality, an adaptability – what Alex called 'the ability to survive rough winter storms' – and therein lay his support for Scottish independence.

'I believe we will be better off as part of an independent Scotland,' he said matter-of-factly, explaining how the idea of Scottish independence has become a pervasive, inescapable part of Scottish politics. 'It's not for emotional reasons, but for practical reasons. There's a lot of disdain with Labour, with Conservatives and with the centralization of power. There's a cognitive attraction towards independence. I don't have a fire in my belly for independence, but I believe that in practical terms it's something we need to pursue.'

I found support for an autonomous Shetland widespread during my stay. The guise which that autonomy is to take, however, seemed very much up in the air. Some Shetlanders want further autonomy within the United Kingdom; others, like Laurie and Alex, believe Scottish independence is the way forward, and everyone wants closer ties with Scandinavia. One of the very few fighting for an outright independent Shetland is Stuart Hill. He doesn't believe the islands are even legally part of Scotland, or the United Kingdom.

Stuart's story is almost unbelievable. He'd quite literally washed up on Shetland's shores in 2001, when attempting to circumnavigate the United Kingdom in a home-made boat. The media nicknamed him 'Captain Calamity', deriding Stuart (probably fairly) for forcing the RNLI to rescue him on numerous occasions. Stuart, who is from Essex and now in his seventies, never left Shetland after his shipwreck, and instead did what borderland eccentrics seem to do best. He acquired the two-and-a-half-acre island of Forewick Holm in the Sound of Papa, a few miles west of Mainland, and declared independence as the 'Sovereign State of Forvik'. Stuart sees Forvik as an experiment, a microcosm of Shetland, because whatever happens there can happen on the Mainland.

When we met in the Isleburgh Hostel Cafe in Lerwick later that morning, I soon felt party to a conspiracy. As we unpacked a satchel bag bursting with documents and photocopies of old treaties and court cases, it was hard not to get sucked in. 'I realized that not everything is as it seems here. The whole establishment is run on a lie,' whispered Stuart, who looked the part of an ageing sailboat captain with his wiry build, grey hair and ragged jumper. Stuart explained how he'd based Forvik's secession from the United Kingdom on Udal law, the old Norse legal system he believes was never rescinded. 'From a legal standpoint, I see no way that either the UK, or Scotland has any authority here. But no one wants to challenge that.'

Stuart has traced his legal arguments all the way back to the 'Dowry', the turning point in Shetland history, when the islands were handed over to Scotland. He says that legally, the land in Shetland remained 'Udal', meaning it was always owned by the people under ancient Norse laws. If that's the case, then Scotland could never have and has never had sovereignty here. He's spent the best part of two decades researching this and has written a whole host of literature on the topic – including his self-published book, *Stolen Isles*, of which he gave me a fifth-edition copy after insisting on signing it – where he sets his arguments out and explains why it matters.

There was a touch of the megalomaniac in his actions.

He stirred up trouble, driving around in a car with homemade number plates ('Sov State 1'), flashing his home-made driving licence to police officers and claiming they had no authority. He was constantly trying to get himself arrested so he could argue his case for Shetland's independence when he went to trial. He'd been in and out of court for years, stacking up fines and not paying them as he tried to prove the authorities had no jurisdiction over him. Shetlanders rolled their eyes when I mentioned Stuart – he was well known (it's a small place) – but several people I spoke with also admitted quietly that technically, he was probably right about the whole Dowry thing.

Given the huge amount of untapped natural resources here, Shetland could indeed harvest a bountiful return if it was to become independent. Stuart's even been sending the wind turbine companies invoices, asking them to pay the 'Sovereign Island of Shetland' – a campaign group he's established and which he says has 250 members – millions a week in rent for the use of Shetland.

Stuart's is an extreme narrative. He believes that Shetland already has its independence, and it just needs to be recognized. In a way, it's the ultimate attempt at decentralization. Even so, Shetland is right now de facto part of the United Kingdom, and locals aren't so disillusioned with the current state of affairs that they're concerned with enforcing ancient Udal law.

If the islands seriously started thinking about independence, though, they'd certainly have plenty of legal arguments to fight their case for secession. Independence is probably a long way off (despite what Stuart says) but the one constant I heard was the need for further autonomy. If Scotland and the

United Kingdom fail to listen, perhaps Shetlanders will take up Stuart's cause more emphatically in the future.

Bressay

The distant lights of Lerwick shimmered across Bressay Sound like the Mirrie Dancers in the dark night's sky. Viking warriors, their long beards ragged in the dim firelight, clasped round wooden shields against blue-turquoise smocks, and stabbed axes and longswords upwards. The frigid air reverberated with gruff roars as the longship ignited in a blazing inferno. As flames licked timbers and paint peeled, the smell of burning wood overpowered the salty aroma of seaweed on the shore.

This was Bressay Up Helly Aa, one of the annual fire festivals marking the end of Shetland's long winter, and the most defining image of Shetland's Norse character. Lerwick's Up Helly Aa – an event which sees tourists from all over the world descending on Shetland's capital as fires and Viking warriors engulf the town – is the biggest, but it's extraordinarily difficult to source accommodation when it's on in late January. Luckily, I'd discovered that the island of Bressay, a seven-minute ferry ride across the sound from Lerwick, hosts a smaller, community-focused Up Helly Aa in March.

Bressay's population numbers no more than 360. A lonely lighthouse sits on the island's southwestern shores, guarding the narrow passage into Bressay Sound. An equally lonely pub sits by the ferry terminal facing Lerwick, where we had time for a pint of Belhaven before the Up Helly Aa began after dusk. Narrow country lanes lead through treeless fields occupied by Shetland ponies and sheep to the main settlement, which is really just a collection of houses, a small marina, a community shop and a school that doubles as a cafe on the island's sheltered western side.

A shuttle bus dropped off the brass band, who'd been shipped over from Lerwick, outside the village hall, where a hundred or so torchbearers merged into a long column. The 'Jarl Squad' – men and boys from Bressay dressed up in their Viking gear – led the march to the longship on the beach. We followed the flaming torches, blending with the crowd as we pulled our scarves tighter and cracked open the tinnies we'd brought along for the spectacle. The Jarl Squad formed a loose ring around the longship. One by one, torchbearers marched past, throwing flaming torches on to an ever-growing pyre of burning timber. There was something primal in the Up Helly Aa. A human need to bring light to the darkness. But while it's inspired by the Norse past, its roots aren't so ancient.

The official history of the Up Helly Aa says it evolved from Shetland's raucous Christmas celebrations in the nineteenth century, when barrels of tar were set alight and rolled down Lerwick's narrow streets. Islanders consumed enormous quantities of alcohol (not much has changed in that respect) and, given their ready access to gunpowder and firearms, proceedings became chaotic, even dangerous. So, locals began to take a more orderly approach to the festivities, adding a touch of early health and safety to lessen the chance of injuries and fatalities. The festival was pushed back later into January to distinguish it from Christmas, and some time in the 1870s, it took on Norse dimensions when locals rediscovered their 'Viking' heritage. By the 1930s, the celebrations had gone full Norse, with the introduction of the Jarl Squad, Viking regalia and the infamous role of the Guizer Jarl (the Up Helly Aa 'leader'). The Guizer Jarl can spend years planning their turn to lead the event, while the Jarl Squad spend hundreds if not thousands of pounds on replica gear and weapons. Whatever its origins, the Up Helly Aa has taken on a fiery life of its own, coming to symbolize a lost Norse culture Shetlanders are now reclaiming.

'You must be Ian!' I shouted at a Viking warrior standing guard by the fire. 'Aye!' he said, looking at me quizzically. 'Ah, you must be Richard!'

I'd just about recognized Ian Harkness from his Facebook photo, even if the trim suit he wore in his profile picture had been replaced with his finest Viking armour, a winged helmet and a sword and shield. Ian was in the Jarl Squad, and he was heavily involved in the day's pyromania. After contacting him online, he'd told me to come along for the night. 'Ach, I've been drinking since 5.30 a.m.,' said Ian, who clearly had a Viking constitution, given he didn't look worse for wear in the slightest. 'It's been a long day, and we're only getting started.'

The Jarl Squad had set off early that morning, and by seven thirty they were at the Speldiburn Cafe in Bressay, singing songs and performing skits for local schoolchildren. They'd hopped on the ferry to Lerwick dressed as Viking warriors, entertaining pupils and teachers in classrooms on the Mainland, too, before returning to Bressay and burning the longship after dark. The day wasn't over yet, though. Ian had reserved us tickets for the now sold out afterparty at

Bressay Hall. 'I hope you have your dancing shoes on,' Ian said with a devilish grin before we followed the crowd back to the village hall. 'Do you know your two-step?'

The police were confiscating beverages from underage drinkers outside Bressay Hall. On the door, a burly bouncer in a dark suit checked tickets and handed out wristbands. Inside – after we'd paid a staggering £25 entrance fee – we found school chairs lined up around what could only be a dancing square.

Mum was convinced the Vikings had ripped us off. 'Does everyone pay this?' she asked, as we found space at the back and the hall filled with people, some dressed in tracksuits, some as Vikings, and others in kilts or suits. 'There's no way people are paying £25 for this!'

'It's like Hogmanay, Christmas and New Year all rolled into one,' I said, as the smell of stovies and boiling beef drifted through from the kitchen. 'We paid £25 for our New Year's tickets in Exmouth. That was in a gazebo.'

The drinks were cheap, and after stocking up on wine from the village hall's bar, we waited in awkward anticipation until the fiddle band announced the entrance of the Jarl Squad. The Vikings came flying in, Ian among them and the Guizer Jarl at their head, singing their Up Helly Aa song before launching into a chaotic rendition of 'Rocking All Over the World'. The Guizer Jarl gave a short speech, and with barely a pause, everyone was up and dancing the two-step.

'This is like a massive stag do,' said Claire, who wasn't that impressed. 'It's just bad dancing and bad karaoke.'

But this was culture, I protested. If I'd grown up in

Scotland, I'd have learnt the two-step at school. My parents had taken me to plenty of ceilidhs when I was a baby, and whether you live in Bressay or Berwickshire, the two-step is burnt into the soles of your feet. The Viking regalia, Norse themes and fire set the Up Helly Aa apart from your normal Scottish ceilidh, but it hardly matters if those traditions were only adopted a century ago. Both the Shetlanders and the Scots from the Lowlands adopting kilts and bagpipes are developing a new sense of self because that's how culture works: it changes, adapts and evolves. This was Shetland reasserting its identity, differentiating itself from Scotland, in the same way Scots have adopted Highland culture to differentiate themselves from their English neighbours.

Still, Bressay Hall was madness incarnate. As the Jarl Squad sang 'Mamma Mia' and a poor cleaner mopped spilt beer from the dance floor, a rival band set themselves up in front of the dismayed fiddle band on stage. Suddenly there were performers dressed as sheep, and a bald Viking sitting in the row in front of us chugging cans of Tennent's turned around and asked us if it was magic mushroom season in Bressay. 'The sheep skit is mental,' he said with a confused shake of his head. 'I don't have a clue what the hell is going on.'

It was well past midnight. Getting more confused as the hall got drunker by the minute, we decided it was time to head back to the ferry terminal. 'Twenty-five quid?' my mum asked again, as we walked back in almost pitch-black darkness to the late-night ferry, which was doing extra shifts until 4 a.m. 'Well, I suppose if it helps keep the traditions going, then that's OK.'

Unst

We rose with the sea haar and bundled into our little red car hire, only slightly groggy from our Up Helly Aa antics the night before. I wanted to end our borderland escapade with a trip to Unst, Shetland's most northerly isle, and with my dad at the wheel, we took the A907 north in search of spaceports and gin distilleries on Britain's final frontier.

Out of Lerwick, big peat banks were draped in mist, and the headlights of oncoming cars loomed through the fog. There was something righteously atmospheric about the weather that day, a touch of the Norse gods grasping out from the past, until the monstrous turbines of the Viking Wind Farm loomed through the mist, announcing Shetland's march towards a sustainable future.

Peaty landscapes were scarred by jagged inlets slicing through the very rock of Shetland. Lochs were churned by winds, old crofters' huts lay empty and scrawny sheep huddled along Dales Voe. In the distance, a bright flare marked the Sullom Voe Terminal oil refinery, a fiery beacon that's refined billions of barrels' worth of crude oil dredged from the North Sea into petrol.

Driving to Unst, which reaches north like a crooked finger into the freezing waters of the Atlantic Ocean, required two ferry crossings each way. My dad had taken it upon himself to time our trip to perfection. He'd pre-booked slots on the car ferries so we could, if all went to plan, just roll on and roll off all the way north. Somehow it did go to plan, and we were soon zipping across the desolate scenery of Yell – 'The Friendly Isle', a welcome sign announced – where the only souls we saw were a taxi driver waiting for who knows who and a few stray sheep. The next ferry sloshed around in the Sound like a tin can lost in the waves, with water spilling over on the cargo deck. On Unst, where long stone walls divided beige, soggy fields, more empty stone crofters' huts lined lonely lochs.

Unst is the third largest island in Shetland, and I saw more human and sheep life here than Yell. The scenery was sparse, but became more forgiving as we rounded Baltasound, the island's largest settlement (population: 600) and stopped for a photo of Bobby's Bus Shelter on the road north. One of the most northerly bus stops in the UK, the wind-wracked red shelter is furnished with all manner of decorations and quirky memorabilia. The theme changes, celebrating events like the late Queen's Platinum Jubilee or the Olympics, and this year's nautical theme meant there were sailor's hats for visitors to try on, and books about the Merchant Navy to read while waiting for your bus.

Occupying another lay-by next to the closed-up doors and windows of the Balta Light public bar, the Last Checkout store was surprisingly busy. You could buy anything up here, in small amounts, be it knitted hats, birthday cards, bottles of Devon cider or plumbing parts for your broken toilet. The community noticeboard advertised work in the SaxaVord Spaceport, a poetry competition called for entries in Shaetlan and first prize in the next raffle was a ticket on the NorthLink ferry to Aberdeen. With the hills rising higher to form the island's granite spine, we stopped once more to peek inside a recreated Viking longhouse and admire a Viking longship, both painstakingly built by the Unst Heritage Centre on the site of a former Viking settlement. History marches on, and as we neared the northern shores of Unst, we found ourselves driving along a single-track road, past an old kirk and into the spaceport.

It was hardly Cape Canaveral. An official sign warned that 'Any aliens will be reported to the space police and transported to Mars.' The spaceport is there, though, and hardy souls are battling against the elements and reaching for the stars above on the most northerly inhabited island in the UK. Located on an old RAF base, Unst was chosen by the private space company SaxaVord simply because if there's an accident, debris is likely to fall out to sea, rather than rain down on an inhabited area. It was rustic, but it spoke volumes of Shetland's ambitions to reach that final frontier. Next to the spaceport's canteen was the SaxaVord Gin Distillery, the most northerly distillery in the UK (but then again, anything up here can claim to be the most northerly something). Unfortunately, the distillery was closed. Beyond lay the villages where the last Norn speakers lived, but with the mist wrapping its tendrils around the spaceport, we made a dash for a viewing point by an old radar station from which we hoped to look out over Unst's most northerly shore.

The single-track lane wound uphill, past an old, barely readable sign warning we were now entering an area governed by the Official Secrets Act. This part of Shetland is so strategic that during the Cold War, the Soviets planned to nuke Unst in the event of all-out war. We didn't beat the mist. The visibility diminished like nothing I'd experienced before, but with the fog lights on we stoically continued uphill, hoping it might clear.

Claire and I braved the weather and hopped out of the car when we reached a chain fence ringing a radar dish. A poem inscribed on a sign by a lonely bench said, '*In dir blue an gold ribbons da Dancers turn'* ('First Snow', by Jack Renwick). On a good day, we would have seen right out to Muckle Flugga Lighthouse. Not far beyond lies Out Stack, a craggy uninhabited islet that's officially the most northerly island in the United Kingdom. Not today. We couldn't see even two metres ahead, and the final boundary marking the end of Britain lay tantalizingly out of sight as the rain began to lash down. That's Shetland, ever changeable, ever unpredictable.

There was little to do but head back south. We'd had a small taste of Shetland's future up here, but the limits that geography and climate impose upon this northern world had beaten us. But despite the foul weather, whether you find joy in the geology, the harbours, the ruins or the wildlife, Shetland is a place so steeped in raw history it continually delights. Old crofting huts litter the countryside, their broken walls holding a thousand unsung stories within a mossy embrace. Pictish stones inscribed in lost Ogham runes are unearthed in backyards, and Viking hoards are discovered buried under white sand beaches. Shetland is an ancient place, but the bright buildings I saw being built to Scandinavian designs showed how the archipelago is looking to secure its future, too. Ancient sheep breeds plodded in the great shadows of wind turbines as Shetland switches to renewable energies, harnessing the powerful winds that can rock slate townhouses to pieces.

So far from Britain's mainland, Shetland might seem like a distant place to discuss the future of the United Kingdom, but it's on borders like these where we find a microcosm of the nation itself. Up here they are debating oil and gas and the future of renewables, as we are all over Britain. They are searching for a sense of self in a nation at a crossroads, wondering whether to break away, or integrate further, just as the rest of Britain debated with Europe, and now with itself. And right at the end of the line, Shetland's unique identity is becoming stronger on the borderlines between Britain and Scandinavia.

We took the ferry back to Aberdeen the next evening. It was even rougher than on the way out. Next, though, would be my toughest journey of all, as I turned my sights to the Irish border.

8

Northern Ireland

And so, I ask you to build on the opportunity you have before you; to believe that the future can be better than the past.

Bill Clinton in Derry/Londonderry, 30 November 1995

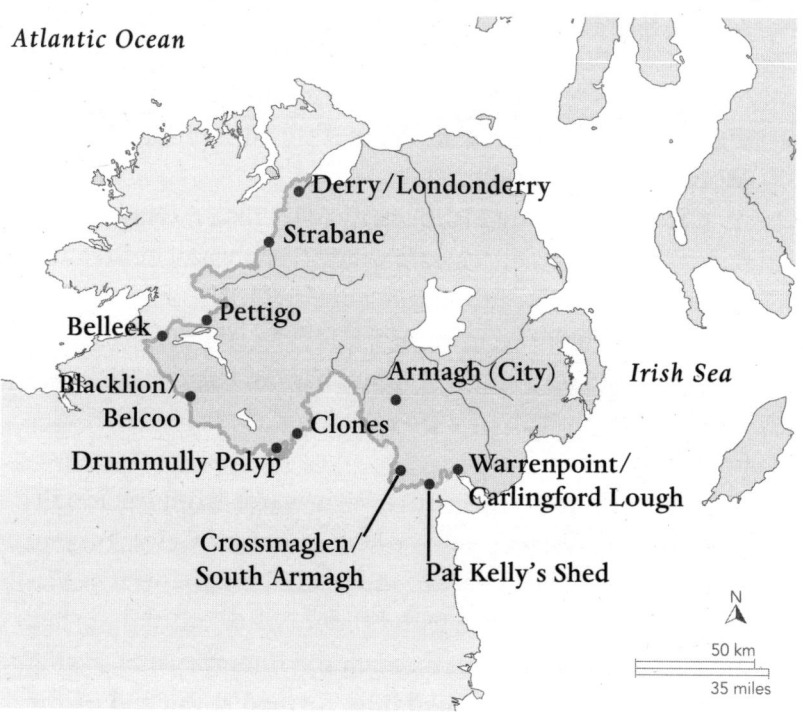

Warrenpoint

I stood on a concrete pier in Warrenpoint. It was mid-October. A light wind rippled across Carlingford Lough's calm waters. Forested banks, wreathed in the dark-brown sheen of autumn, lined either side of a glacial channel leading to the Irish Sea. The Mourne Mountains rose on the lough's northern side. My phone pinged between UK and Irish carriers, the signal carried from metal pylons placed high atop the Republic of Ireland's mist-swathed Cooley Mountains to my south.

Carlingford Lough is the seaway to Ulster. One of four historical Irish provinces – alongside Connacht, Leinster and Munster – Ulster's nine counties are divided. Three of these counties are in the Republic of Ireland. Northern Ireland, the United Kingdom's smallest home nation, has the other six, located to the north of a 310-mile-long international border beginning here.

Following the Newry River westwards from the lough-side town of Warrenpoint – where murals of Celtic folklore and Irish Republican heroes add a splash of colour to a Victorian promenade – the Irish border twists and slithers like a dazed adder thrashing through the underbrush. Carving apart drumlins (egg-shaped hills, formed at the end of the Ice Age), loughs, rivers, forests, mountains, towns, villages and even farmhouses, the border reaches out for the Atlantic Ocean but never makes it. County Donegal holds the Atlantic coastline for the Republic of Ireland, and the border shoots north along the River Foyle, stranding Derry/Londonderry in Northern Ireland before concluding on the muddy banks of Lough Foyle.

My next journey would take me along the length of the United Kingdom's only international land border. I would road trip westwards into Northern Ireland's County Armagh, traverse the enclaves and exclaves of County Monaghan in the Republic and trace this enduring boundary through the watery landscapes of County Fermanagh (Northern Ireland) and County Cavan (Republic of Ireland). I would then turn north, ending my journey in Derry/Londonderry, where the Troubles began among the north's divided Catholic and Protestant communities in the late 1960s.

It would start, though, amid Warrenpoint's brooding Gaelic landscapes, where damp moss glistens emerald green in the rare sunlight and I felt a spectre of the ancient. Ireland's history runs as deep as Carlingford Lough, where Vikings once settled a fjord-like channel that reminded them of home. But the Irish border is far from ancient. Roughly drawn along county boundaries in 1921, the border divided Ireland between the newly independent Catholic-majority Irish Free State in the south, and the Protestant-dominated north, which remained in the United Kingdom.

From the moment Northern Ireland came into existence on 3 May 1921, discontent simmered among disenfranchised Catholic minorities left in the north. In August 1969, the Battle of Bogside in Derry/Londonderry sparked the Troubles, a decades-long sectarian conflict pitting the volunteers of the Provisional Irish Republican Army (IRA) – fighting for Irish reunification – against Northern Ireland's police, Loyalist paramilitaries ('Loyalists' are those loyal to the Crown, who want Northern Ireland to remain in the United Kingdom) and the British Army. This was a war about a border. A border Loyalists wanted preserved; a border the IRA wanted torn down.

The borderlands became a war zone. The deadliest IRA attack of the conflict occurred a mile west of where I now stood, outside the ragged sixteenth-century stone walls of Narrow Water Castle. On 27 August 1979, shrapnel peppered Carlingford Lough's quiet waters and plumes of black smoke filled the horizon when the IRA's South Armagh Brigade detonated a 360-kilogram homemade fertilizer bomb on the northern bank of the River Newry. The IRA watched and waited from across the border, detonating a second fertilizer bomb when British Army reinforcements arrived to help the convoy caught in the blast. Eighteen British Paratroopers were killed that afternoon, and an innocent bystander, William Hudson – a Londoner visiting family in County Louth – was killed by a stray round when British soldiers fired back over the border. During thirty years of violence, 3,600 people were killed and thousands wounded. In 1998, the Good Friday Agreement brought peace, a chance for reconciliation. Most hoped the hard border, with its watchtowers and customs posts – a symbol of conflict and division – would never return.

Today, a granite 'peace boulder' stares longingly over Carlingford Lough from Warrenpoint's seafront. A yappy Jack Russell broke the silence, its owner skirting around me as I gazed across the quiet water. Republican flags fly in Warrenpoint; musicians sing mournful Gaelic songs in cozy pubs packed with Guinness drinking tourists. Times have changed, and a generation has grown up knowing peace, not war. But this remains a raw borderland. Brexit reignited fears of a resurrected land border, and with ever-changing demographics – there are now more Catholics than Protestants in Northern Ireland – calls for Irish reunification have only grown stronger.

Like the New Zealand cabbage palms along Warrenpoint's seafront, I too was about to be planted well out of my comfort zone. This is the border I knew least about, and to understand its history, I had to get out there and hear, first-hand, the stories of the people who call this borderland home. Accompanied by my equally ignorant English friend Tom, we would travel the border's length from here to Derry/Londonderry. I wanted to see if a hard border would ever be revived, or if the future of Ireland lay in reunification, rather than continued division.

Pat's Shed

We found Pat's Shed a half mile south of the border in County Louth, in the Republic of Ireland, a half-hour drive west from Warrenpoint. The white, green and orange flag of the Republic of Ireland flew lazily in the chill autumn wind. Rusting rolls of barbed wire lay strewn among weather-beaten 'Road Closed' and 'Customs' signs, once found all along the border, and now stacked in Pat's farmyard. Pat, a grey-haired farmer with an unshakeable grin, may or may not have been in the IRA. We didn't ask. He didn't say. But there was no debate where Pat's loyalties lay. 'We say the

"North of Ireland" up here,' he said in a firm but friendly tone, after he'd quieted the barking dogs alerting him of our arrival. 'It's *never* "Northern Ireland".'

Pat stood a head shorter than me, but his mischievous smile, worn, moustachioed face and gruff Irish accent meant I wouldn't be arguing semantics. We stepped inside the cold, cavernous shed he'd crammed floor-to-ceiling with relics from the border. Pat immediately started showing us his firearms. He'd propped rusting Lee–Enfield rifles against bicycles that once cycled through border checkpoints, dressed mannequins in IRA and Ulster Special Constabulary uniforms and filled every inch of wall space with newspaper clippings, photos, maps, postcards, letters and posters. Tom – an old friend I'd met during my University of Nottingham days, whose love for politics had him begging to join me on the Irish border – raised an eyebrow. 'Where the hell have you brought me?' asked his quizzical look.

Pat grew up on this very farm. We'd only found it by chance the night before while sinking Guinness in Warrenpoint. Scanning the wiggly lines of the Irish border, 'Pat's Shed' suddenly appeared on Google Maps. Hidden away in an empty-looking stretch of borderland, Facebook pictures showed the man himself posing by his 'Road Closed' signs with tourists and minor celebrities, including Spider from the Pogues. Pat seemed like exactly the right person to give us a fiery introduction to what life was like on the Irish border – particularly during the Troubles, an era of history many in England know so little about – so I'd WhatsApped him, asking if he was around the next day.

He replied instantly, saying he'd have coffee on the boil

in the morning. He'd forgotten about the coffee when we showed up, but he did have a moonshine-like whiskey distilled from potatoes. 'Have you ever tried *poitín*?' Pat asked, pulling an unlabelled bottle down from a dusty shelf. 'Who's driving?' Luckily I was, and Tom grimaced as he stoically downed the shot in one.

Pat pulled out a crinkled British Army border map from 1978. I traced the route we'd taken from Warrenpoint via Newry – where Republic of Ireland flags and Sinn Fein (the Irish Republican Party, which is active on both sides of the border) campaign posters marked the small Northern Irish city out as Republican – then skirting the base of Slieve Gullion, a mist-wrapped mountain overshadowing the border, which Pat said was once home to a monstrous army observation post.

An air of militant mystery surrounded Pat. During the Troubles, the Garda (the Republic of Ireland's police force) had once found unlicensed firearms in the boot of his car. 'Don't worry, it's deactivated,' he said with a devilish grin, handing me a pistol from his collection and taking a photo for the shed's Facebook page. 'It's a black powder gun. It won't fire any more.' I asked Pat if this was the sort of weapon the Garda had found on him. He laughed heartily, said nothing, but soon handed me a semi-automatic Armalite rifle. Abruptly, he then pointed out a photo of Gerry Adams, Sinn Fein's former president (who claimed to never have been in the IRA) stood in the same damp shed we were in now.

Pat wasn't so much interested in telling us about the border as showing us. Next, he pulled out a newspaper clipping from the seventies, pointing out the black-and-white photo of a digger tearing into a British Army border barricade built from concrete and barbed wire. 'That's me driving the digger,' he said with his happy grin. He'd spent his youth knocking down barricades. For him, the north was all Ireland, and the barricades stopped him from travelling freely into what he saw as his country. 'The British Army would block the road up there on Mondays. I'd turn up on Tuesday and dig it up. It had to be done. I'm proud I was involved in that.'

Pat had the brooding confidence of a man who'd happily defy the authorities if he believed it the just thing to do. The true extent of his defiance was never clear, but as we explored his shed, each newspaper cutting or memento revealed a story, usually involving him in some roundabout way. In 1981, for example, Pat's horsebox was stolen. The IRA later used the same horsebox in the infamous Shergar horse kidnapping. Pat also had a piano he said belonged to the mother of Bobby Sands, an IRA hunger striker who'd died in the Maze prison outside Belfast in 1981.

'Maggie Thatcher was a dickhead. Letting the hunger strikers die,' he said, without his characteristic laugh. 'You know, I quite liked the Queen, though,' his chuckle returning, as he pointed to Queen Elizabeth II's photo on the wall. 'Charles is all right. Andrew's a fuckhead. The Pope's a dick. I'm Catholic myself but I've no interest in it. More people have been killed in the name of religion than anything else. It's mad.'

Pat dispassionately told us stories of the Troubles, often paired with a deadpan laugh and wry humour. He told us of an SAS man who, despite having an Oxford-English accent (according to Pat), tried to pass as an Irishman, singing

Republican songs in Republican pubs along the border. 'He was a bad bastard,' said Pat. 'The IRA kidnapped him, took him over the border and shot him. They're still trying to find his body in the bogs.'

Pat had a bullet-riddled 'Sniper at Work' sign from Crossmaglen, a town a few miles north in South Armagh, a border region in Northern Ireland known as 'bandit country' during the Troubles. 'That's Miss South Armagh,' he said with another hearty chuckle, pointing out a female mannequin dressed up in a gas mask and combat fatigues, another Armalite rifle in her plastic hands. 'You have to laugh at these things!'

Pat's humour was dark. He was moved to tears of laughter when Tom pulled on the Royal Ulster Constabulary's heavy, blue woollen coat, donned the dark navy-blue hat with its harp emblem and posed for a photo with a Lee–Enfield rifle. The RUC – Northern Ireland's police force from 1920 until 2001 – was accused of numerous atrocities throughout the Troubles and were replaced by the Police Service of Northern Ireland following the Good Friday Agreement.

Pat had saved an Ulster Volunteers Force (UVF) flag, with its brutish red fist on an orange and purple field. The UVF was a Loyalist paramilitary group, fighting against the IRA to preserve Northern Ireland's place within the United Kingdom. In 1974, the UVF detonated bombs in Dublin and Monaghan, a border town in the Republic of Ireland ten miles from here, killing thirty-four civilians on one of the bloodiest days of the Troubles. 'People walk in and ask what the fuck am I doing with these flags,' Pat said, also pointing out a tattered Union Jack. 'But you have to show both sides of history.'

Pat didn't forget those times, but these days, he's more

concerned with music. He eagerly showed us album covers and signed photos of the Mary Wallopers, an Irish folk band hailing from Dundalk, a few miles away, who played Glastonbury in 2024. They're regular visitors to the shed, playing gigs and drinking with Pat. 'One of them fell asleep in the torture chair once,' he said disconcertingly of a rusting dentist's chair in the corner. 'We had a right laugh with him.'

Pat was called back to the border during Brexit. The RUC uniforms came in handy, and he helped organize mock customs posts as part of a project called 'Border Communities Against Brexit'. A reminder of what had come before, and what could be again.

Pat's Shed was the raw introduction to the Irish border we were looking for. There was much he said that I promised not to write, and what he left unsaid spoke as loudly as the stories he did tell. Pat had shown us the polarizing dangers of a hard border, and the ghosts that linger in a borderland where conflict was once embedded in daily life. He rued the day Ireland should ever return to violent times. For Pat, the border should never have been drawn and should never be drawn again, a sentiment we would encounter daily as our journey continued.

Bandit Country

Pat pointed us north. Into bandit country. Speed limits switched from kilometres to miles per hour and road markings from yellow to white as we followed a lonely road over the same border into Northern Ireland, where a young Pat had once bulldozed barricades.

Our next stop was Armagh, County Armagh's only city, which was a half-hour drive north of Pat's Shed in a border region once at the deadly heart of the Troubles. But Armagh has been the ecclesiastical capital of the entire island of Ireland since the fifth century, and the primates of Ireland, Catholic and Protestant, are both based there. If Ireland were unified, Armagh would no longer be near an international border, but right in the centre. I wanted to know if the city – home to two cathedrals, one Catholic and one Protestant, where the same saint is revered – could inspire unification, rather than division.

On the way, we drove through green farmland punctuated by barren drumlins. Stretching north from the Irish border to the banks of Lough Neagh, County Armagh typifies Northern Ireland's sectarian divides. The county's south is largely Catholic and Republican and the north Protestant and Unionist. The divides go back centuries. In the 1600s, King James I and VI established 'plantations' (colonies) after the defeat and exile of Ulster's Irish earls.

Protestants from the Scottish Lowlands and England (many of them exiled Border Reivers) settled in Armagh's fertile agricultural lands, displacing the native, Irish-speaking Catholics into the sparse, mountainous lands now along the border. Once the most Irish of provinces, Ulster became the heartland of the Protestant Ulster Scots.

In 1795, the Orange Order, a masonic-like Protestant society, was founded in the County Armagh town of Loughgall. Named for Protestant King William of Orange, who'd ushered in the Glorious Revolution, the Orange Order formed as a Protestant defence movement, and its members (who are almost exclusively male) pledge to 'defend the King and his heirs so long as he or they support the Protestant

Ascendancy'. 'Orangeism' remains hugely influential; from 1921 until 1972, every single First Minister of Northern Ireland was an 'Orangeman'.

County Armagh's northern towns, including Portadown and Craigavon, are fiercely Loyalist, and known for the staggering bonfires (some built two hundred feet high) lit on Eleventh Night (11 July), a fiery spectacle celebrating the Protestant victory over the deposed Catholic King James II at the Battle of the Boyne in 1690. Orange marches then take place on 12 July, when kerbs are painted red, white and blue, and marching bands beating goatskin drums lead Loyalists through neighbourhoods decked out in Union Jack bunting.

Driving through South Armagh's villages, Irish Republican flags betrayed competing loyalties. Tom, who was looking at Google Maps, said we were close to Crossmaglen, the border town where Pat's 'Sniper at Work' sign had come from. One hundred and sixty members of the British Army and Northern Ireland's security forces were killed in South Armagh during the Troubles, often by snipers shooting from across the border. There were 1,255 bombings, many more shootings, and countless IRA informants and victims have yet to be found after they were shot and dumped over the border in bogs (the Disappeared, as they're now forlornly known). The violence earned South Armagh its bandit country moniker, a term coined by Northern Ireland secretary Merlyn Rees in 1974. Many of those caught up in the spiral of violence and revenge attacks were farmers, whose isolated farmsteads made perfect targets or hideouts for both sides.

The sun was drooping over the border to our west as a rutted lane strewn with potholes brought us to one such farmstead sprawled over muddy fields divided by brambles and barbed wire on the outskirts of Armagh. Tom had booked us into an Airbnb, and Frank, dressed in farmer's clothes, wearing wellies, beige trousers and a waxy jacket met us in the courtyard. He'd taken the place over a few years before, he said in a jovial voice echoing off the flagstones. His ancestors had worked the farm for generations, but he stressed he wasn't a farmer. He left the farming to others more knowledgeable than him, running another business from his farmhouse office instead.

Frank showed us into the barn conversion and asked if I had any Irish ancestry. I said I'm probably an eighth Irish, but instead of tracing genealogy like many of the tourists he sees, we were following the border. Frank's eyebrows raised with intrigue. When he was young, his dad moved his family away from Northern Ireland to escape the border's violence. He grew up removed from the Troubles but heard awful stories on summer trips back home.

'My cousin was killed by the IRA on his farm. He was one of the first to die. He was the son of a farmer,' he said with a sad look in his eyes. 'Most of the people killed along the border were farmers or farmers' sons. Some were involved in the paramilitaries or the IRA. Not everyone. The IRA killed the sons of farmers so Protestant farms would be sold to Catholics. They wanted to change the demographics of the border. But the plan never worked.'

Protestant border communities were hit hard. Bloody incidents like 1976's Kingsmill massacre near Newry – which left some ten Protestants dead on the side of the road after the IRA forced them off a bus and shot them – are still recalled with a shudder. But Frank recognized how easy it is to remember only one side of the story in a polarized borderland. While the IRA made the headlines, he told us, Loyalist paramilitaries were out there killing Catholics. In 1975, in one tragic incident, the UVF shamefully murdered three members of the Miami Showband – one of Ireland's biggest pop acts – at a fake roadblock north of Newry, right after they'd played to screaming crowds in Belfast.

'There's still bad blood,' Frank said. 'A lot of ill feeling. The people that did the killings, on both sides, they're in government now. All the perpetrators are in Stormont! But we're all talking, at least.'

'The way of the gun won't work,' he continued, with an off-the-cuff but heartfelt speech. 'It never does. There will never be a united Ireland forged through violence. It must be democratic. And I think that will happen in my lifetime. The communities here are moving closer together. You just think, no. You never want to return to those dark days.'

'Leave the boys alone!' Frank's wife jokingly scolded him. She'd heard his booming voice from across the farmyard and popped over with cake, jam, clotted cream and extra blankets. They left us to settle in before moonlight lit up the farmyard. The next morning, mooing cows woke me with a start. Another chill autumn day brought crows squawking through brambles and chaffinches calling out from trees. It was hard to imagine living here, in fear, during the Troubles. We hopped in the car, drove slowly back to the main road, and headed into Armagh to discover what unites, rather than divides, these borderlands.

Curving Georgian terraces twinkled with the pinkish hue of Armagh limestone. Some eight miles north of the Irish border, Armagh is set around *Ard Mhacha* – the 'Heights of Macha' – a grassy, egg-shaped drumlin steeped in Ulster mythology. It's an ancient place associated with Macha, the Celtic goddess of warfare, horses and sovereignty, whose story is passed down to us through mythical medieval sagas like the Ulster Cycle. Macha's husband is said to have boasted of his wife's godlike speed, and the King of Ulster forced Macha, who was heavily pregnant, to race his finest horses to prove the boast. She beat the king's horses, only to give birth in agony to twins on the finishing line. Macha cursed the men of Ulster. In their greatest time of need, they'd suffer the same pains of childbirth, and in later tales, the 'Debility of the Ulstermen', as it became known, would incapacitate Ulster's finest warriors on the eve of battle.

The curse echoes through the centuries. Atop the Heights of Macha, where Saint Patrick founded his first stone church in 445, I saw the ungainly Norman tower of St Patrick's Cathedral, which is Protestant and Church of Ireland. Half a mile away, on a smaller hilltop opposite the Shambles Market car park where we'd pulled up, the striking neo-Gothic spires of the Catholic St Patrick's Cathedral faced off against the Protestant spires. This is the only city in the world with two cathedrals dedicated to the same saint, a simple summation of Armagh's divides.

Approximately 67 per cent of Armagh City's population defined themselves as Catholic in the last census. The Irish tricolour flew from lamp posts, graffiti called for a united Ireland, 'IRA' was scrawled across a road sign, and flags draped from shopfronts read 'Good Luck Armagh' for the All-Ireland Gaelic Football Championship. I was struck by the outward support for nationalism, but in Northern Ireland, flags allow you to orientate yourself, to know which neighbourhood you're in. Unionist neighbourhoods often paint their kerbs red, white and blue, and a wrong answer to the question, 'What colour are your kerbs?' could have got you killed during the Troubles. Enter a Loyalist area and you'll see the Union Jack flying alongside Israeli flags. Republicans fly Palestine's flag. In Ireland, people are used to choosing sides.

Republicanism has a long tradition in Armagh. Michael Collins, an Irish revolutionary who fought in 1916's Easter Rising in Dublin, gave fiery speeches at the Charlemont Arms Hotel in the city centre. He was elected Armagh's MP in 1921, and was assassinated in 1922 during the Irish Civil War. Armagh is a place of contradictions, however. Ian Paisley – perhaps the most divisive Protestant political character in Northern Ireland's recent history – was born here in 1926. Staunchly Unionist, Paisley opposed the Catholic Civil Rights Movement, and his inflammatory speeches from the pulpit stoked Protestant fears of a Catholic takeover of Northern Ireland. Paisley founded the Democratic Unionist Party (DUP) in 1971, a frighteningly conservative, right-wing Loyalist party that still holds large numbers of seats in government. Armagh grapples with these conflicting histories and identities – as evidenced by its two cathedrals – as it attempts to build a modern sense of self across centuries-old divides.

Donna, who we met back by the Shambles, grew up on a farm near the border, like the one we'd spent the night at. She works in tourism, an industry that's boomed more than any since the Good Friday Agreement allowed tourists to visit in safety. Wearing a jazzy silver puffer jacket to battle the October chill, she told us about her upcoming Halloween ghost walks where she would bring the ancient and often macabre history of Armagh back from the dead (it was Donna who told us the legendary tale of Macha). But the border's recent past is just as ghostly, and perhaps more terrifying, than anything that came before it.

Donna remembers the checkpoints from her childhood in the 1970s. She'd wait hours to cross the border, just to visit a restaurant or cafe in Monaghan. Cars were inspected, number plates checked and at night, the spotlights were blinding. 'I remember waking up one morning to find soldiers along our road. They'd raided a farmhouse,' she recalled of the constant military presence. 'There was a funny relationship. My mum gave the young soldiers tea and cakes. She'd say, "They're someone's son." Other times you'd be stopped by paramilitaries in ski masks. That was scarier. You never knew which side they were on.'

Donna gave us a whistlestop tour of Armagh. She pointed out a plaque on the high street dedicated to John Gallagher, a Catholic civil-rights protestor shot and killed by police in August 1969. The plaque was in Irish, and Donna proudly showed us the Cultúrlann, a Gaelic community centre where she was learning Ireland's native language. She's somewhat of a linguist, speaking French and German, and felt it inappropriate she'd never learnt Irish.

In 2021, around 12 per cent of Northern Ireland's population declared some knowledge of Irish on the census (0.3 per cent identified it as their primary language). It wasn't until 2022 that Northern Ireland recognized Irish as an official language, alongside English and Ulster Scots. Donna said there's an Irish-medium primary school in Armagh, while other Irish traditions – like the Mummers, whose wicker hats and frightening masks are part of local Halloween celebrations – are being revived, and Gaelic sports taken up by people on both sides of the divide.

Despite this embrace of Irish tradition, Northern Ireland remains segregated in ways I couldn't comprehend, particularly in terms of education, with Catholic schools teaching an Irish curriculum and Protestant schools teaching a British curriculum. Donna knows from experience that integrated education can break the divides. She described herself as 'lucky enough' to have gone to a rare mixed school. It gave her a more inclusive outlook on life. Out of over a thousand primary and secondary schools in the country, though, only seventy are classed as integrated.

The spectre of sectarian conflict runs deep. 'My parents' generation's social lives were very segregated,' said Donna, as we stopped outside the site of the former City Hall, opposite the Claremont Arms, an eighteenth-century hotel which was bombed three times during the Troubles. 'The City Hall was the only real cross-community place to meet. But it was bombed. I think it was an IRA bomb,' she added in the hushed tone I'd come to expect. 'They never caught who did it.' Now, the same site is occupied by the North South Ministerial Council Headquarters, a cross-border body established after the Good Friday Agreement to debate all-Ireland issues like agriculture and tourism.

Donna believes Irish reunification will happen within her lifetime. 'If you'd asked me that before Brexit, I'd have said no. But Brexit changed everything. It pushed us towards a united Ireland,' she said excitedly, before explaining how the fear of a hard border returning when the UK left the European Union made many in Armagh believe that reunification was the future. 'The demographics are moving that way, but you need both sides of the island to agree, and it won't be smooth sailing when it happens. Watch this space.'

For Donna, Irish reunification was inevitable, but that's one side of a polarized issue. The DUP is diametrically opposed to reunification, so I'd arranged a meeting with local DUP councillor Scott Armstrong in the Craic'd Pot cafe that afternoon.

I agree with hardly any of the DUP's policies. The Unionist party is anti-Irish language, anti-same-sex marriage, anti-abortion and evangelical in its Christian beliefs. Frankly, they're xenophobic, homophobic, misogynist fundamentalists. Still, they're incredibly popular in Northern Ireland's Loyalist communities, winning five out of eighteen seats in the 2024 general election (only Sinn Fein, with seven seats, won more).

Armagh's DUP councillor was a fresh faced 26-year-old. Armstrong is a strong Border Reiver name, and Scott was Ulster Scots to the core. He had short, trimmed hair, and with the white collar of his shirt poking over the top of a smart black jumper, he had the air of a student about him. He'd grown up in Armagh, knowing only peace, he stressed, having been born in the late 1990s. He explained how his politics took shape at Ulster University, where he was a conservative in an extremely liberal environment, but also realized his voice was as legitimate as any other. He then worked as a chef for several years, before pursuing his true ambition of a full-time political career.

Tom and Scott chatted easily about politics. Tom, who is originally from Lancashire, is a Conservative councillor in his adopted London suburb of Wimbledon. He'd studied politics at university – where he was involved in his first and only political scandal as president of the Conservative Society after running 'Port and Policy' evenings that made the front page of the university newspaper for their drunken debating – and I recall he once had a cardboard cutout of Margaret Thatcher in his bedroom (I'm still not sure if it was ironic or not). I'd been surprised at Tom's overt level of patriotism when we first met – he loved all things British, be it the Queen, Last Night of the Proms or a jug of Pimm's – but despite our often-differing political views, we'd bonded over real ales and a shared love of the pub.

Even for Tom – who'd worked in Parliament and written speeches for Tory MPs – the DUP's politics were too conservative. Scott explained that while yes, the DUP were right-wing on social issues, he didn't necessarily agree with everything about them. He'd joined them because he 'disagreed with them less than with the other parties', and was primarily drawn by their fundamental goal of retaining the Union with Britain. 'We used to say I'd rather be an Ulster man than anything else in the world,' he said over the hiss of a barista machine. 'Your heritage is so important, and Britishness is a shared history we look upon fondly. It's an inherent bond between me and you.'

For Scott, Britishness is primarily represented by the monarchy, which provides a continual link through British history. He also listed more tangible 'advantages' of the United Kingdom, including being part of the world's sixth-largest economy, and British institutions like the NHS (which

I agreed with). Scott looked to the past, though, in a way I didn't, glorifying the monarchy, the British Empire and a 'value system' he said was exported to the rest of the world. 'What makes you British a hundred years ago,' he said, rather vaguely, 'is the same as what makes you British today. We're loyal to our king and loyal to our country. What makes me British makes you British.'

Although Loyalist neighbourhoods in Northern Ireland can feel more 'British' than anywhere in Great Britain – on Belfast's Shankill Road there are big murals of Queen Elizabeth II and King Charles III – this idea of the Union seemed based on a glorified past. It's the same psyche I've seen in places like Gibraltar, where patriotism in the form of red postboxes and fish and chip shops distinguishes Gibraltarians from the Spanish (and where a hard border imposed for thirteen years by the Spanish dictator Franco only served to cement a sense of British patriotism in Gibraltar). In the same respect, Scott's Loyalist identity seemed very much a product of living in a contested borderland, where heightened ideas of nationalism and identity are moulded by conflict, tension and fear. Here in Northern Ireland, I didn't recognize Scott's vision of the United Kingdom.

Brexit strained the connection between Great Britain and Northern Ireland. The Northern Ireland Protocol, as it's termed, placed the customs border between the European Union and the UK in the Irish Sea, to avoid resurrecting the land border between the Republic of Ireland and Northern Ireland. While this means goods and people can pass freely across the island of Ireland, it's served to effectively cut Northern Ireland off from mainland Britain.

Loyalists would've preferred the Irish border to have

remained on the island itself (the 'natural border', Scott called it), rather than in the Irish Sea where the customs border now lies. Unionists feel forgotten about; Scott felt they're ignored, shunned by the country they love. Not just because of Brexit, but because of the Good Friday Agreement, too, which brought a blanket amnesty to those involved in the Troubles. For Loyalists like Scott, this amnesty means that many of the crimes and murders committed by the IRA, who they see as terrorists, will never be brought to trial.

'Travel to the border villages,' he said, raising his voice so we could hear him over the loud Taylor Swift music the cafe had started playing, 'and the trauma's still raw. We're just twelve miles from where the Kingsmill massacre took place. There's never been any justice for that. Unionists feel isolated, as if the British government doesn't care about justice. Ask any Unionist politician over the last one hundred years if they feel forgotten, and they'd say yes. We always feel we give back and get nothing in return. We feel forgotten. You walk down a street here and people are more British than someone in Somerset, but it's like we don't exist.'

The danger is that Unionist voices like Scott's, now in a minority, are lost in a scramble to unify Ireland. But throughout my travels in Northern Ireland, I was surprised at the polarization of attitudes towards reunification. It felt as if people lived in their own bubble. It was either inevitable or never going to happen. There was no middle ground.

'Reunification won't happen in my lifetime,' said Scott without hesitation. He didn't think enough people want it. For Scott, who'd grown up without a border, without war, there was no reason *not* to keep the status quo. 'We've kept the peace,' he said, as we wrapped up our conversation. 'You forget that twenty-six years ago we were at war, now both sides are in Stormont.'

Clones

The dull thud of shotguns (from a game shoot, rather than a borderland skirmish, I hoped) carried on the wind as we packed up the hire car in the morning drizzle. We left Armagh behind, the A3 turning into the N12 as we crossed the border into County Monaghan. I wanted to understand how communities divided by an international boundary were now building bridges, rather than burning them, so we made our way forty minutes west to Clones (pronounced 'Clone-ess'), which sits in the Republic of Ireland, less than a mile from the border with Northern Ireland's County Fermanagh.

Clones' history stretches back to the sixth century, when Clones Abbey was established by Saint Tigernach (or Tiarnach, if you're Protestant), who raised the Archbishop of Armagh from the dead. We found the abbey in ruins, with 'No public drinking' signs posted on its crumbling archway. In the twelfth century, the Normans built a motte, now overgrown and covered in rubbish, on Clones' outskirts, before Protestant settlers laid down the town centre's 'diamond' plan, a typical cross-shaped pattern embraced by Ulster Scots in the Plantation era.

The grey spire of St Tiarnach's Protestant church overshadowed a weather-beaten Celtic cross in the square, where for centuries, farmers brought goods to market from fields now spilling over the Irish border. Irish tricolours and Palestinian flags flew from grey townhouses, and after a quick stroll through Barry McGuigan Park – named after the All-Ireland boxing world champion from Clones – we walked to St Tigernach's Cemetery, where a twenty-metre-tall sandstone tower rose above gravestones dotted with purple wildflowers.

We were looking for the old Victorian schoolhouse opposite the cemetery. A recipe for 'Famine Soup' – calling for turnips, water and cabbage to feed hundreds at a time – was printed on an information board in the garden. Between 1845 and 1852, some one million people perished in the Great Famine, a bleak episode of Irish history still lingering in the collective consciousness of the nation. Blight struck potato crops and wealthy landowners hoarded grain. The shameful inaction of the British government left individuals – including Cassandra Hand, an Englishwoman from Surrey, who arrived in Clones in 1847 – to provide what little relief they could. Cassandra established Clones' lacemaking industry, offering work and charity to desperately starved locals. She invested profits back into community projects like the schoolhouse, which was founded in 1859. Now restored, the schoolhouse is home to the Cassandra Hand Folk and Famine Centre, a museum and community centre where tourists can trace their Irish genealogy and learn about *An Gorta Mór*, the 'Great Hunger'.

Inside, the smell of burning wood greeted us, as Anne, the curator, fought the autumn cold with a log fire. The crackling of flames echoed off polished oak floors, where school desks stood eerily empty in a recreated Victorian classroom. Anne had arranged for us to meet with two Clones locals who knew the border well. She told us the story of Cassandra, Clones lace and the famine, before Pat, a Sinn Fein councillor, and Donald, a local businessman involved in cross-border development projects and peace commissions, burst through the Victorian doors a few minutes later.

Pat Treanor gave Tom and I thick handshakes. A soft-spoken man in his seventies, his green tweed jacket and trousers made him look every inch the rural borderer. A quiet fire within Pat spoke of his Republican side. He'd spent the best part of thirty years as a political activist. He's a pacifist at heart, but he'd dismantled plenty of border barricades in his time. 'I hope you made it safely over the border today,' chuckled the other man, who was wearing a big orange fleece, even though he was a Republican. 'My name's Donald McDonald.' True to his almost unbelievable name, Donald McDonald was larger than life, his big frame and loud voice matching his big personality.

Anne laid out a table and chairs for us, leaving us to chat after setting down biscuits and tea. Long before the Troubles, said Donald, this was a borderland between Irish kingdoms, a place where clans battled and cattle were rustled. The first boundaries followed the rivers, streams and drumlins. The earliest archaeological evidence for a man-made border remains in the ditches and earthen mounds marking Black Pig's Dyke, an ancient Iron Age boundary stretching across Ulster. Donald and Pat proudly called themselves 'border people', speaking of a millennia-old border identity straddling political divisions thrown up by Partition.

Partition occurred on 3 May 1921, when Ireland – which had been ruled as one island from Westminster, since the Act of Union in 1800 – was divided into the Irish Free State (the forerunner to the independent Republic of Ireland) and Northern Ireland, which remains in the United Kingdom to this day. I visited several Orange Order and Protestant-run museums during my journey. The overriding Loyalist sentiment I gleaned was that the creation of Northern Ireland was the logical outcome to a 'Home Rule Bill' – a proposed Act of Parliament which would have granted a devolved government in Dublin the power to rule over both the north and south of Ireland – opposed by the majority Protestant north.

The six counties feared the oppression a Catholic-majority government in Dublin might bring. For Unionists, self-determination meant staying in the United Kingdom. The creation of Northern Ireland, which would be ruled from Stormont in Belfast, allowed them to uphold their Loyalist identity and Protestant traditions, including Orange marches and fraternal Protestant organizations like the Orange Order. Equally, Loyalist-dominated Stormont refused to respect the self-determination and traditions of Catholics and Republicans within Northern Ireland's new borders. Northern Ireland had the first devolved parliament in the United Kingdom, but it failed spectacularly when in 1972, Westminster stripped Stormont's powers and placed it under direct rule. The parliament wouldn't be reinstated until the Good Friday Agreement, with both sides agreeing to share power and enshrine the rights of Catholics and Protestants alike in law.

Donald described Partition in simpler terms as a messy solution for an island divided between Republicans and Loyalists. A hatchet job of division tore apart communities, farms and even, in Donald's case, his house. 'I lived in a farmhouse on the border. I could sleep with my feet in the north of Ireland and my head in the south of Ireland,' he reminisced with another chuckle. 'The border went through my living room. If I moved from the living room into the kitchen, I crossed the border. My postal address was Northern Ireland. I paid for electricity and water in the south.'

Donald said he shared more in common with borderers who lived five or six miles over the border than the rest of the Republic of Ireland, or Northern Ireland for that matter. He described the defining commonalities of borderers as resilience, fortitude, tolerance and creativity. A cross-border loyalty transcends Loyalist or Republican ideals. 'It's never been about a flag, or an emblem, but about collaboration,' he said firmly. 'As border people, we see integration and equality of opportunity as keywords for the future.'

'I agree,' said Pat, explaining how, even if there were regular customs checks on goods along the border before the Troubles, people could move freely across it. 'Our friends and relations are over the border in County Tyrone or Fermanagh. We've always had a cross-border culture. We relate with them more than people from Cork or Kerry.'

The Troubles tested these shared bonds. Pat said they faced blatant discrimination driving through border villages. Soldiers at checkpoints held guns to their faces, saying 'Go back to your own country'. The border was fraught with danger. In 1994, Pat guided a group of Swedish journalists to see what he'd called an illegal British Army roadblock on a road leading north. He was arrested on suspicion of terrorist offences, and in an unhappy coincidence, was in the back of a police car when the IRA sprung an ambush later that day, just weeks before a ceasefire.

Pat was quieter than Donald, but politically astute. Road closures, checkpoints and barricades never worked. He said to look at Israel, whose blockades in Gaza cause death and deprivation. Here on the border, where so many Palestinian flags fly, Republicans empathize with the Middle East's conflicts. 'The Israelis don't seem to get it,' Donald added. 'Keep your boot on the throat of your neighbour, eventually your neighbour bites back. I was in Beirut twenty-five years ago. All those casualties simply became martyrs for the cause, their photos on every street corner. They were heroes.'

I'd seen the same thing myself when I visited Beirut in 2022: an endless cycle of violence with no end in sight. After a time, even pacifists find their fire. For Pat, that time came during the hunger strikes in the 1980s. 'We became much more accepting of armed conflict,' he said with a sad look. 'After the hunger strikes.'

During the hunger strikes, ten IRA prisoners starved themselves to death protesting British internment policies in Northern Ireland. Bobby Sands was the first to die, but not before he was elected as an MP for Newry, even while dying in jail. One hundred thousand people attended his funeral, and worldwide media attention transformed Sinn Fein (the IRA's political wing) into a legitimate political force to be reckoned with.

Donald and Pat didn't just hate the border for the lives it took, but also for the economic stagnation the borderlands suffered because of it. Pat was in the egg industry. With suppliers and customers on both sides of the border, the barricades and roadblocks bled his business dry as costs mounted and the movement of goods and people were restricted. Donald said there'd always been more deprivation and less investment in the borderlands than elsewhere in Ireland, but when the border did come down, the borderlands found a new lease of life. Donald likened it to spending your whole life carrying a four-stone bag of spuds on your back everywhere you went, then it's gone. 'Suddenly, the roads were open, there's peace, and it's like you've tossed that bag of potatoes away,' he said, jumping out of his seat for emphasis. 'And can you imagine, you stand up, and you can stand tall and straight for the first time in your life!'

The Good Friday Agreement created opportunities to bring the borderlands together again. Pat talked about institutions like ICBAN (Irish Central Border Area Network), consisting of councillors and businesspeople (like Pat and Donald) from both sides of the border. ICBAN was established to promote cross-border cooperation in key areas like water quality, agriculture, the environment, healthcare and energy. They're building bridges, as Pat put it – in some cases literally, as bridges demolished during the Troubles are rebuilt – and improving quality of life, often through simple initiatives like fire services responding to incidents regardless of which side of the border they're on. These are practical things, necessary things, but they unite, rather than divide. Communities like those in Clones or Armagh, where cooperation isn't a luxury, are at the forefront of this, paving the way for a united Ireland.

'I hate the bloody border,' Donald said after a silence. 'I never wanted it. But it's made us more resilient. I'd love to see an Ireland without a border; I'd like to see the border abolished. A united Ireland.'

'I'd love to think in my lifetime that Ireland would be unified,' echoed Pat. 'But you need to be clinical about these things. You can't stoke things. We need to find a way to share this island.'

By looking to the borders, to the 'border people' who've

long shared a cross-border space, perhaps Ireland can find a way to unite, if that's what the island desires. 'How do we do that? How do we move forward?' asked Donald, as the fire crackled in the old schoolhouse. 'You've got to get people looking back at those last hundred years of Partition and saying, it didn't work. If it was an experiment, then it certainly failed. The predominant theme from the last century will be of loss. So, let's find another way of sharing this island and working ahead together.'

Drummully Polyp

Rain pelted the windscreen. 'That's the first crossing,' said Tom, as the Republic of Ireland's N54 turned into Northern Ireland's A3 a few miles west of Clones. 'That's the second,' he added, ten minutes later, the A3 turning back into the N54. 'We're in the Drummully Polyp now.'

I'm fascinated by geopolitical oddities – strange border phenomena existing for geographical or political reasons. From tiny microstates like San Marino and Andorra to Ceuta and Melilla, Spain's African exclaves, I've visited oddities the world over. I was excited then, to discover that the next step of our journey to Blacklion and Belcoo – twin villages in Cavan and Fermanagh divided by the border an hour's drive west from Clones – would take us through the Drummully Polyp, where we could experience the ridiculousness of the Irish border in all its unnecessary absurdity.

An Irish peninsula surrounded on three sides by Northern Ireland, Drummully Polyp is as peculiar as the name suggests. Although not an exclave in the strictest sense of the definition, the River Finn marks Drummully Polyp's southern boundary (rather than the international border), meaning the only way in or out is through the United Kingdom.

'That's the third crossing,' Tom continued as the N54 once more turned into the A3 and we left the Drummully Polyp as quickly as we'd arrived. 'How many crossings are there?' he asked with bewilderment, scanning a mass of wiggly borderlines dancing around one another on Google Maps like scorned lovers.

It was difficult to say. Sometimes the tarmac changed abruptly from grey to black, signalling our re-entry into the Republic. Short stretches of pristine road suddenly became potholed, betraying our re-arrival into the UK. A mass of petrol stations, currency exchanges and roadside fireworks shops were clear markers of a borderland, but with prices advertised in euros and pound sterling, they didn't always give away which side we were on.

The messiness of the border, once traversed by a trainline which crossed the border untold times on its way from Dundalk to Enniskillen, demonstrated the ludicrousness of Partition on an island where infrastructure was designed for an entire landmass rather than two separate nations. With up to 275 potential crossing points, the entire border could never be manned, and it was lonely roads like this that whip between north and south that the British Army simply barricaded with concrete breeze blocks or blasted full of craters.

'That's number five,' said Tom, as we crossed from County Cavan into County Fermanagh, where vast landed estates divided the Gaelic earth once the border straightened itself out. We followed the A509 north towards Enniskillen, but quickly turned west again, where the scenery changed from damp fields into undulating, tree-lined avenues resplendent in shades of red, brown and gold, as Marble Arch Road sped us back towards the border.

The border between Fermanagh and Cavan goes right over the immovable, boulder-strewn summit of Cuilcagh Mountain (at 666 metres, the highest mountain on the border), where the River Shannon, the longest river in the British Isles, begins its winding 224-mile journey south. Shared mountains, waterways and roads speak of an island refusing to be divided. Yet it is. Humanity had torn this rolling landscape asunder with boundaries. As we made our sixth border crossing since leaving Clones, just twenty miles away, and sped along the southern banks of Lough MacNean into Blacklion (population: 175) in the Republic of Ireland, that human need to divide fascinated and scared me in equal parts.

Blacklion looked like any other Irish village between Malin Head and Cork – there was an emerald-green post office, a darkened pub named Maguire's and Flynn's the Butcher ('Flynn's for Flavour', said the sign outside) – but I was drawn here because few other villages are so distinctly divided by an international border. The rain drizzled endlessly as we parked up and strolled on to a short bridge, located between Blacklion and Belcoo and spanning the narrow, frothing river connecting Upper and Lower Lough MacNean. The map told us we were right on the border, so we spent a rainy minute taking selfies with one foot in Ireland and the other in the United Kingdom.

There were flags on the bridge. Not the Irish tricolour or Union Jack, but the Four Provinces flag, a suitably medieval livery depicting the four coats of arms of Ulster, Leinster,

Munster and Connacht. An all-island flag. No signs said welcome to Ireland or the United Kingdom. They simply said '50', *An Blaic*, Blacklion', speed limit in kph, and '30', 'Belcoo', speed limit in mph.

Belcoo (population: 540) begins where Blacklion ends. When the Irish Boundary Commission surveyed the new border between 1924 and 1925, they recommended that Catholic Belcoo be seceded to the new Irish Free State. The commission made similar recommendations across the length of the Irish border. Its findings were ignored, though: it quickly became apparent Northern Ireland would need to surrender large tracts of land in majority Catholic areas like this if the border were drawn along accurate demographic lines.

The result of Partition is that places like Blacklion and Belcoo, which had coexisted quite amicably until that point, were divided. When the border came down, the twin villages reconnected. Now the old Customs House in Belcoo, a few metres from the border, is a hotel and restaurant where we had a room booked for the night, rather than a checkpoint. In Belcoo, I spotted a BT phone box, the UK's familiar black bins, Neighbourhood Watch signs, and, on the front of a corner shop, the Royal Mail emblem. It wasn't these familiar symbols of Britishness that made Belcoo feel normal (to me anyway); it was the lack of national flags. There were no Union Jacks, no Israeli flags, no Irish tricolours or Palestinian flags to be dampened by the rain. It looked British, but Belcoo is 89 per cent Catholic, so I knew this had to be a Republican village.

There are few flags because there's no need to display loyalties here. Blacklion and Belcoo should be one town divided by a river, not two villages divided by an international border, but which side of the river you lived or worked on determined your tax rate, your access to healthcare, schooling, and any other myriad micro-details of life never pondered further away from the border. The absurdity of the border was apparent in the rival institutions on either side, the need for two post offices, two police stations, two schools. In Belcoo, there's even a second pub named Maguire's.

The Maguire's in Belcoo was open until 3 a.m. that Saturday night. 'Please be patient with the bartender,' said a sign behind the bar. 'Even a toilet can only serve one asshole at a time.' We ordered pints of Smithwick's and chasers of Powers whiskey, listening as a makeshift musical group held their weekly practice session on one side of the pub – playing flutes, acoustic guitars and pipes and singing in English and Irish – while punters watched Premier League football on the other. The floors were sticky, the bar stools creaky, and the drinks cheap. It was Tom's last night on the border, since he was flying back the next day when we made it to Derry/Londonderry, and we settled in to spend the remainder of his Ulster banknotes.

'Where are youse from?' asked one inebriated but jovial man when he heard our accents at the bar. 'Devon, where the fuck's that?' he asked with a confused look. 'Are youse feckin lost?' asked his older mate, who came over to join us. They swayed at the bar as I told them we were following the border. 'Well, I guess you're exactly where you need to be then,' said the older man with a chuckle. The slightly younger man asked us if we thought Belcoo was British or Irish. I said it looked British but felt Irish. He said Britain had deserted them. This was a Republican village, through and through.

We drank more whiskies and pints of Guinness with the local lads. The night got hazier. The clocks went back while we were still in Maguire's. A blessing and a curse. An extra hour in the pub and a well-earned extra hour in bed the next morning. We shook off the hangovers with an Ulster Fry and hit the road in the early afternoon. From Belcoo, we followed the B52 west along the northern banks of Upper Lough MacNean, the worsening rain contributing to the already waterlogged scenery. Our route zigzagged in and out of Ireland and the United Kingdom for the next two hours as County Donegal (in the Republic) collided piecemeal with County Fermanagh, then County Tyrone. We drove through Republican villages like Belleek (the most westerly settlement in the UK, famed for its artisanal pottery), and majority-Protestant villages like Pettigo, where the Britton's pub sits in the Republic of Ireland, on the wrong side of the border.

We followed the Mourne River into Strabane, where Irish tricolours and IRA murals revealed a 95 per cent majority Republican population, again on the wrong side of the border. For the next seven or so miles, the Irish border cuts northwards along the middle of the River Foyle, then sweeps westwards in an unnatural arc, strangling Derry/Londonderry in an embrace that, historically, hasn't been warm. The city sprawls across both banks of the River Foyle. Catholic neighbourhoods are centred on the west bank of the river; Protestant neighbourhoods are centred on the east bank.

A few miles north, the border runs to a muddy conclusion on the wide, estuarine banks of Lough Foyle, where both nations have claimed sovereignty over brackish waters since Partition. County Donegal extends further north, until the

Atlantic Ocean crashes into the 400-million-year-old quartzite cliffs of Malin Head, the most northerly point on the island of Ireland.

I dropped Tom off at the airport outside Derry/Londonderry for his flight back to the mainland. He had gained not only a new appreciation for the Irish capacity to drink, but also an appreciation for the United Kingdom's nuanced identities and history he'd never known before. The next morning, I set about discovering how a segregated city was coming together.

Derry/Londonderry

Stroke City

The morning breeze rustled fallen leaves along Derry/Londonderry's coarse schist walls. From eight-metre-high bastions which encircle the Diamond for over a mile, I peered down a grassy embankment to Free Derry Corner, where bright murals depicting gasmask-wearing protestors and masked IRA gunmen adorned rows of council houses. Beyond Bogside, the city's main Catholic neighbourhood, the Donegal Hills marking the Irish border were draped in low-hanging clouds a few miles west.

I continued along the seventeenth-century walls, past lads in tracksuits vaping by an iron cannon aimed at Bogside and council workers in hi-vis jackets laying down green, orange, yellow, red and purple lights for the Halloween trail opening that evening. On the other side of Bishop's Gate, high metal fences – the type of riot fence you see dividing ultras in

European football stadiums – protected a row of red-brick houses. Peace walls, they're called in Northern Ireland.

I jumped aside as a large tour group led by an umbrella-holding guide coursed past. 'To your left is the Fountain,' I overheard her say. 'A Loyalist exclave on the western bank of the Foyle.' I poked my head through crenellations. Big letters spelt out 'Londonderry', the Loyalist name for the city. I made out dull red, white and blue kerb stones. Another sign said 'West Bank Loyalists Still Under Siege. No Surrender.'

Derry/Londonderry is a mess of interweaving border-lines, enclaves and exclaves, riot fences and stone bastions. I wanted to unravel them. Pick them apart, straighten them out and piece them back together. This is a city of borders, a city with multiple names, each holding political, historical and cultural meaning. The name Derry is taken from the Irish word *doire*, meaning an oak grove. Derry's origins go back to the sixth century, when the Irish missionary St Columba founded an island monastery on the Foyle surrounded presumably, by oak groves. Once the realm of Irish kings, the Protestant plantation was funded by London merchants in the 1600s, who paid for the walls. The settlers – who exiled native Catholics to the boggy western peripheries – renamed the city Londonderry in their honour.

The stout walls were tested during successive Irish rebellions marked by bloody massacres on both sides. The most revered episode in Ulster's Protestant history occurred here in 1688, when a Catholic army, led by the deposed English King James II, besieged the city. A group of thirteen young 'apprentice boys', drawn from guilds and merchant houses, went down in Protestant folklore when they barred the gates on the king. The defenders raised the cry of 'No Surrender', which is still the cry of Loyalists today. Although 72 per cent of Derry/Londonderry identifies as Catholic, this is a city Loyalists could never relinquish. When Partition split Ireland, the border was drawn three miles west of the city, rather than along the banks of the middle of the River Foyle as done elsewhere, capturing Derry/Londonderry within Northern Ireland's boundaries.

Divides run deep. But things are changing. On the facade of Badgers Bar, beneath the walls on Orchard Street, I saw a building-sized mural of the Derry Girls, dedicated to the hit comedy show, which follows the trials and tribulations of Derry schoolkids during the Troubles. The mural was painted by UV Arts, cross-community creatives who've ringed the city centre with new apolitical artworks, including another of the Undertones, the Derry punk rockers who defied sectarian divides to play music.

The Troubles may have started here in 1969, but the expression of comedy and art, alongside the mass of tourists visiting for what's now the largest Halloween festival in Europe, showed how Derry/Londonderry – or 'Stroke City', or 'Legenderry', if you fancy being neutral – is moving on. To find out more, I'd signed up for a Bogside walking tour.

Bogside

I walked through Shipquay Gate and found Macrae among a throng of tourists in front of the Grade-A listed Guildhall, which suffered multiple bombings during the Troubles. A short man in a chequered jacket, corduroy trousers and smart brown shoes, his flat cap barely contained his bushy grey hair. Rounded glasses and a Palestinian flag pinned to his lapel gave him the look of a scholarly freedom fighter, but despite having a touch of Che Guevara about him, he had never been a militant.

Macrae, a big woollen scarf pulled tight around his neck, hadn't yet reacclimatized to the Irish autumn. He'd spent the best part of three decades in the sunnier climes of the Basque Country after escaping his native Bogside during the Troubles. He'd returned, a prodigal Derry son, to lead walking tours of his neighbourhood, a progression he'd never imagined possible when he was younger.

The group of fifteen or so tourists, including visitors from as far afield as Australia and Argentina, and as close to home as Donegal and Dublin, were utterly transfixed by Macrae's stories, told in a mellow Irish accent, as he led us out from the Guildhall Square, through a Halloween market where food stalls sold bao buns and empanadas, and on to the quieter corner of Wellington Street and William Street. The pavement was damp underfoot, the air chilly, but Derry was a buzz of activity. Macrae raised his voice as a group of excited skeletons, vampires and zombies headed into Tracy's Bar, telling us how the Bogside of the Troubles was far removed from the scenes we saw now.

'I remember my dad always smelling of petrol,' said Macrae, who was five years old when his dad joined Catholic civil-rights demonstrations – railing against endemic gerrymandering and disenfranchisement – which were regularly confronted by Loyalist paramilitaries and increasing police brutality. 'The Battle of Bogside is when the Troubles really escalated.'

The Battle of Bogside was fought from 12 to 14 August

1969. Things had come to a head during the annual Apprentice Boys Society Parade, when Protestants march around Derry's city walls celebrating their ancestors' victory in 1688. Catholics pelted Loyalists with rocks, running battles were fought in the streets and barricades went up across Bogside, which became a no-go zone for the police, Loyalists and British Army soldiers drafted in to restore order. 'Free Derry' was declared, a separatist state effectively existing independently of the United Kingdom until 31 July 1972, when the British Army invaded with armoured cars and bulldozers in *Operation Motorman*.

Macrae grew up in a war zone. 'I saw dead soldiers in the streets when I was a child. It was normalized,' he said, still bewildered, decades on. 'Women were tarred and feathered by the IRA. People were kneecapped. There was a sadness with the paramilitary takeovers. You had to conform. My parents had eleven children; they had to do what was needed to survive.'

Macrae led us down William Street to 'Aggro Corner', a borderline marking the entrance to Bogside where protestors and rioters regularly gathered to confront the police and army. On 13 January 1972, paratroopers fired into the crowd, killing thirteen outright, wounding a fourteenth who later died and injuring a further twelve unarmed protestors.

Macrae was eight years old on Bloody Sunday. He remembers panic and gunshots. He led us along what's now the B527, where the Rossville Flats, a council estate where many were killed that day, once stood. The bottoms of lamp posts were painted orange, green and white, and stickers informed us we were now entering 'anti-fascist, Free Derry'. Macrae brought us to a stop by the Bloody Sunday Memorial.

'If I was older, if I was eighteen or so at the time,' he said solemnly. 'I'd have been in the march. I could've been shot. Killed. Most of those killed were teenagers. It's morbid, I know. If I'd then survived the protest, there's no doubt I would have joined the IRA.'

Some Bogsiders stayed to fight, but many more left as the Troubles deepened. 'I'm from a typically Catholic family,' he said, as we walked towards Free Derry Corner, which sits on a traffic island at the end of the same road. 'Five sisters and five brothers. But we weren't born to be warriors,' he laughed. 'Eight of us left because of the Troubles. I never believed I'd come back from Spain, but seven of us have returned.'

The Bogside, which is still predominantly Catholic and Republican, remains a fierce gallery of political murals and sectarian slogans, but violence has dissipated since the Good Friday Agreement. Where youths once threw up barricades and police lobbed tear gas, walking tours now occupy street corners. The edgy sense of activism might never leave Bogside, and Free Derry Corner – where the words 'You are now entering Free Derry' were immortalized on the side of a council house during the Troubles – is preserved as both a memorial, and a canvas for political struggles.

Painted across Free Derry Corner's white facade were portraits of Palestinian activists killed in Gaza. On the grassy reserve dividing the B527, memorials remember the IRA hunger strikers and IRA volunteers killed in action. A wooden sign facing traffic said 'Sovereignty, not Stormont', hinting at simmering political tensions. A pro-Palestine banner on the frontline of houses facing towards Derry's city walls, which loom large above Bogside, read, 'Two nations, one struggle.'

Macrae's younger self could never have envisaged how curious tourists now walk the no-go zone. Tourism is one of Derry's biggest industries. '200,000 people will be here for Halloween,' said Macrae, slightly astounded by a figure which is double the city's resident population. 'Biggest show in Europe! But the main thing is that Protestants and Catholics are finally getting on. Some are even getting married. Derry is a fine example of how communities can come together!'

Waterside

The wind ripped across the River Foyle. I followed in the footsteps of Bill Clinton, Tony Blair and the Dalai Lama as I crossed the snaking white spans of the pedestrianized Peace Bridge to Ebrington Square in Waterside, the traditionally Loyalist side of the city on the eastern bank of the river. Once the site of a British Army barracks during the Troubles, the square is now flanked by a craft brewery and a multimillion-pound hotel project. A Union Jack and Northern Irish flag flew on the corner of King Street and Columba Terrace, and I couldn't miss the bright red, white and blue kerbs as I walked along Glendermott Road and into the Democratic Unionist Party's Waterside Centre office.

In 1998, the Good Friday Agreement brought a tentative end to the Troubles after an all-island referendum (71.1 per cent of voters were in favour of it), but the DUP walked out on peace talks. I wanted to know why, so I'd arranged a meeting with Gregory Campbell, a Loyalist DUP politician who as of 2024 held the distinction of being Northern Ireland's longest current serving MP.

I was buzzed into reception. Gregory, wearing a sleek suit with a red poppy pinned to its lapel, explained how he's been East Londonderry's MP since 2001 as he met me with a firm handshake. I was nervous about meeting Gregory. Not because of his long political career, but because I knew he'd spoken negatively about everything from same-sex marriage and abortion to the official recognition of the Irish language in Northern Ireland. Gregory and the DUP take the 'values' of the Protestant faith and Loyalism to extremes, and I just didn't know what we'd agree on.

The Troubles had hardened Gregory's political stance. He was there when it began, a teenager in the Apprentice Boys Parade attacked by Catholic rioters in 1969. As part of Londonderry's minority Protestant community, he'd felt his identity, history and way of life were under siege. That drew him to the DUP when Paisley founded the party in 1971. Gregory understatedly described the Troubles as 'exceptionally difficult'. The saddest indictment was the normalization of violence. There was no escaping it. He always checked under his car for bombs. Whenever there was an incident, it was inevitable he'd know someone personally involved.

It's easier to comprehend how hard-line political views form when you know that people like Gregory had friends and family who were injured or killed. Gregory said a hard border was necessary to stop IRA activity, to find weapons and bombs that killed people. For Loyalists, the border existed to save lives. Ironically, he added, the border which the IRA wanted dismantling only existed because of the IRA.

'The border was much more significant for Protestant communities,' he said in a tone hardened by decades of conflict within a city he felt he was protecting. 'We didn't cross the border. Most of the police or army personnel came from our communities. The IRA would have shot them if they found them in the wrong place. They were in extreme danger of being murdered if they crossed the border. Many who did were. A sizable section of our community wouldn't go near the border, even if they just wanted to cross for a day trip to the beach in County Donegal.'

For Gregory, the IRA weren't freedom fighters, but murderers and terrorists. That's why it was difficult coming to terms with a peace process exonerating them. 'Imagine,' he said, turning his fierce gaze directly upon me. 'Being in a position where you need to negotiate with people who've broken into your house, stolen goods, beaten up your family. And some people say, "Well, look, they're committed to never doing it again. If you'll sit down, you can talk with them about living peacefully beside each other." I think most reasonable people would say, well, I want to see tangible evidence they're not going to do it again. That's what proved difficult.'

In Unionist communities, the Good Friday Agreement was more controversial than the resounding 'yes' vote lets on. Only 57 per cent of Protestants voted in favour of the deal. Some were morally opposed to sharing power with people they'd seen as terrorists: people like Martin McGuinness, a Bogsider who'd risen high up in the IRA and played a significant role in the peace process. The release of prisoners terrified both sides. Republicans and Loyalists were rightfully concerned that paramilitaries on both sides weren't going to simply give up their weapons after thirty years of war. The DUP even went as far as to walk out on the peace talks when Sinn Fein, the IRA's political wing, joined, showing the depth of feeling many Unionists felt towards Republicans.

'Add into that mix that while we Unionist communities were using peaceful means to try and achieve our objectives,' said Gregory, without a flicker of irony. 'McGuinness and his cohorts used violence and murder against us to achieve theirs: that made things toxic, very toxic indeed.'

It's not quite true that Loyalist communities used peaceful means to achieve their aim of staying in the United Kingdom. Of the 3,000 deaths attributed to the Troubles, Loyalist paramilitaries were responsible for over 1,000, the majority of whom were Catholic civilians, often killed in revenge attacks. Until Loyalists like Gregory truly recognize this side of history, divides will remain.

It's remarkable, though, how the Good Friday Agreement was not only pushed through – largely through the work of the Ulster Unionist Party on the Loyalist side, and the Social Democratic and Labour Party on the Republican – but has kept the peace. Gregory agreed with this. 'We're undoubtedly in a much better place,' he said, the first hint of a smile flickering across his otherwise stern face. 'When that end came about, that was when hope started to reign supreme, we said, things could be better.'

Still, Gregory wasn't too keen on a unified Ireland. 'For reunification to happen, it needs to happen by consent,' said Gregory when I asked his opinion. 'And there's no way Loyalist communities will give their consent for that. There's not even a remote prospect of a united Ireland. It's not going to happen.'

ALONG THE BORDERS

The Holywell Trust

Long after the border checkpoints were dismantled and the Armalites decommissioned, segregation still pervades Derry/Londonderry. But one man bringing people together is Gerard Deane, director of the Holywell Trust, who whisked me to the rooftop of the social enterprise's headquarters on Bishop Street later that day.

Founded in 1988, the Holywell Trust is a neutral, non-aligned space hosting cross-community events and promoting cross-community projects. Gerard was wearing a light olive-green jumper, the collar of his shirt poking out the top, and he shivered in the bracing wind that whipped across the rooftop garden. The city was arrayed before us. He pointed out St Columb's Cathedral (the first Protestant cathedral in Northern Ireland), the Apprentice Boys Memorial Hall and Derry City Football Club's stadium, home ground of a team forced out of the Northern Irish league to play in the Republic.

'This is a borderland,' he said, pointing at misty landscapes to our west, before quickly returning his hand to his pocket as rain scoured the rooftop. 'We're border people. The organization is named after Holywell Hill; it's through the mist somewhere, right on the border. So, we're a cross-border organization by our very nature. In Derry, we're always conscious of being on the periphery. Being on the borders, we're so far from state support, we're far from state powers in London, Belfast, Dublin and Brussels. We're right on the edge of Europe.'

Gerard wanted me to visualize the physical borders in and around Derry, and he explained how the border follows the middle of the River Foyle everywhere but here. If the border had been drawn practically when Ireland was partitioned, we'd be standing in the Republic right now. 'But Derry is so significant to Protestants, they didn't,' he said with a shrug, before we turned downstairs to escape the cold. 'Now we all live across borders, so it's vital we build a cross-border future.'

Gerard was calm and collected. He spoke methodically but purposefully, and throughout our talk I felt that here was a man of reason in a society that, based on opinions I'd heard so far, often seemed to want nothing more than to bury its collective heads in the sand. He knew his own biases (calling the city Derry was the first giveaway), and his goal was to help others understand theirs. He wanted Northern Ireland to consider its future empirically, looking at facts and figures, rather than basing decisions solely on identity. His greying hair, though, hinted at the frustrations the Holywell Trust faces. Change doesn't come quickly or easily here.

Gerard, a Derry local, has worked on cross-community projects for most of his professional life. After seeing his schoolmates leaving their home city, searching for opportunities elsewhere, he realized that Derry/Londonderry needed the best and brightest to stay and build the best society it could, to seize upon the opportunities presented by the peace process in a city always at the top of the wrong tables in terms of poverty, unemployment and NHS waiting lists.

One of the biggest contributors to these rankings is segregation. Segregation is expensive, and borders, whether international or inter-community, limit opportunities. There are multiple sports centres or health facilities for different communities, when only one might do, for example, while millions of extra miles of car journeys are made every year as parents drop their kids off at Catholic or Protestant schools, rather than at the closest ones. Decisions aren't made on a fiscal basis but are dictated by identity. 'It sounds ridiculous,' added Gerard with another shrug. 'But it's true. It's just not the way to run a country.'

The economics of segregation are astounding. Four in five Derry/Londonderry households take more in benefits than they contribute in tax. Northern Ireland has run a deficit every year since 1966, which sits at around £10 billion, or £5,000 per capita. That's larger than any other region in the United Kingdom, larger even than the annual membership fees the UK paid to be in the European Union (around £9 billion). The Republic of Ireland, on the other hand, had a surplus of around €20 billion Euros in 2024.

Gerard says people put up with it so long as peace is maintained. Now that it has been kept, they need to have objective conversations about how things can change. 'They need to look at the system and ask, "Is that what we've been doing all these years?"' said Gerard, amazed that segregation was *still* occurring. 'It's happening, slowly, but there's resistance because there's no trust yet.'

One of the most important projects the Holywell Trust works on is called 'Future Relationship Conversations'. It's a project taking important constitutional questions, like that of Brexit or a border poll for a united Ireland, and facilitating discussions about those questions – concerning the future of Northern Ireland, the Republic of Ireland and the United Kingdom – between groups of people that wouldn't normally even talk.

The Holywell Trust sources facts and figures that people can assess outside of their traditional family, community, political or belief circles, so decisions are made on empirical evidence, rather than because of existing loyalties. One of the major problems it faces, though, is the continued existence of paramilitaries. Several Republican splinter groups, including the Continuity IRA and the New IRA, never gave up the fight, while some Loyalist paramilitaries – including the UVF – never disbanded. I'd seen billboards in Armagh and Derry/Londonderry warning locals against paramilitary influence. Rather than dealing out political violence like they used to, they now try to control communities through moneylending and drug dealing, as part of organized crime rackets. Other major problems include a lack of trust between different parts of society, and the tendency for people to vote along community lines.

'We need to create a new normal,' he said, sitting back in his chair with a sigh. 'I hate that term, the traditional divide,' he added, saying how it normalizes segregation. 'People are people, and you need people to think they're not traitors to the cause. My generation never had the chance to change. But the next ones will. We need to improve this place, and the vast majority of people are willing to work together and engage with each other.'

Gerard, true to the Holywell Trust's neutrality, didn't comment on Irish reunification. 'Whatever we choose to do next,' he said. 'We need to do it together.'

Northern Ireland remains a nation of borderlines. In Belfast, high peace walls divide neighbourhoods. In Stormont, political parties, including the DUP – which is inherently opposed to reunification – and Sinn Fein – Northern Ireland's largest party, whose MPs refuse to take their seats in Westminster – are fundamentally at odds with each other. Polarization is endemic. Ask a Republican if reunification was going to happen, it's inevitable. Talk to a Loyalist, it's an impossibility.

The hard Irish border remains in minds and memories, even for those too young to know the checkpoints. Fear lingers, and many of those I spoke to in hushed tones at the back of bars and cafes asked me to change their names or later asked me to cut their stories completely. But things are changing. Economics and a simple desire for peace ensure people now look beyond traditional loyalties, and the resounding truth is that no one wants a border on the island of Ireland again.

In the 2021 UK census, for the first time in Northern Ireland's century-long history, there were more people who identified as Catholic than Protestant (46 to 44 per cent). The Good Friday Agreement allows people to hold both British and Irish citizenship, and ideas of identity are shifting, too. In 2011, 48.4 per cent of Northern Ireland's population identified as British. In 2022, this was down to 42.8 per cent.

The Good Friday Agreement also laid down a potential path towards reunification through an island-wide referendum, which can happen when the conditions for a 'border poll' are met. The conditions for this are somewhat vague, admittedly, and the secretary of state for Northern Ireland can call a referendum when they believe a majority of people would vote for unification. Given the uptick in Irish citizenship north of the border, this condition could arguably have already been met.

Despite this, Northern Ireland taught me more about

what being British means than anywhere else. By looking to the Irish border, I'd discovered what the Britain I know back home isn't. My own love for Britain comes not from a glorified past, the Union Jack nor the monarchy. While I understand the DUP's desire for self-determination, I see its stance on social issues as fundamentally un-British. Equally, I agree that great institutions like the NHS are at the core of our modern British identity.

I also realized the level of indifference that much of the rest of the United Kingdom has for Northern Ireland. This is our country, too. My passport says the United Kingdom of Great Britain and Northern Ireland, and I'm ashamed I knew so little about it before my journey. The fact is, if Britain remains indifferent to Northern Ireland, then we'll have made the decision for many people. Loyalty only stretches so far, and despite ardently professing their love for Britain, there may come a tipping point when even the most diehard Unionist questions why they bother.

When I set out on this journey, I was exploring how the United Kingdom can keep itself together. I hadn't truly factored in Northern Ireland. From what I'd seen on the border, I now believe the time will come when Ireland does reunite, when the conditions for a border poll are met. And I hope that happens democratically. Derry/Londonderry is moving forward. The very fact conversations are taking place is a sign of that, and I have every faith the next generation will make the right decisions, in whatever the best interest will be for the majority in Derry/Londonderry, and in Northern Ireland.

That faith was compounded on my last evening in the city. It was Halloween. Derry/Londonderry's Halloween festivities started by accident in the Castle Bar pub in 1985 when a fancy-dress party spilt over on to the streets. It quickly became a welcome distraction from the Troubles, a chance for both sides to come together and, even if just for one night, forget the war raging around them.

Now, it's outgrown the Troubles. It's a thing of its own. The streets were packed with families and students. The sound of steel, not orange, drums echoed off grey kerb stones. There were skeletons, demons, cats, pirates, vampires and the odd teenager in army fatigues and a ski mask. There were neon drummers, Ghostbusters in a foggy haze of dry ice, a huge spinning wheel holding a jazz band within its strange steampunk-like contraptions and monstrous mechanical puppets. It was madness incarnate. Like Day of the Dead on LSD. But it was a good madness.

After hearing so many terrible stories along the border, I'm not ashamed to say I shed a tear among the crowds on the banks of the River Foyle. As fireworks exploded into the night sky above the Peace Bridge, I knew there was hope after all.

9

The Kentish Border

The English Channel is a mere ditch. It will be crossed as soon as someone has the courage to attempt it.

Napolean Bonaparte

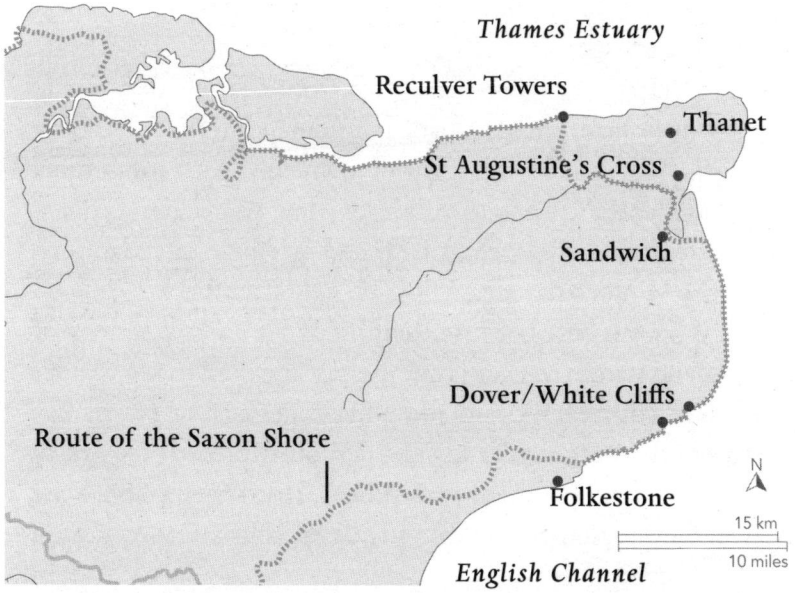

The Saxon Shore

It was late on a December afternoon when we cycled along a cracked concrete promenade east from Herne Bay. I say late – it was barely 3 p.m., but the sun cast long shadows across the Thames Estuary's brackish waters, where container ships lumbered into the North Sea and wind turbines spun loosely in the distance.

'Cycled' is a loose descriptor, too. Claire's dad – who now lives far from his Cornish homeland in the hills above Herne Bay, in a Kentish seafront town lined with amusement arcades and Victorian townhouses – lent us his flashy ebikes. We'd breezed under chalk cliffs and up single-track lanes on a crisp winter's day when the rain held itself back.

We were here because Kent holds the earliest history of England within its ever-eroding coastline (and to see Claire's dad, of course). We parked up five miles east of Herne Bay where two rectangular towers, perilously placed on a grassy knife-edge atop a sheer escarpment, rose sharply above the weather-beaten edifice of a medieval church, its roof long since caved in.

The Normans raised the Reculver Towers in the twelfth century to guide ships into London's dockyards, and as the frigid North Sea breeze whistled through fallen masonry, layers of history stirred in the chalk beneath our feet. These twin signal towers were built on the hallowed ground of a sixth-century Anglo-Saxon monastery, itself built by a

THE KENTISH BORDER

Kentish king on the foundations of a Roman fort, of which all that remains are ankle-height bricks.

From the fourth century, with Rome's military overstretched, barbarian warriors pillaged Britain's coastline, burning villages, sacking villas and taking off with gold, silver and slaves. As the empire was besieged in its dying century, the Romans constructed an immense line of fortifications along Britain's eastern and southern coastlines, including at Reculver. Along the *Litus Saxonicum*, or 'Saxon Shore', Roman legionaries stamped their cold sandals in the same damp ground we walked over now. Sharpening spears around the dim embers of signal fires, they awaited 'barbarian' ships from across the dark seas. When the legions left Britain in the fifth century, Angles, Saxons and Jutes carved new kingdoms from the ashes.

Today, Reculver Towers are part of a long-distance hiking and biking trail named the Saxon Shore Way. Starting in Gravesend, not far to our west, it passes Roman forts and medieval ports on its 163-mile-long route around Kent's bulbous coast. Looping south to the white cliffs of Dover, it crosses into East Sussex to end outside the Roman walls of Pevensey, where William the Conqueror landed in 1066. Roughly following the Saxon Shore Way south to Folkestone by bike, car and on foot, my final journey into Britain's borderlands would see me traversing the same frontier at which the earliest Anglo-Saxon settlers arrived so many centuries ago.

I would be looking as much to the present as to the past, because the earliest history of the English people echoes in the political battles now waged by populist right-wing politicians like Nigel Farage, whose talk of refugee landings and invasions of small boats has transformed Britain's maritime border into a modern-day battleground.

But people living on a frontier spilling over the English Channel into Europe understand the need for empathy in a divided world. Travelling the Saxon Shore Way, I'd find a sense of steady, welcoming pride, rather than the flag-waving nationalism of UKIP or Reform. On Kent's shores, I'd find the deeper ideals of the English and British identities: ideals which I know can unite the nation through a progressive, rather than bigoted, vision of the future.

'We should get going,' Claire said when a quick Google search told us the sun was setting at 3.55 p.m. 'We haven't got any lights. Even on turbo mode it's a twenty-minute ride to Herne Bay.'

There was one boundary I had to see before we ebiked back. 'The River Wantsum should be over there,' I said, striding off along the gravel path running alongside a section of Roman wall now sprouting weeds. 'Give me a minute!'

Even without the wind turbines and pleasure piers, Kent's coastline would be unrecognizable to the Romans once stationed here. At the mercy of battering floods and violent storms, coastal erosion whittles away sheer cliffs that drop like chalky blades to the lapping shores of the Thames Estuary below. Once a navigable channel, the River Wantsum marooned the Isle of Thanet from Kent's mainland, providing a shortcut for ships to sail from the English Channel into the Thames Estuary. By the thirteenth century, the waterway had all but silted. Today, there's almost nothing left of this formerly mighty channel. It's a particularly unremarkable geographical feature, and all I found was a narrow drainage ditch with fields on either side masquerading as a river, before petering quietly out on to a shingle beach. Still, this muddy boundary between Thanet and the rest of Kent is where England's story truly begins.

If we're to believe murky chronicles from the Middle Ages, some time in the fifth century the British king Vortigern permitted two Anglo-Saxon brothers named Hengist and Horsa to settle the Isle of Thanet after they defeated a marauding Pictish army who'd crossed Hadrian's Wall. Hengist and Horsa soon came into conflict with the Britons they'd saved. Hengist was killed in battle, and Horsa in turn killed Vortigern. According to the Venerable Bede – who recorded this semi-mythical foundation story in his eighth-century work, *The Ecclesiastical History of the English People* – Horsa established the first Anglo-Saxon kingdom on what became English soil.

Gildas – a British historian who wrote *On the Ruin and Conquest of Britain* earlier in the sixth century – scathingly blamed Vortigern for opening the floodgates and causing the downfall of Romano-British civilization, as Angles, Saxons and Jutes landed in ever larger numbers, and established kingdoms in what are now Kent, Sussex, Essex, East Anglia and Northumbria. The Wantsum Channel, the first border between Anglo-Saxons and Britons, was crossed, and for the native Britons, this was the point of no return.

It's curious to think that here in Kent, a place I've always seen as quintessentially English, Brythonic languages once rolled across green hills and white cliffs. I wonder if the story of Hengist and Horsa is still ingrained deep in our psyche. Here, where England's history starts with Anglo-Saxon warbands, Thanet was the first and only region ever to elect a majority UKIP council when it voted the right-wing, anti-immigration party into power in 2015. The same year, Nigel Farage narrowly lost when he stood in South Thanet at the general election. He then later won a seat for Reform in Clacton, just over the estuary in Essex, in 2024. As our Anglo-Saxon ancestors displaced the people that lived here, do we fear being displaced in turn by another people arriving from the sea?

The sun dipped lower. I hurried back. Claire was waiting, helmet on, by the ebikes we'd secured to the railings outside the King Ethelbert Inn next to Reculver Towers, a pub named for the Kentish king who'd founded the sixth-century monastery here. Ethelbert was converted from paganism by St Augustine, the Apostle of the English, who brought Christianity to the Anglo-Saxons. St Augustine had also landed in Thanet before establishing nearby Canterbury as the centre of English Christianity. Like the very coastline we cycled in the dying light, Britain has changed irrevocably over the centuries, and it will change again in the not-so-distant future.

Sandwich

The next morning, I traded the ebike for the car and followed the A299 through farmland swathed in winter fog. Dull green fields were hidden beneath frost, and I stared curiously at the unusual conical silhouettes of red-brick Kentish oast houses (old kilns once used to dry hops) as I drove through the 'Garden of England'.

Claire had stayed behind to hang out with her dad. My next stop on the Saxon Shore Way was Sandwich, a medieval town an hour's drive southeast of Herne Bay. Once one of

England's most important harbours, Sandwich was one of five towns along the southeastern seaboard granted the coveted medieval status of a Cinque Port, granting special privileges and tax exemptions in exchange for not causing the king trouble and defending the maritime border.

Enshrined in culinary lore by the fourth earl of Sandwich, who famously asked for his roast beef to be served between bread in the late eighteenth century, I would unashamedly dig into a sandwich in Sandwich when my mission that day was complete. Before that, I wanted to discover the extent to which the town's modern character, and that of the wider Kent coast, had been shaped by exiles, migrants and refugees, be they Anglo-Saxon warbands, Huguenots fleeing religious persecution or German Jews escaping the Nazis.

First, the A299 – a stretch of which is named the Hengist Way – brought me into Thanet. After driving past the grey runway of Manston International Airport (which closed in May 2024, and has since been used as an emergency lorry park when Brexit disrupted border crossings to France), I turned south for a pitstop at Richborough Fort, where stout walls, an amphitheatre and a triumphal arch remember the Roman landings in Britain almost two thousand years ago. The Romans knew this land as Cantium, a Latinized version of the Celtic name, which loosely translated means 'on the edge'. The name 'Kent' holds whispers of a borderland identity, and this Celtic etymology survived, while surrounding counties like Essex ('Land of the East Saxons') and Sussex ('Land of the South Saxons') derive theirs from Germanic languages.

The Kingdom of Kent was largely independent during the Anglo-Saxon era. A long line of Kentish kings led the

'Kentish Men' until Wessex dominated much of what became England in the ninth century. William the Conqueror never technically conquered Kent by force. The Kentish folk struck a bargain with the Norman invaders, gaining autonomy in exchange for laying down arms. Today, the county motto '*Invicta*', meaning 'unconquered', remembers this past.

This independent streak survived into the twenty-first century. After Brexit, Kent found itself in a peculiar position wherein Westminster politicians regarded the county's internal boundaries (its borders with East Sussex, Greater London and Surrey), as Britain's international border with France. In response to growing queues and tailbacks at customs checkpoints in ports like Dover, Michael Gove (then transport secretary) confirmed in 2020 that lorry drivers would face a 'de facto border' in Kent, meaning they couldn't cross into the county unless they'd sorted their paperwork beforehand.

This seemingly trivial act of bureaucracy raised myriad geopolitical questions. Was Kent to remain in the European Union? Was this now French territory? Or was Kent a nation of its own? Brexit continued to divide the United Kingdom by resurrecting unnecessary borders, and some in Kent (only half-jokingly) responded with calls for 'Kentish independence'. I found one Instagram account stating: 'Kent shall be independent, and oast houses shall be everywhere.' Another group of Kentish freedom fighters printed mock Kentish passports for Kentish citizens looking for a new nationality.

A few miles south of Richborough Fort, Sandwich exemplifies Kent's independent-mindedness. I'd never visited before, but amateur historian and local tour guide Terry Palmer enthusiastically agreed to show me around his home town, advising me to park outside his house on the eastern bank of the River Stour if I wanted to avoid the overpriced medieval car parks.

I knocked on the door and Terry – a volunteer tour guide with the local-history society – thrust a steaming hot mug of tea into my hands and ushered me into his study. 'We get so many tourists, but all they want to do is take a photo of themselves eating sandwiches in Sandwich,' he said with a look of disdain, so I kept my own plan to eat a sandwich quiet. 'It's nice to focus on the real history for a change. I won't knock them, but there's so much more to see. In my humble opinion, Sandwich is the best-preserved medieval town in England.'

Before we set off on our walk, Terry, who was already well prepared for the gloomy weather in his robust walking trousers, heavy fleece and hiking boots, cleared his desk and laid down two maps: a modern OS map of Sandwich and a reproduction of a medieval map. Side by side, the scale of Sandwich (population: 4,000) has changed little in eight hundred years. The coastlines, however, differed drastically.

The sea is now over two miles away, but Sandwich once overlooked the southern entrance to the Wantsum Channel. On the medieval map, the sea encroached right up to the town's gates. Terry explained how the geography changed remarkably over the centuries due to coastal erosion, often caused by what he called 'tremendous storms', including a particularly dramatic one in 1287 which ravaged the coastline from here to Sussex. As cliffs fell away into the sea, debris and sediment built up, causing harbours to silt and rivers to change course – a reminder that England's southeastern frontier is continually in flux, at the mercy of the elements.

'The story of Sandwich begins right outside my house,' said Terry, as we finished our cuppas and pulled on raincoats, in case the dreary grey clouds burst during his tour of Sandwich. 'So, this is really a very appropriate place to begin. And not just for the free parking. A few centuries prior, all this land was underwater.'

A brisk five-minute walk took us from Terry's home to the narrow banks of the River Stour. Terry's enthusiasm for Sandwich's past was matched only by his preparedness, and he showed me a fat binder full of weatherproof notes that accompanied him on every tour. ('It's only a backup!' he made sure to tell me. 'You never know when someone's going to surprise you with a question about the Battle of Sandwich in 1217.')

Leaning on the white, wrought-iron railings of the old Toll Bridge opposite a restored thirteenth-century gateway with a chequered stone facade and red-tiled roof, Terry claimed in his chirpy English tones that in the thirteenth century, this was the second-busiest English harbour after London. Now, the shouts of sailors and the clank of industry have been replaced by quacking ducks and the buzz of light boat engines. Small, river-going craft bobbed around in the water and a few algae-covered pontoons swayed around beyond a stone esplanade. Long gone are the days when channel-going sailing ships and flat-bottomed Thames barges moored up to unload cargoes of wine, pilgrims and soldiers.

Terry listed the many celebrities who'd passed through this English gateway, including Thomas Becket, Eleanor of Aquitaine, Richard the Lionheart and Edward the Black Prince. 'An elephant came through here once, too,' Terry added with an air of mystery as we walked through the gate,

THE KENTISH BORDER

emerging into a small square surrounded by red-brick buildings (many of them pubs) that lay beyond the walls of this stout border town.

A small town with a mighty history, almost all of Sandwich is under a preservation order, and as we turned right on to Strand Street, I was met by a wonky line of timber-framed buildings with precarious, wooden overhangs stretching lazily over narrow pavements. Painted in the black-and-white Tudor style, tiles had largely replaced thatched roofs, but Terry was proud to announce this was the longest block of timber houses still standing in England. Now taken over by estate agents and cafes, these medieval houses had once lodged international pilgrims journeying to Canterbury.

The breeze carried a salty tang, a reminder that Strand Street was once the seafront before the storms changed everything, wrecking the coastline and floundering the harbour miles inland. Economic stagnation couldn't, and still can't, dent local demand for Kentish ale, and Terry was immensely proud of the fact there were once thirty-six pubs in Sandwich, one for every hundred or so Sandwich citizens. Many are still standing, including the Mermaid's Locker, New Inn and Old Drum, which date back to the thirteenth, fourteenth and fifteenth centuries respectively, and once teemed with Venetian wine merchants and Dutch woollen traders.

We skipped into the sixteenth-century Kings Arms for a toilet break. Back outside, Terry explained how St Mary's Church – which comprised patchy stonework packed with bricks and masonry of varied sizes, and shades of grey and black – was rebuilt by the Dutch after a fire. Sixteenth-century Sandwich was a beacon of hope for oppressed religious groups in Europe, particularly the Huguenots and Dutch Protestants, who were known as 'the Strangers'. After biblical storms and perpetual border conflicts, European refugees brought Sandwich back to life, with the population doubling from 2,500 in 1565 to 5,000 in 1600, as arrivals from France and the Netherlands brought new weaving, masonry and agricultural skills with them.

'After the fire, the Dutch said, "Don't knock the church down, we can rebuild it,"' Terry said, as we walked into St Mary's Church, where the wooden beams had been salvaged from the refugees' ships. 'They sourced stones, flints, different building materials they knew how to work with that you now see all over Sandwich. We also have the Dutch to thank for "market gardening". Kent is the Garden of England, and we have refugees to thank for that!'

As we strolled deeper into Sandwich, Terry pointed out red-brick houses on the high street designed in a distinctly Dutch style, with large windows providing ample light for weaving. He was taken by the abundance of flint walls in the town centre, a style of building work the Dutch were masters at, and which can be found across Kent, including Canterbury Cathedral.

At first, I'd seen the timber frames and red-brick heritage of Sandwich as typically English in their medieval style, but now I realized how continental influences are deeply ingrained in the very fabric of Sandwich. Indeed, many of the wider architectural styles you see in historic English cathedrals, stately homes and other institutions originated in Europe. The baroque style (the University of Oxford's Radcliffe Camera library being one famous example) developed in Rome, and Gothic architecture in France (Westminster

THE KENTISH BORDER

Abbey and Canterbury Cathedral are just two examples of the 'English' Gothic style).

I'd always seen the wider county of Kent as a bastion of Englishness, too. The white cliffs linger long in the memory of English folk crossing the Channel; Kent's green fields are straight out of the pages of an Enid Blyton book; and the Battle of Britain was fought in the blue skies above the county. Kent is a place that's sculpted the popular imagination of what England means, and what it means to be English, for both us and the wider world.

But beneath the Englishness, the history of Sandwich is inextricably linked to immigration, be it that of Roman invaders, Anglo-Saxon settlers or French Huguenots. Sandwich, Kent and England have all been shaped by different peoples, speaking different languages, practising different religions and bringing unique trades, skills and outlooks across borders. Far from being the most English of places, dig a little deeper into Kent's rich soil and you find the very notion of Englishness constantly redrawn by the myriad peoples who've called this borderland home.

We arrived at the Guildhall with frozen hands and red cheeks, our breath misty as the frigid morning turned into a frigid afternoon. The Cinque Port coat of arms – three golden lions next to three wooden ships – hung above a heavy, black door set against red bricks. Above, the black-and white-timbers gave the sixteenth-century building a resounding Tudor look as it loomed over a town square decked out with Union Jack bunting.

Terry said goodbye, recommending the cafe on the opposite side of the small square if I did, after all, decide that I should try a sandwich in Sandwich. I pushed through the oak door and into the Guildhall Museum, where I found Hank, who held the fantastically archaic title of 'Guildhall Master'.

Hank, who was heavily involved in the town's ceremonial side, had agreed to show me around the Guildhall and explain more about Sandwich's many curious traditions, which I knew would be a microcosm of England's peculiar love for bizarre and downright strange customs.

Hank met me with a finger-breaking handshake. A sturdy man with a straight back and neatly trimmed moustache, Hank was stern in tone as he showed me around the Guildhall, where there were a mock Victorian courtroom and an exhibition on the Huguenots. Hank's borderland attitude came to the fore immediately, when he spoke rather disparagingly of our cross-channel neighbours. 'We say *"sink"*, not *"sank"*, when we talk about the Cinque Ports,' Hank said, so I had no doubt as to the local pronunciation. 'We don't say it the French way. We were always fighting the French, and we still are really!'

This great English rivalry with France was born along England's maritime frontiers. I'd seen it in far-western Cornwall, where towns were burnt and raided, and now here it was in Sandwich, where in 1457, the town mayor was killed in a French raid (all of Sandwich's mayors since have worn black robes in remembrance). While this rivalry is all in good jest these days, the age-old practice of building a national identity by defining yourself in opposition to someone different is still readily apparent in our collective disdain for our French friends.

'This is the invasion coast,' he said, explaining why Sandwich, here on the border, is so important to English history. 'Romans, Hengist and Horsa, William the Conqueror. Every major invasion of England happened here. The history of this country is here in Sandwich. Every single king or queen has been here. The Spanish Armada and Battle of Britain are better known, but the Battle of Sandwich in 1217, when the French tried to land a fleet to fight King John, is just as important even as the Battle of Trafalgar. Without it, we could have been speaking French.'

Hank's straight-talking demeanour came from his thirty years in the RAF. He'd returned to his Sandwich roots after retiring from the service, becoming fascinated with local history after tracing his ancestry here back centuries. He was proud to be descended from the 'freemen' of the town – merchants who held positions of power within local guilds and trades – and told me in lofty tones of what he called 'the good old times in Sandwich', although he wasn't clear when exactly that was.

Hank looked back through rose-tinted glasses at the town's medieval heyday, centuries before either of us were born. Indeed, Sandwich had such status that Hank wasn't surprised when a rare copy of the Magna Carta, proven to have been made in the thirteenth century, not long after it was signed, was uncovered in 2015 in the Guildhall archives by its caretaker.

One of England's defining documents, Magna Carta is still quoted by politicians today, providing the basis for many English laws and ideals we hold dear, including the right to a fair trial and the right to be tried by a jury. We should be proud of its democratic legacy, but I also knew this 800-year-old treaty – forced upon King John by angry barons – did little for the common medieval man, let alone woman. The Magna Carta enshrined the 'rights' of the barons to rule over the peasantry, and Britain wouldn't see universal suffrage until well into the twentieth century.

Their copy of the Magna Carta was on display on the other side of the Atlantic in Washington DC when I visited Sandwich, but they did still have their prized 'Moot Horn' in the Guildhall Museum. Traditionally, this twelfth-century horn was blown when the town was attacked, to call meetings or when the reigning monarch died. The 'Hornblow', as the blowing of the Moot Horn is known, is one of many traditions the town upholds. Every evening, St Peter's Church rings the 'Curfew Bell' at 8 p.m. sharp, a medieval practice signalling townspeople to put out their fires for the night. In celebration of the Battle of Sandwich in 1217, children run around the outside of the Church of St Bart's on 24 August and are rewarded with a specially baked biscuit (what that has to do with victory over the French, Hank didn't really know). Once a year, Sandwich Town Council, as a Cinque Port, still tries to collect 'ship money' from nearby villages like Sarre. For equally inexplicable reasons, Hank explained how representatives of these Cinque Port 'limbs', as they're known, still turn up at the Guildhall every year with new and creative reasons as to why they can't pay their dues.

These traditions are literally medieval in origin, rooted in the same world that spawned the Magna Carta. They also show how English culture is very much still alive. I've taken English culture for granted my whole life, I realized, and this journey has given me a new appreciation for our often-strange practices, which are undoubtedly a pillar of England's national identity. Many of these traditions are hyperlocal, unknown outside the county or even the village where they're steadfastly celebrated.

THE KENTISH BORDER

As Hank showed me the Huguenot exhibition, he also reminded me that English culture has taken much from overseas in its time, just as Terry had explained earlier. As we stood under the timber-framed roof of the Guildhall, looking at the lavish coats of arms and colourfully stitched flags that are brought out whenever there's a parade, Hank also brought up another contrasting, almost contradictory side of the Kent border's past, and present.

Hank explained how in early 1939, as many as 4,000 Jewish refugees from Nazi Germany – the same population as the town itself – were readily welcomed into Sandwich. The refugees were mostly men, their wives and children meant to follow once they'd made Kitchener Camp – an old army base outside Sandwich where they were housed – habitable. The Second World War broke out in September of that year, though, and sadly, many never saw their families again.

Despite the hardships and tragedy, the 'Kitchener Refugees', as they were known, reciprocated the hospitality they received. I've seen black-and-white photos online of refugees holding musical concerts in Sandwich. Many found ready work on Kentish farms and formed football teams to take on the locals. Some 887 volunteered for service in the British Army. The vast majority moved out of Kitchener Camp as the war progressed, but their descendants haven't forgotten the warm welcome they received in Sandwich. In 2019, the Association of Jewish Refugees unveiled a blue plaque in Sandwich to commemorate the eightieth anniversary of the refugees' arrival on Kentish shores.

At the same time, though, Sandwich was also home to a frightening number of blackshirts, British fascists led by Oswald Mosley who would happily have welcomed Nazis over the border. 'There was a blackshirt headquarters on Strand Street,' Hank said in a hushed voice. 'Some have said that during the Second World War, the reason no bombs ever fell on Sandwich was because it was a blackshirt base. Goering apparently went to Mosley's wedding, so he knew all the henchmen who lived here.'

History is short, and in 2022, a Kent Conservative councillor was pictured wearing a blackshirt uniform at fascist events. Borders draw out the best and the worst in people. Sandwich is at times a magnet for far-right politicization. Other times, it's supremely welcoming, and it's benefitted greatly from providing this hospitality, be that from the market gardeners or the Dutch architects who rebuilt the town. It was a suitable time to make my exit. On the way out I bumped into the caretaker, Kevin, who happily showed me some more flags and tapestries hidden away upstairs. 'I'm only the Guildhall caretaker, but somehow it's going to be my responsibility to look after the Magna Carta too when it's back here,' he said with humble understatement. 'To top it off, one of our cleaners is leaving, so I'm taking on four public-toilet shifts while looking after one of England's most important documents!'

Before leaving town, I stopped off in the cafe opposite the Guildhall, finally digging into a sandwich in Sandwich before hitting the road south to Folkestone.

Folkestone

My phone switched to French time. Runners, braving the cold on their Saturday morning parkrun, weaved around bandstands and cabbage palms on the Leas, Folkestone's

THE KENTISH BORDER

Victorian promenade, below. Instant coffee in hand, I peered across busy shipping lanes from the rusting metal struts of my 'balcony room', which I'd spent all of £10 upgrading to at the weary two-star Southcliff Hotel. I'd hoped to wake to a view of France, which lay across thirty miles of busy shipping to the south, but morning fog blanketed the English Channel. The Saxon Shore Way bypasses Folkestone's seafront to the north of the town as it continues eastwards, but I'd travelled here from Sandwich because this is where worlds collide.

While Folkestone's seafront resorts are dated and worn, the town's colourful streets are alive with craft breweries, boutique shops and quirky art galleries as the town reinvents itself as a creative hub, fuelled by an exodus of middle-class Londoners looking for a seaside escape. Then, on the outskirts of town, is Napier Barracks, where refugees arriving on Kent's shores are held in squalid accommodation while courts decide their fates. It was a calm day, and I knew that out there – even in the winter fog – coastguard patrols and RNLI boats would be searching for small boats drifting dangerously across the English Channel.

The so-called small-boats crisis, the breaching of Britain's borders as it's seen by many in England, contributes just a small, almost insignificant number of migrants to the total entering Britain each year. Yet it's become one of Britain's intensely politicized issues. While I understand concerns, be they economic or the fear of terrorism (the latter is certainly overplayed, given how Parliamentary research I dug into showed that in 2021–22, 78 per cent of people arrested on terrorism charges were British nationals), I also know it's all part of a larger populist narrative, an attempt by the right to create an enemy, an 'other', to divide us. It's a medieval method. When things aren't going well at home, stir up trouble on the border. Find someone else to blame.

Given that Folkestone bears the brunt of these landings, you might presume locals would be against refugees. But the story isn't quite so simple. I finished my coffee and headed down creaking stairs to find a border town that's far more welcoming than I'd imagined.

In the nineteenth century, Folkestone was one of England's most popular resorts. Queen Victoria holidayed here in its heyday, and Charles Dickens, writing in 1859, gave a glowing review: 'The situation is delightful,' he wrote. 'The air is delicious and the breezy hills and downs, carpeted with wild thyme and decorated with millions of wildflowers, are perfect.'

The air that day wasn't quite so delicious, given the pungent tang of cigarette smoke coming from a pair of early-morning drinkers sat on a blustery park bench, but I could still see why King Edward VII had been a regular at the Grand Hotel just along the seafront, the same place Agatha Christie holed up writing *Murder on the Orient Express*.

'Your grandparents didn't vote for fascists, they shot them,' said scrawled graffiti on Harbour Street, where I stood in the hulking shadow of the Grand Burstin, a monstrous boat-shaped Britannia hotel looming large over Folkestone's old stone harbour. A miniature house painted pink with purple doors floated on still waters in the harbour opposite (an art installation, I later discovered). Fishmongers in yellow aprons sorted through prawns and packed plaice and bream into boxes by an open-air fish market, while the enticing smell of seafood chowder (only £3 a pop) drifted over from Bob's Seafood.

THE KENTISH BORDER

Carbon-fibre boats and stacks of barnacle-encrusted lobster traps lined pebble shores next to Folkestone's long harbour arm, a concrete pier and former train station now dedicated to taco stands and champagne bars, where Londoners can live the seaside life with all the comforts of the capital. If it hadn't been 9 a.m., I would've stopped for a pint at the shipping container turned craft brewery on the beach. Instead of sipping on pale ale, I walked back through the harbour and towards the white cliffs rising to the east. Ferries and container ships spun their course on the English Channel, but refugees don't have the luxury of such safe travel. Among beachside art installations, locals hold seaside vigils for those lives lost crossing the open waters.

A National Coastwatch lookout stood on Folkestone's chalky eastern cliffs, a place lined with barbed wire and gun emplacements during the First and Second World Wars. On Folkestone Warren's grassy verge, I found Martello Tower Number three, one of seventy-four defensive forts built to defend Britain's coast during the Napoleonic era. It was said that from these cliffs, you could see the canvas tents of a French army massed between Calais and Boulogne, a time when Napoleon famously said: 'The English Channel is but a ditch, and anyone can cross it who has the courage. Let us be masters of the strait for six hours and we shall be masters of the world.'

Napoleon was all bluster. He only crossed the Channel when he was taken aboard HMS *Bellerophon* after the Battle of Waterloo, before he was shipped off to die in exile on St Helena's barren shores. The threat of invasion was very real, though, as it was again in the First and Second World Wars, and it seems to me that calling a few dinghies an invasion force is a huge disservice not just to refugees, but to the people who endured the real experience of war here.

I headed back to town when a red danger sign on the cliffs warned of landslips and a retreating Britain. I found myself on a high street home to taprooms and art galleries, faded British staples like Poundland and Wetherspoons and a cannonball fired by the English during the siege of Boulogne in 1544. Folkestone Museum, located within the town hall, was hosting a 'Folkestone on the Front Lines during the World Wars' exhibition. The town's long pier, down by the harbour, is where Belgian refugees arrived in 1914 when the German army crossed their neutral border. 65,000 Belgian refugees passed through Folkestone and some 15,000 stayed until the conflict ended. A painting hanging in the museum (by Fredo Franzoni, a refugee himself) depicts locals welcoming the Belgians in their thousands. Some 20,000 arrived in one day alone. That was the record day for refugee arrivals, dwarfing the hundreds arriving daily in the twenty-first century.

Folkestone has made a tradition of welcoming those in peril. To find out more about the local attitude towards refugees and migrants, I'd arranged a meeting with Patrick Marrin in his antiquarian bookshop.

'I have an old guide to the Saxon Shore Way you may find of interest,' Patrick said in a deep voice as I squeezed into his bookshop. 'Have a look around. I'll be with you in a minute; I just need to package up a few maps.'

Patrick was a broad-shouldered chap who must've found it harder than I did to squeeze through the narrow, overfilled wooden cabinets of frayed and well-thumbed books lining the precariously stacked shelves of Marrin's

Bookshop. A musty smell lingered in the air, not unpleasant as such, more a reminder of the history held within frayed pages. The chemical twangs were pungent, however, as Patrick tried to beat back dust and grime that could damage priceless literary relics with heavy-duty cleaning solutions. Price tags were exorbitant. Tens of thousands of pounds for a first-edition Charles Dickens, hundreds for a rare book by Milton and a first edition by Beatrix Potter probably worth an entire Saxon hoard.

'I tried to arrange the travel section like a world map,' Patrick said from his desk, as I searched in vain for the guidebook he'd mentioned. 'Mexico's in the middle. America and Canada above. The mountaineering section is at the top. I assume anyone climbing mountains is happy to reach for the top shelf.'

Patrick, his wispy grey beard wizard-like, wore a Victorian-esque waistcoat and a dark trilby. A jazzy shirt revealed the antiquarian's vibrant undertones, but as he sat wearily among piles of books at his wooden desk, he said he was in ill health. 'I've had a rough year,' he said forlornly. 'Open-heart surgery and then a kidney removed. I'm alive, though.'

Born in Hythe, just along the coast from Folkestone, Patrick had sold books for fifty years. His first shop was called the Cinque Ports Bookshop, then he took over Marrin's Bookshop, a repository for rare tomes, from his father some years ago. His ailments couldn't stop his passion for bookselling, not when books had the power to inform and change narratives. One of those narratives so concerning Patrick was the perception and treatment of refugees.

Patrick worked tirelessly with pro-refugee groups in Folkestone, organizing and partaking in anti-fascist protests and campaigning to improve the living conditions of refugees. There are multiple refugee charities and community groups in the town, including Napier Friends (named after the barracks), who have a team of forty or so volunteers providing English lessons, cooking sessions and even art and gardening classes. In turn, they also encourage refugees and asylum seekers to volunteer in the local community, join sports clubs or take part in social activities to help them integrate into their new home.

Ever the antiquarian, Patrick felt he had a personal stake in the story due to his ancestry, and he explained how he knew much about his own refugee lineage, thanks to a chance encounter with a very distant relative who walked into his bookstore one day.

'I didn't know I was a Huguenot until a man turned up and said, "I'm Charles Marrin, you're my 261st cousin removed, or some drastic number," Patrick said from his chair. 'He was from America. A lawyer in a big San Francisco firm. In his retirement, he'd tracked down Marrins all over the world.'

Fleeing religious persecution in France, the Marrins were among some 50,000 Huguenot refugees who sought sanctuary in southeastern England in the 1600s, from where they emigrated across England, Ireland and the United States. Patrick enthusiastically explained how the Huguenots had an enormous impact on the south coast, bringing with them weaving skills and starting the silk trade in places like Spitalfields in London. 'They were industrious; many became very wealthy,' Patrick said, beaming with pride at his ancestors' exploits. 'There's a long list of people we see as being English to the core, but they're all bloody foreigners. Descended from French Huguenots no less!'

THE KENTISH BORDER

Patrick recognizes those same hard-working traits in the refugees arriving in Folkestone today, who toil to gain a foothold in their new country. Give people a chance and they show you the best, was his ethos. 'To say I didn't already have a soft spot for refugees is wrong. I did, even before I knew my own family history. You can't choose where you're born. All this nonsense every year about there being record numbers of refugees arriving in England,' he said, his voice reverberating around the bookshop. 'The numbers arriving here in Britain are minuscule compared to migrations elsewhere and other times in history.'

He's not wrong. Britain has a deluded sense of self-importance when we look at the number of refugees we take in. The Syrian civil war, for example, saw millions flee the country. I've been to Istanbul and met with refugees, who number in the hundreds of thousands in Turkey's capital alone, many of them doomed to a life of exile, with little chance to advance themselves or return home. Britain, by comparison, accepted around 99,000 asylum applications in 2024, a quarter of whom had arrived by small boats.

'We get vigilante groups "patrolling" the cliffs, and I've heard people saying we should throw them back into the sea,' Patrick continued with contempt. 'The far-right groups holding rallies here aren't even from Folkestone. They take the train here.'

The attitude of locals couldn't be more different. Living on the border exposes you to something beyond partisan politics. Here, you begin to understand refugees aren't just numbers, but people, with lived lives or lives that could have been lived. Patrick understood that, which is why he was so against the demonization of refugees. For him, this positive mindset was a product of living on the border, of close intermingling with the continent, with different cultures and people, in a town that spills over the English Channel.

In contrast, the rest of England, away from the border, can seem short-sighted, with an inability to look beyond its own borders to understand that Britain can't isolate itself from the rest of the world. It never has and never can. We were invaders ourselves, and deep down, we know that the history of Britain is the history of the movement of people. To resist that is to resist the tides of the English Channel themselves.

Sadly, I later discovered that Patrick passed away not long after I'd met him in Folkestone. A true Englishman, descended from French Huguenots, he helped me understand that being English or British is about the values you adopt and the stances you take, not where you're from, what religion you profess, the colour of your skin or how high you fly your flag. I'm honoured he gave me his time towards the end of his life, when his concern wasn't himself, but the poor souls landing on our shores.

The soy sizzle of chow mein cut through the sweet smell of masala chai when I stepped into Kathmandu House on West Terrace to find Bridget Chapman, a tireless campaigner for refugee rights, waiting for me at a table by broad, bright windows. I wanted to bust the prevailing myths about refugees. Bridget – who at the time, worked as the media liaison for the Kent Refugee Action Network (KRAN), a non-profit helping young refugees in Folkestone who arrive here without family after dangerous journeys across Africa, the Middle East and Europe – was the perfect candidate.

A neighbouring table feasted on tandoori chicken, while large platters of dhal bhat (a staple Nepali curry) took me straight back to the Himalayas. I'd found Bridget on Twitter, where she called out commentators spouting nonsense about the refugee crisis. She'd been busy that week giving interviews to the press, she said, which largely consisted of her telling the *Daily Mail*, time and time again, how these were not record numbers of refugees. That record was made when 20,000 Belgian refugees arrived at Folkestone pier in 1914.

Bridget started dealing with media enquiries for KRAN in 2019. I could see why. She was firm, a straight talker with facts and figures to back everything up. I was amazed at her stoicism; she continued telling the press exactly what they didn't want to hear, yet saw them print exactly the opposite of what she'd told them. I'd thought she'd put me down as just another journo, but she was genuinely intrigued in a project showing border towns like Folkestone differently to the regular headlines about small boats.

'Approximately four hundred refugees arrived in small boats yesterday,' Bridget, a spiky-haired Londoner who'd escaped the capital a few years before, explained. 'But you know, I'm an economic migrant. I'm from London. I moved down here because it was too expensive there. I brought no real skills with me. I was lucky to be born here, to have that little red passport – now a blue passport. I can go to Calais and back safely whenever I want.'

While Bridget might never truly understand the lived experiences of refugees, she could try to help. She explained how KRAN works with minors and young refugees no older than twenty-four, providing legal help, mental-health support, employment training and English language education. Refugees endure atrocious journeys, often escaping war-torn home countries. She knows young refugees who've been raped and abused, seen their friends shot, executed, blown up or drowned before they ever get near the English Channel. 'They get here, for the final crossing,' she said, welling up slightly. 'And I'm amazed they make it here because they've been through so much.'

The last stretch of that journey is extremely hazardous, even on clear, calm days, and at least 234 lives were lost in the English Channel between 2018 and 2024, according to the International Organization for Migration. 'People often ask me, "Are you on the beaches welcoming dinghies?"' she said. 'The reality is we can't know where they land. People are shoved into boats in France and told to aim for the lights of Dover, the closest point. But small dinghies are swept around by the winds and tides. They can end up anywhere between here and Hastings and Deal. It's a huge area. Usually, people are picked up by coastguard patrols or RNLI boats. They call 999 because they want to be picked up by the authorities. They want to regulate their status, go through official channels and eventually have a normal life. Nobody wants to be here illegally.'

Those refugees that do make it in small boats are sent to processing centres in Dover, where they're health checked and screened, before they're sent to the Napier Barracks in Folkestone (if they're over eighteen), or to hostels and hotels across the country while they await a decision on their refugee status. There are never enough foster placements to care for underage arrivals, and these youngsters, aged sixteen or below, end up living in cramped, shared accommodation, or in dilapidated private homes that aren't marketable, homes that few would want to live in anyway.

Bridget described young refugees as incredibly focused on their education. She sees them growing up and heading to college. Many then find employment in vital industries begging for dedicated workers, including the NHS or care homes. 'My attitude is that we are lucky to have them,' said Bridget without a shadow of doubt. 'These young people are willing to work. People I work with would happily be HGV drivers, for example, and we need more of them in the economy. It's controversial to say, but I want them here.'

A common misconception is that refugees are economic migrants, rather than fleeing conflict or persecution. That's why people get annoyed hearing how refugees are housed in hotels or private homes and given food allowances at taxpayers' expense. As Bridget said: 'This line put forward by people like Farage is wrong. They aren't economic migrants, and they aren't stealing homes.' In comparison, net migration – the vast majority of which comprises legal, economic migration – reached a peak of 764,000 in 2022, when it was only 184,000 in 2019. Some job Brexit did securing our borders.

The number of refugees arriving is manageable for the world's sixth-largest economy, where refugees make up just 0.26 per cent of the population. Given the number of Reform votes in 2024's general election, I suspect many people won't agree with Bridget. I do, but then again, I understand how important it is to be able to move across borders, whether for safety or for economic reasons. Like Bridget, I too could never afford to live in London, or even in Buckinghamshire where I grew up – not on a freelance journalist's wage. I'd made a career of moving from one place to the next, one country to another, and I could only do it because I had a strong passport and the backing of a strong pound. Because I've lived all over the world, and so easily, I genuinely believe everyone should have the opportunity to live and work internationally, across borders, particularly if you've endured war and conflict.

Paradoxically, many of the people living in Folkestone who Bridget sees as 'racists' (she doesn't mince her words), who are opposed to migration, are people who've moved here from other parts of the UK. 'They're what I like to call "white flights",' she said. 'They left London because London was too multicultural for them. They expected to find that Folkestone was not multicultural, but their world was shattered. It wasn't what they were expecting.'

Folkestone is far from monocultural. Earlier that day, I'd found myself strolling past a mosque and the Folkestone Islamic Cultural Centre (founded in the late 1980s by Bangladeshi restaurant owners), a short walk from the town's Catholic church. There were Turkish barbers, Syrian pizza shops and an abundance of Nepalese restaurants like the one we were in, often run by retired Gurkhas who'd served in the British Army. 'Go to the Bell and have Sunday lunch,' Bridget said. 'Your Yorkshire puddings are made by an Afghan. Take a taxi and you'll meet Kurdish drivers.'

Bridget stressed how Folkestone, for the large part, embraces its diversity. 'Folkestone is welcoming, despite what the media might say,' she said, adding that the town's demographics are changing. 'When I arrived, everything was Conservative. Now it's Green and Labour. A huge change. That's positive. People here are speaking up about their refugee heritage or taking pride in their Huguenot past. They know the myths aren't true.'

Bridget highlighted a welcome event they'd held at Napier Barracks in support of refugees. The local council pressured them to cancel, fearing it would be a magnet for far-right extremists and that it would descend into violence. They went ahead anyway, and the event attracted hundreds of pro-refugee supporters. The opposition march staged against them attracted just twenty-seven people.

'It's the unemployed nutters who're obsessed with people arriving,' she said of the twenty-seven. 'They said refugees should go home. That we should put machine guns on the clifftops, spray the Channel with bullets, set petrol on fire in the water. But they're a minority.'

Wild anti-immigration plans from the Home Office when the Conservatives were in power – which spouted mad ideas about floating walls, wave machines, armoured jet skis and the infamous Rwanda deportation scheme – had encouraged anti-refugee protests in Folkestone. Talk of invasion incites people towards violence, as I'd seen in Tamworth, particularly when there's something deeply ingrained in our island mentality about defending the Channel.

'The central government agenda has amplified these voices. When you shriek about record numbers, people get scared. You have this fear of being overwhelmed by people of fighting age, hiding in the hedgerows waiting to spring sharia law on people. That's just not true. The people I know don't want to impose sharia law on anyone. They just want a KFC,' said Bridget, before summing up the other side of the story. Many of Kent's coastal towns suffer serious deprivation, high unemployment levels, rising house prices and a lack of GPs.

It's sadly a similar story across the United Kingdom: a cost-of-living crisis, empty high streets, stagnating industries and the decline of institutions like the NHS which once brought us together. Politicians blame migration. They say we've lost control of our borders. They'll ignore the lack of democratic reform, cronyism in government, limited investment in infrastructure and the unequal distribution of wealth and opportunities across the country. For the Conservative government, it was simpler to blame these problems on the people arriving in small boats, rather than trying to fix the issues themselves.

It's easy to stir up hatred from afar, but on the border itself, it's Folkestone's welcoming side that quietly cuts through the noise, hinting at a selflessness that we as a nation should be proud to embrace. Rather than the shouty approach of the far-right, this is a quiet form of patriotism, one we can easily equate with the long-held British quality of stoicism. We don't need to wave flags when we have nothing to hide. We don't need to be blindly patriotic when we'd do better to have a little self-reflection. True British patriotism is about being self-critical; it's about making the country we live in a better place.

Bridget does a fantastic job providing a voice to the voiceless. If anyone could change the public's mind, it would be her, and I was pleased to see she later went into politics, when she was elected as a Labour councillor for Folkestone. I left Bridget to her work and walked back to the seafront. By the war memorial, still covered in wreaths from Remembrance Sunday a month earlier, there was another memorial to refugees who'd died in the Channel. Bridget had humanized the refugee story, making me appreciate they weren't numbers or figures, but people. They're also people that Britain needs, people willing to work hard and make the country better. The moment refugees and migrants stop turning up on our doorstep is the moment we know Britain has failed.

Dover

The next morning, a Southeastern train whisked me eleven minutes east from Folkestone to Dover as rare beams of winter sunlight glinted off the English Channel. The largest town on Kent's coast, Dover is another of the old Cinque Ports. It's a place where the imposing flint and ragstone towers of Dover Castle, which sits on clifftops hollowed out by tunnels and air-raid shelters, overshadow drab council flats.

Huge works of Napoleonic-era engineering, including citadels and gun bastions, now overgrown, hem in the town centre. To the west, the famous white cliffs of Dover hang dreamily above a monstrous port, where lorries belch fumes as they drive on to P&O ferries. The closest point on Britain's mainland to France, this would be my last port of call, and I wanted to end my journey on the chalky cliffs of the Saxon Shore Way.

I stepped on to the platform, recalling the curious memories Dover Priory station holds for me. When I was at university, with just £200 in my bank account and a thin sleeping bag bundled into a battered hiking pack, a friend and I hitchhiked here from Buckingham in the summer break. The stationmaster let us spend the night on the waiting-room floor, where we were joined by weary-looking characters stopping over on their way to who knows where.

We had planned to hitch a ride across the Channel, naively assuming this would be easy. But this was 2013, the height of the Syrian civil war. Even if we were going the opposite way to the tides of people travelling through Europe, no one wanted to take us over the border. We coughed up for the ferry fare, hitchhiked to Spain and blew what little money we had left in Pamplona. The trip opened my eyes to the refugee crisis. We spent short nights camped out in parks with refugees, sharing boxes of cheap French wine or plastic bottles of sangria bought in the Carrefour. Police dogs chased us out of Gare du Nord in Paris at 4 a.m. A Syrian doctor broke down in tears telling us the plight of his home country as he drove us to Montpellier.

For the first time in our cushy lives, we'd seen just a little of what things were like for refugees. We knew we were there by choice, though, that we'd never ever truly understand their experiences. We had our British passports. We could cross the border back home to the United Kingdom whenever we wanted. For many, the UK's maritime border is a life-threatening place. The distinction boils down to where you're born, what documents you have.

Noting with a wry smile where we'd slept on the grimy station floor, I exited Dover Priory and clocked graffiti, scrawled across the walls of an underpass, that said 'The real enemy travel by private jet not by dinghy.' It was cold, bitterly cold despite the sunshine, and I shivered as I walked the steep road uphill to Dover Castle. Built by King Henry II in the twelfth century, Dover Castle is the 'Key to the Kingdom of England', and woe betide anyone who dares scale its wall.

THE KENTISH BORDER

Through medieval walls ringing the hilltop, I found a Roman Pharos, or lighthouse, stood on a cliff's edge by the red bricks of an Anglo-Saxon church. One of only three Roman lighthouses left in the world, its flames once directed ships along the Saxon Shore, where they'd pass into the Wantsum Channel and then follow Reculver's lights into the Thames Estuary.

Down in town, Dover is one big transit hub, a true border town with a mass of petrol stations, cargo facilities, and Premier Inns and Travelodges where weary travellers and truck drivers rest before early-morning ferries. I've spent a lot of time in border towns around the world; it comes with the job. There's always a gritty edge to them. Borders attract illicit activity, and Dover was described in the past as a 'villainous den infested with atrocious smugglers'. Smuggling won't ever stop, borders only encourage it, and I know plenty of people caught with carloads of cigarettes on their way back from France. Border towns are dangerous in places, too – darkened crossings in Central America still give me the chills – but even so, I have a strange soft spot for their dingy bars and bare-bones hotels, places where the world fleetingly meets, passing through like ships in the night.

Small fishing boats lay on the shingle shore along the promenade, and I followed Dame Vera Lynn Way past endless queues of backed-up lorries with European number plates. Under chalk cliffs a line of battered houses led to the First and Last Pub, shuttered long ago. The road continued to a ferry terminal surrounded by vicious razor-wire fences watched by security cameras. I followed the coastal path upwards, counting four P&O ferries in the harbour below, and found myself back on the trail of the Saxon Shore Way.

Out of breath atop Langdon Cliffs, and with white

ALONG THE BORDERS

chalk underfoot, I saw the frontier below me. 'Oh, this is so English!' some American tourists hurrying past exclaimed as the rain suddenly worsened. My phone switched to French time again. But I was indeed standing on the most English of all landmarks, the white cliffs of Dover. Ahead, clouds had rolled in and enveloped the English Channel, a geographical border that separated us from continental Europe over one hundred thousand years ago when sea levels rose, obscuring any further chance I might've had of seeing France.

Is it here I'm meant to feel patriotic, I wondered? While the famous cliffs stretched eastwards, I was fixated by the industrial monstrosity below, where ferries spouted smoke, chains clanked and a thousand engines roared in unison. Below was the stinking business of borders in all its primordial antagonism. Passport checks, queues, smuggling and smog. Beyond lay modern-day terra incognita. We have boundaries because we fear what's ahead of us. We fear the unknown. This is my land, not yours. You can only cross that frontier with the right visa, the right passport, the right nationality. Only when you board the ferry and look back at the white cliffs with a rosy glow do you say, 'Oh, England looks glorious.'

Here I was on the border of Britain, the end of my journey, but in a strange way, I felt trapped by the very frontiers I'd set out to understand. To me, it seems as if the ancient boundaries that dotted this island are rising once more. Brexit enforced the divide between us and the continent, while a surging tide of nationalism – in Cornwall, Wales, Scotland and England – only serves to heighten a sense of ominous division. It felt as though the borders were closing in around me.

THE KENTISH BORDER

Britain's borders are ancient, but why can't we leave these medieval mindsets behind us? Why do we continue to blame others, people on the other side of these boundaries, for our problems? I realize now, after travelling across the United Kingdom, that this island nation – my home nation – will only improve when we look beyond the walls, not when we build them higher.

A ray of sunshine cut through the clouds. Dover was strangely beautiful in a golden haze of light, as were the green fields behind me. We need tough love in Britain. We need to change if we want our motley bunch of nations to remain united. To do that, we need to transcend the ancient borders intended to divide us, not resurrect them. And then perhaps, we can create a united nation, one that all our nationalities, ethnicities and peoples are proud to call home.

Epilogue

When I was researching the Irish border in Monaghan, I met an enthusiastic curator named Liam. Dare I say it, but the Irishman was even more of a border fanatic than me. Liam lived and breathed the Irish border. He crossed it no less than four times a day – sometimes more, depending on the route he took – driving to and from his job at Monaghan's museum. He was a borderlander. He lived his life across borders. And he was fascinated by the borderlines around him.

He told me how those borderlines weave their way through time and place, right back to the earliest hunter-gatherers who congregated into groups and attempted to make sense of the world around them. Those hunter-gatherer groups evolved into communities. They planted roots. Marked boundaries. They began believing in different gods, ideals and ways of life. They compared themselves to other groups, defined themselves in opposition to the community on the other side of the valley. They built hill forts. They carved great dykes across the landscapes, constructed castles and divided the land. Kingdoms fell, empires expanded and modern nation states were born. Ireland was partitioned and ancient boundaries were lined with barbed wire. Then it all came down. But the borders are still there. They've always been there. And perhaps, borders will never disappear.

EPILOGUE

Borders have two inevitabilities. The first is that people will build them. The second is that people will cross them. It was this story, one of inevitability, that Liam tried to tell through his museum's 'Borderlines' exhibition. He showed me a photograph of a bridge spanning a river, the same bridge he crossed every day. He described how one moment he's in the European Union. He drives over the bridge. In his car, nothing changes. But outside, everything changes. As he moves over the river's no man's land, he crosses multiple borderlines, both man-made and geographical. He sees the gradient of the road changing. The broken yellow lines become a straight white line. The tarmac changes from dark black to mottled grey. Suddenly, he's not in the EU. He's in the United Kingdom. There's a different currency, different laws, different governments, 'different everything'. Borders are paradoxes. Nothing changes, except everything does. The border changes the physical world, but it doesn't change him. He's still the same person on both sides. People make borders. But borders don't make people.

'I don't see a reality where we don't have lines,' Liam had told me on a moody morning in Monaghan. 'But people have been moving over lines for millennia. History shows that people change, they move, and trying to stop it is a fallacy. There's no point. There's more that binds us than separates us.'

When I set out to write this book, I believed in finding ways to smash down the barricades and borders I saw being resurrected across Britain. Without those borders, though, the multitude of identities they nurtured would never exist. Liam, whose entire existence has been moulded by the myriad borderlines of community, faith, politics and

EPILOGUE

nationality in Monaghan, wants us to see the borderlines woven all around us differently.

He doesn't want to remove them, because he knows we never really can. After all, the history of humanity is one of borders. A search for definition. There will always be some echo of those differences across the divides that have been, and the ones yet to come. Those lines in the sand help us to understand our sense of place and identity in the world. Instead, Liam wants us to meet in that no man's land in the middle, that hazy space where you can see the border clearly for what it is. Rather than trying to blast barriers apart or tear down walls, he wants people to simply step through, to step over to the other side. When we recognize the separation between us, we can start making connections, find common ground, forge identities spanning the borders meant to define us. That's how borders are bridged, how boundaries are crossed.

Borders are designed to separate us, and yet, as I'd found on my journey, borders are what brings people together. By looking to the borderlands, I'd discovered the essence of what Britain is and what it isn't. What it has been and what it can be. That last great question still hangs in the balance. As I sit here writing this epilogue in the comfort of my Devonshire living room, not far from the River Tamar where my journey began, across the Atlantic US President Donald Trump has declared a 'national border emergency'. That's no surprise. Borders exist to be politicized.

Trump's actions have encouraged politicians in the United Kingdom to call for the same, to shout for our international borders to be closed, boarded up and lined with razor wire. For boats in the Channel to be sunk and migrants deported.

EPILOGUE

Hatred exploded on to the streets of Northern Ireland in June 2025 – not violence between Catholics and Protestants, but with 'natives' turning on their Eastern European neighbours in Ballymena, burning houses where foreign-born families live. Is this the Britain we want? Where pogroms engulf red-brick Victorian streets, and foreigners fear for their lives? That's the terrifying side of borders, the terrifying side of nationalism. When borders are raised higher, it's a sure sign you're enduring a crisis of identity, and that much is clear in Britain.

Much has changed since I started writing a book about Britain's borders. The pandemic is a distant memory. Cornwall has devolution, but not a parliament; the Scottish National Party were almost wiped out in Westminster; and the Conservatives were ousted. But borders remain the defining topic of twenty-first-century politics, and none of the fundamental questions asked by Britain's borderlands have been answered in government. Questions of sovereignty, devolution, migration and identity remain. The very future of the United Kingdom still hangs in the balance, like the crumbling Kentish coast awaiting the next ravaging storm. The Reform Party has gone from strength to strength off the back of anti-immigration rhetoric; Northern Ireland's future remains uncertain; and Welsh nationalists march in Cardiff. Time will tell if we decide to pursue our regional identities at the expense of Britain, if we will fortify our borders and discard our sense of Britishness. Or we can step through the borders, see what's on the other side and build a stronger nation.

Britain, as I'd discovered, has some of the most ancient borders in the world. I'd hoped to learn what they could

EPILOGUE

teach us about our nation. But now, after my journey by bus, boat, train, plane, car, bike and on foot, through hundreds of miles of borderlands, I realize that the story of Britain's borders *is* the story of our nation. Our nation's very identity is echoed in its cross-border identities and the changing borderlines that never sit still. Britain *is* a borderland, a place where people, like me, hold multiple identities that are constantly shifting.

The one constant of all borderlands is change. The question is, how do we react to that change? Do we burn down hotels, man the barricades and fight for a past that never existed? Or do we accept change, look ourselves in the mirror and march onward? To sit still, to fester behind our walls and build them higher, to stop people from stepping through – that would be the downfall of the United Kingdom.

No matter how much barbed wire you put down, people find ways to cross borders. That's human nature. And that's also the essence of the British nation, a nation which holds so many borderlines and mixed identities within its grasp. Ultimately, what separates us unites us. Together, we can all thrive and prosper, so long as we push past the borderlines, look to the other side to admit our flaws and mistakes, and come home again, stronger for it.

Richard Collett, January 2025

Acknowledgements

First of all, I have to thank my partner, Claire. She stoically endures my long absences and journeys to often strange, sometimes dangerous and inevitably remote destinations. More often than not, she even accompanies me. Without her unyielding enthusiasm, encouragement and support, *Along the Borders* would have remained buried somewhere in the depths of my Google Drive. I have to thank Claire's dad, Paul, for inspiring my travels along the Cornish border, which in turn inspired the rest of this book, and the rest of Claire's family – Sal and Sophie – for supporting it.

Many more thanks go to my parents, Paul and Belinda, who inspired my love of travel by moving us to Muscat when I was young. They've continued to support my often-questionable travel and career choices ever since. Thanks to my siblings, Sarah and James, their partners Oli and Brigid, and my niece and nephew, Abigail and Rupert. Thanks to my grandma for her lifelong support. I'm only sorry that Grandad, Nanny and Grampy never had the chance to read this.

Thanks to friends who've also supported me in life, travel and writing. To Joe and Kev, for guiding me through their beloved Leicester. To Tom, for enthusiastically accompanying me to a few too many pubs along the Irish border. To the Irving family, for inspiring my travels into the Debatable

ACKNOWLEDGEMENTS

Lands, and to all of my Notts and Bucks friends (you know who you are) – but especially Jack, Jordan and Hannah.

Thanks to my excellent agent, Amberley. You've been so enthusiastic from the moment I pitched you out of the blue. You shaped a rough idea into something concrete, and were indispensable in guiding an unknown travel writer into the publishing world. Thanks to Sharika, my equally excellent editor at Doubleday. Your enthusiasm, encouragement and editorial vision helped shape *Along the Borders* into what I hope is the best it could be.

Thanks to the rest of the team at Penguin Random House – proofreaders, copy-editors, fact checkers, mapmakers, cover designers – who readied *Along the Borders* for publication. Thanks to the Society of Authors and the Authors' Foundation, whose much-needed grant allowed me to focus on writing when I most needed to. Thanks also to the British Guild of Travel Writers, and the many travel writers and editors who continue to support my work and travels.

Finally, a special shout-out to all of the *many* borderlanders I met on my journey, who helped shape, inspire, critique and inform this book. I interviewed and spoke with well over a hundred people between Land's End and Shetland, and it would be impossible for me to name everyone who played their part. Thanks to all of you in the borders – tour guides, publicans, councillors, politicians, shopkeepers, historians, antiquarians, booksellers, geographers, editors, teachers, volunteers, charity workers, hoteliers, re-enactors, fishers, artists, farmers, museum curators. You all played your part in this book, and in making the British Isles such a fascinating place to live.

About the Author

Richard Collett is an award-winning travel journalist who regularly contributes to major international publications, including *National Geographic*, *BBC Travel*, *CNN Travel*, Lonely Planet and the *Telegraph*. His award-winning travel blog *Travel Tramp* explores the world through its borders. Born in Scotland to English parents, Richard is now intent on discovering a sense of identity in his ever-changing homeland.